The BEST YEARS BOOK

Books by Hugh Downs

YOURS TRULY, HUGH DOWNS

A SHOAL OF STARS

RINGS AROUND TOMORROW

POTENTIAL: THE WAY TO EMOTIONAL
MATURITY

30 DIRTY LIES ABOUT OLD

The BEST YEARS BOOK

HOW TO PLAN FOR FULFILLMENT, SECURITY, AND HAPPINESS IN THE RETIREMENT YEARS

HUGH DOWNS & RICHARD J. ROLL

A DELL TRADE PAPERBACK/ELEANOR FRIEDE

A DELL TRADE PAPERBACK/ELEANOR FRIEDE

Published by Dell Publishing Co., Inc.
1 Dag Hammarskjold Plaza, New York, New York 10017

*This book is dedicated to parents and children,
for they share
in each other's hopes, dreams, and aspirations*

ACKNOWLEDGMENTS

THIS work involves the help and participation of many people. Our greatest debt of gratitude is to Steve Morgenstern, whose tireless dedication and painstaking research contributed much to shaping the ideas in this book; and to Joyce R. Manes, whose insightful cross-country interviews contributed the critical dimension of how real people experience the retirement years.

Special thanks are owed to the dozens of retired and semiretired men and women across the country who in many cases shared with us their innermost thoughts, their victories, and their fears. We would also like to thank the following people who reviewed or assisted with parts of the manuscript: Pat Bergen, registered dietician; Dr. Dorri Jacobs; Bradley King, Esq.; Jack London, Esq.; J. Martin Obten, Esq.; Caroline J. G. Russell, Blue Cross/Blue Shield of Greater New York; Judith Sachs; Judy Salwen; Sam Schiff, Insurance Information Institute; Sally J. Stewart, YMCA of Greater New York; Robert Waldron, American Council of Life Insurance; Paul Wasserman, C.P.A.; and Jack Wynn, Manufactured Housing Institute. Thanks also to Mel Berger, our literary agent; and to a skilled and dedicated team behind the scenes at the PBS television series *Over Easy,* from whom one of the authors, as host of that program, learned much.

Indebted though we are to those mentioned above for their help and support, the responsibility for the material in this book, and its shortcomings, is ours alone.

TABLE OF CONTENTS

INTRODUCTION   1

The BEST YEARS BOOK

INTRODUCTION

PEOPLE sixty-five and over have one thing in common: They've all reached one particular age bracket. And there the universality ends. They do not all like the same things; they do not all look alike. Which makes them pretty much like the population in general—different needs, different interests, different abilities. What *your* life will be like after sixty-five is largely up to you, and it depends on how well you prepare for it. And the first step is to evaluate all aspects of your life *today*—whether you're forty-five, fifty-five, or sixty-five—to develop a plan of action for retirement: what you want to do, what means you have to do it, and how you will accomplish it. This book will show you the best way to create your own plan.

To most active people in their forties and fifties, retirement is a tomorrow thing, not worth worrying about. But that attitude can prove disastrous. The time to begin planning for retirement is *at least ten years before you turn sixty-five*—early enough to avoid the three major pitfalls that can befall retirees: financial insecurity, uncertainty about where to live, and post-retirement letdown, which can turn your well-earned reward into a tedious agony.

My decision to leave the *Today* show in 1971 was made three years in advance. That isn't much for retirement planning, but then I hadn't really thought of it as retirement. I thought in terms of quitting New York and regular broadcasting, and not having to hear the alarm go off at 4:15 A.M. I had visions, I guess, of doing specials and other forms of broadcasting, but not on a regular basis. This would allow me to live in Arizona, and to teach, write, lecture, and do a lot of other things I wanted to do. So I moved and I carried out my plan. But in a way it amounted to retirement, even though I resisted the word. Once the press picked it up, the news was spread that I had retired.

I anticipated the shock of losing my "amplified voice." I knew that when I cut that off, I would feel it. And even though I planned for it, I *did* feel it. I remember the second day I was in Arizona, I tuned in to the *Today* show and noticed they did something that wasn't quite right. My first thought was, "Tomorrow morning I'll correct that." But then I realized that I couldn't. Sure, I could call Barbara Walters and mention it to her, but that was all the say I'd have on the subject. I was going to have to live a more proportional human existence, and my spheres of influence would be much more local, rather than national.

There was a feeling of letdown. It wasn't intolerable; it didn't make me *terribly* unhappy. But it was there, and even having planned for it, it surprised me that I felt it. Fame and national attention were more important to me than I had realized. Maybe the letdown could have been avoided had I planned more thoroughly and done some research into what the transition is like. I thought I knew myself well enough, but it didn't happen exactly as I thought it would. And I think that is true for a lot of people, even those who retire by their own choice.

The sensible person doesn't really retire. He or she changes activities or occupations. One who retires to do something else, to live life in a positive new way, is still in command. One who has "been retired" is a victim.

Unlike other societies, the United States has yet to institutionalize a proper role for its older citizens. So each retiree in America has the challenge of creating his or her own lifestyle. This can be a problem or an opportunity, because there are many subtle issues involved in retirement. This book will help you identify the options and help you make the necessary decisions so you can get the most out of life after sixty-five.

After the practical, specific concerns are resolved—such as housing, finances, and legal affairs—the next question is, "What does fulfillment mean to me at this stage of my life?" Research on the life development patterns of men and women has highlighted the late middle-aged years as a period of *renewal of purpose*. People who are most successful in the transition to later life are those who can let go of old roles, open themselves to a broader personal perspective, and reach out with a firm grasp to new opportunities.

When I left the *Today* show, my intention was to "repot" myself, just like a plant that needs relocation every now and then. Ruts are comfortable, and they can be good, but they're still ruts. As much as I enjoyed doing the *Today* show, I felt confined—the schedule was too unremitting. There were many other things I wanted to do that would only be possible when I left the show.

If you derive satisfactions from accomplishing, from being respected, needed, and busy—and most of us do—then you'll want to be armed before facing retirement with activities and interests that will enhance *your* chances of achieving these goals. A person with a sense of security, sound physical and mental health, self-motivation, and multiple interests is certainly no candidate for oblivion on retirement.

Retirement can be an open field if you are single, and it is an experience to be shared by husband and wife if both of you are in the picture—and then your plans must take the needs of both of you into account. Indeed, sometimes a person's retirement is harder on his spouse. As Casey Stengel's wife said when he finally hung up his uniform in his seventies: "I married him for better or for worse, but not for lunch!" Then there's the case of the business executive who jumped into a private consulting business upon reaching mandatory retirement age, and from there to additional business ventures. He still insists on making time for his hobbies, however—golf, gardening, and photography. "My wife says that she wanted me to retire, but now that I'm retired she complains that she never sees me," he reported.

Retirement planning takes time and thought. You are about to undergo a definite change in lifestyle and living patterns which, like any change, requires flexibility to be most effective. Sound planning will help you do it well, and sound planning is what *The Best Years Book* is all about.

HUGH DOWNS
New York City, 1980

1

PLANNING
FOR
RETIREMENT
FULFILLMENT

1

WHY PLAN
FOR
RETIREMENT?

Thinking always ahead, thinking always of trying to do more, brings a state of mind in which nothing seems impossible.

HENRY FORD

THE day is coming when, through some combination of personal desire, employment policy, family pressure, and the state of your health, you will step away from your daily job to enter a new stage of life. Retirement is full of exciting possibilities as well as potential problems. You have a choice—you can *let* retirement happen *to* you, or *make* it happen *for* you.

To ignore the important changes on the horizon will leave you at the mercy of circumstance and luck, but planning ahead will put you in control of your own future, so that you can shape it in a satisfying, self-fulfilling way. These years are potentially the most pleasurable and rewarding you will ever spend.

The purpose of this book is to help you identify the issues and options presented by retirement and give you the tools you need to build a better future. You will be called upon to make some major adjustments, but on the other hand you will be free for the first time of many of the bonds which determined your past and present lifestyle. Just think for a moment about how totally your career now shapes the way you spend your waking hours. You spend time getting ready for work, reaching the place where you work, and putting in your hours at work. Your job largely determines where you live, what leisure activities are available to you, how you relate to your family and friends, and even how you feel physically. Add to these formidable limitations the responsibilities involved in raising children, and you'll find you haven't ever had much of a chance to make choices based solely on your own desires.

I know that for Ruth and me it was immensely liberating to have the kids grown and on their own. It was honeymoon time again. Before we had our children, my wife and I had traveled together and enjoyed each other, and when the kids came along we loved them very much but we had to adjust to a different way of life, one that was much less carefree. I don't think we realized it until after they grew up and went off on their own. And then suddenly we began doing the same things we had done at the beginning of our relationship, and that's been great.

It's possible in retirement, as it was for us, to remove many of the constraints which have governed your life in the past. With careful planning, for example, you can achieve a substantial degree of financial independence in your later life and be free of the restrictions of full-time employment. With children grown and out of the house, there is probably little to pin you down to a particular activity or geographical location. While no one can guarantee you will be vigorously healthy in retirement (or for that matter any other stage of life), the fact is that most of us *will* be blessed with sound minds and bodies long past age sixty-five, free from restricting illnesses or disabilities. In short, the path is largely yours to chart—life is yours to be lived the way you want to live it. The problem now is often an embarrassment of choices, which can be tricky to handle if it's something you've never experienced before.

So it requires some thought. Maybe the best way—and the most enjoyable—to figure out where you're going at this stage of your life is to allow yourself the luxury of some old dreams and fantasies.

What do you want to be when you grow up?

Remember that question? How many times did you hear it when you were a youngster and some older person was trying to make conversation? How many times did your answer change over the years?

Now may be the time to ask that question again, rephrasing it slightly: "What do you want to do, now that you're grown up?" You're still changing, capable of picking out goals and doing what has to be done to reach them. You've grown older, but that doesn't mean you shouldn't reach for just what you want instead of settling for what other people have in mind for you. Retirement is the right time to pursue dreams.

Too often we put our dreams aside completely, accept our position as unchangeable, and leave the dreaming to our children. But as much as you enjoy your children's achievements vicariously, it can't match the pride and satisfaction of your own successes. Acknowledging this doesn't mean you are greedy or self-centered. It means you need to feel the purpose of your own life and must learn to understand that your loved ones can be as proud of you as you are of them.

Now ask yourself—where have you shortchanged yourself in the past? Did you put off your own education because you were too busy raising children? Did you take a job as an accountant instead of pursuing an interest in acting? Has travel always seemed like an indulgence you had to forgo in order to provide security for your family? Make a list of the dreams which you have not fulfilled so far. Ask yourself what you would do if you were free to do whatever you wanted. Have you ever said to yourself, "Just once before I die, I'd like to ———"? Now is the time to consider it seriously.

When you've finished the list, look it over with these questions in mind:

- Why didn't I do that? Was I too busy? Too afraid of what other people would say? Not really that interested in the first place?
- Which of these can still come true? How difficult would it be? What could I do now to start the ball rolling?

- If the dream is really impossible, can I come close? How can I adapt that distant goal to make it feasible?

Some of your dreams may be unrealistic, but don't be too quick to cross anything off your list. For instance, let's say you'd always wanted to be a lawyer, but circumstances prevented you from going through all those years of education. Of course it isn't easy to start a career as an attorney in your fifties or sixties, but it has been done. We know of at least one case of a fifty-nine-year-old man who began taking correspondence courses in law, passed his bar exam when he was sixty-two, and established a small, successful practice which at this writing is still thriving.

Whether you're thinking of opening a restaurant, writing a play, sailing a yacht, or whatever else, there are books on the subject available in your library; more important, there are people involved right now in doing what you would like to do who can give you a firsthand account of ways in which you might pursue your goal and reinforce your interest at the same time. The key to this type of dreaming is not to leave your thinking process at list making, but to get out and make the phone calls, write the letters, and set into motion your own chain reaction of enthusiasm and progress.

There is probably a niche for each of us within the field which has always attracted us, if we will only take the time to go out and find it. The frustrated actress can join a community theater group, the would-be astronaut can develop his expertise in astronomy, and the college football hero who wistfully remembers past glories can coach a school football team. The trick to turning your fond dreams into rewarding reality is to:

- *Be imaginative* in coming up with a set of options.
- *Consult other people* to help you come up with possibilities and provide an up-to-date, realistic picture of their own fields of interest.
- *Get started* in the direction you choose now, rather than putting off fulfilling your desires, as you may have done in the past.

Dr. Dorri Jacobs, a New York-based consultant on change, psychotherapist, and author of a book on coping with change, has done extensive research on the way people use their dreams to help them establish a new lifestyle. "At retirement, you have to develop a whole new program for living," she says. "Most people in their adult years don't consciously *create* a lifestyle, but fall into it, through work, through marriage, through living in a particular neighborhood.

"So here you are retiring, with no idea of what it means to create a lifestyle from scratch. Unless you look at retirement planning way ahead of time as a valuable way to learn how to do this—and as an important beginning instead of an ending—you could be completely unprepared."

Some people try to avoid thinking in advance about retirement because they feel that retirement indicates the end of their useful years. These fears are deeply ingrained in our society, even though retirement has gone through a veritable revolution in the past two decades. I'd like to see us get over the rampant cliché that retirement automatically kills you. That's simply not true. Retirement *today* is very definitely the beginning of a new, lengthy, important stage of life, rich with promise and well worth planning for.

Retirement used to be a rarity before the 1940s. Even though Social Security was in effect, pension programs had grown, and there was a viable program for retirement, most people didn't stay around long to enjoy it: the average life expectancy by World War II was just under 65.9 years. When you said goodbye to Joe as he retired from work, very likely you went to his funeral a few months later. By 1977, though, the average life span of Americans at birth had reached 73.2 years. Retirement is not only feasible, it's something to look forward to. Today, if you have survived to society's traditional retirement age, you can look forward to another sixteen years of life, and this number is still increasing. What these statistics *don't* show is that not only are we living longer, but we're staying healthier longer as well. So the idea that retirement means the end of active, vital living is as outmoded today as the Victrola. Since you're likely to continue living a long while as an active, capable adult, it's well worth deciding how you are going to use this hefty proportion of your total life span.

Another important point is that many more people these days are turning age sixty-five, making the older population a more powerful, influential group than ever before. Since the turn of the century, the total population of the United States has nearly tripled, but the number of people over age sixty-five has multiplied sevenfold! Today about one out of every ten Americans is over sixty-five, and by the year 2040 that figure is expected to be one out of four. This means that older people can no longer be pushed to one side, their needs and desires ignored. You will still be in the minority when you reach retirement, but retirees are rapidly becoming a strong and influential minority, made up of people with money, votes, talents, and the energy to forge new roles for themselves.

Myths About Aging and Health

Some of the most dangerous misconceptions about aging are the popular beliefs about the physical and mental limitations of older people. You may be inclined to give up planning for activities which you enjoy just because you have bought a lot of old myths about inevitable inadequacy. By the time you realize that your expectations were wrong you may already have cut down on your opportunities for a full and varied lifestyle. But let me firmly state that the following old wives' tales are hogwash—pure and simple:

Old People Are Helpless. Statistics show how untrue this statement actually is. Eighty out of one hundred Americans over sixty-five have no difficulty getting around, while only 8 percent report some difficulty, and 6 percent require some mechanical assistance. This totals 94 percent, all active and mobile, and these figures cover the entire range of seniors, including those with illnesses and the extremely old. Only 6 percent are incapacitated or bedridden.

The idea that getting old means being abandoned in an institution has no doubt been exacerbated by the fear of nursing homes. These facilities have received a good deal of bad publicity in recent years, but the odds are you'll never have to find out for yourself anyway. Less than 5 percent of the aged in America live in nursing homes, and while even this figure is higher than it would be in a country which provided adequate support facilities for its older citizens, it must be remembered that there are sick people who need round-the-clock care in any age bracket. If you are healthy, you will be able to take care of yourself, and with adequate planning for a personal health program, you will have few worries on this score.

Old People Are Senile. The term "senility" is used incorrectly, and dehumanizes the elderly. The whole notion of senility has rightfully come under attack in recent years, and if people are interested enough to listen, we may be able to wipe out the concept completely and deal instead with the societal forces underlying it.

The first definition of the word "senile" in *Webster's New Collegiate Dictionary* reads as follows: "1: of, relating to, exhibiting, or characteristic of old age ⟨~ weakness⟩; *esp:* exhibiting a loss of mental faculties associated with old age." When people use the word, though, they mean "crazy, incapable of self-control." Senility is a comfortable label generally used by young people who have given up on treating their elders for their problems, or even treating them as human beings. The loss of mental faculties should be associated with brain damage rather than with age. The brain can be damaged by injury, blood-nutrition deprivation, anoxia, cell loss. There are brain-damaged children and brain-damaged middle-aged people, but brain-damaged people are called "senile" only if they are past retirement age.

Mental illness is possible in the old just as it is in the young, but it is *not,* in fact, more prevalent in the old. Gerontologist Alex Comfort has reported that less than one percent of older people can expect to become demented, and he includes in this group those affected not only by organic brain diseases but by "alcoholism, depression, and ordinary insanity as well."

Old People Are Less Mentally Capable Than the Young. Does your brain really "dry up" as you grow older? Irreplaceable cells are lost daily, but it would take several hundred years to destroy an average brain at this rate. Suppose you lost 5 percent of your brain cell supply by age ninety. It has been estimated that we do all our thinking and remembering with about 20 percent of the brain. So since you start out with a good 80 percent unused, you can afford the gradual loss without impairing memory or rational functioning, provided you do not experience the kind of loss, through disease or injury, which affects whole areas and harms reasoning ability or memory.

We don't really need statistics and biological studies to prove the lifelong mental abilities of human beings—we can just look at the evidence all around us. A glance at the roster of great artists, writers, performers, and business and government leaders who have continued their highly creative crafts into their eighth and ninth decades should be proof enough of the continuing capabilities of the human being. And you don't have to stop with celebrities. Skill and experience gained over the years in every realm is a valuable asset in any endeavor.

Then we have intelligence measurements. Recent data indicate that people do not decline in intelligence as they age. Dr. Francis J. Braceland reported in 1979 in the *Journal of the National Association of Private Psychiatric Hospitals* that, "Longitudinal studies—those that follow the same people over a long period of time—clearly show that the intellectual abilities of healthy people grow greater through the years rather than less."

People Lose Interest in Sex as They Grow Older. Here again, society's ingrained prejudice is the culprit. Men and women do *not* become biologically incapable of sexual relations. A variety of prominent Americans have gained reputations as sexy seniors. Senator Strom Thurmond of South Carolina, for example, married a woman in her twenties when he was sixty-six and had three children with her, the last born when Thurmond was seventy-six. Fred Astaire was eighty when he became engaged to thirty-five-year-old jockey Robyn Smith. And to go back a bit in history, Ben Franklin was a notorious lady's man. When he was in his seventies, he had an affair with Madame Helvétius, who was then in her sixties, and he was accompanied on his travels by two French girls young enough to be his granddaughters.

A few other sexually active seniors? Entertainers Charlie Chaplin and Artur Rubinstein, artist Pablo Picasso, and Supreme Court Justice William O. Douglas. Study after study reveals that sexual activity continues into our advanced years, despite the public image of older people as asexual.

Masters and Johnson and other researchers in the field have shown that older men and women go through the same stages of sexual excitement as they did when they were younger—it just takes a little longer. A man will not achieve an erection as quickly as he once did, but then he is less likely to achieve orgasm as quickly either, so the sexual act can be prolonged. A woman who has gone through menopause may prefer certain changes in sexual technique, and possibly wish to use a vaginal lubricant, but her capacity for sexual pleasure and her need for sexual intimacy are undiminished by passing years. Penetration and intercourse are generally regarded as feasible more or less indefinitely. And of course the range of sensual, loving activity is limitless. Some people find they grow more creative sexually as they grow older. If you take a mature attitude toward your sex life as you grow older, you will be able to enjoy physical intimacy for the emotional joy it brings as well as for the continuing sensual pleasure.

UNDERSTANDING THE APPROACHING CHANGE

Any major change in our lives sets up a crisis situation: major decisions are required, emotions run high, and tensions can mount. Your graduation from school, marriage, and the birth of your children were all crises, as is retirement. It is precisely these times of adjustment, of intense feeling and increased activity, which can be the most interesting, exciting, and memorable times of our lives.

Why is retirement particularly stressful? Dr. Dorri Jacobs offers her assessment: "You're facing the void of 'If I'm no longer who I thought I was, and I'm going to be a new person, what do I keep and what do I throw away?' You feel very vulnerable and undefended, and it's not clear that you're going to get a new definition, or one that you like. Here you have a chance to live the way you *really want to live,* and that would be terrifying even at twenty or forty years old."

Faced with this new stage of life, you may find that you've lost all the excuses you always used for not living up to your ideals—being what you really wanted to be, and doing what you really wanted to do. *That* can be very stressful. You must now be totally honest with yourself and ask, Do I have what it takes to shape the life I've always said I wanted but couldn't have because of all my responsibilities?

The stress involved at retirement or other times of change doesn't have to be a problem—it can be the spice which adds zest to everyday life. The key to enjoying the situation is to accept the fact that there is going to be a certain amount of tension involved and get on with the business of exploration, preparation, and decision making which will let you fill the approaching years with planned pursuits, passions, and pastimes. Retirement is in a sense like moving into a new home—it's going to be a lot more comfortable and inviting if you take time and energy to clean, paint, and furnish it *before* you move in.

For the more than three dozen people across the country we interviewed about their retirement, it was often planning which made the difference between comfort and disquiet. Let's take a look at the experiences of some who did it right and others who are still picking up the pieces.

Some Winners, Some Losers, and Why

When we asked Warren Anderson, "What's the best way to plan for retirement?" he replied without blinking, "Plan *never* to retire."

Mr. Anderson, who at eighty-two still consults actively with former accounting clients, has maintained basically the same interests he had when he was younger. But he's shifted gears somewhat, allowing the work he enjoys to fill up just the time he is willing to give it instead of the time it used to demand of him. He thrives on his personal formula for happiness and is not bashful about giving advice to others.

"Plan to make your life a continuous, active life from day to day, and don't plan for a day when you have nothing useful to do," he says. "The important thing is to feel needed—in my case, by my clients, and by my friends."

Anderson said he tried volunteer work but found he didn't have the temperament for organizational politics. So he stuck with what he likes best, his work, and consults with attorneys and other accountants on tax planning and estate matters about twenty hours a week.

"I can still put in a ten- or twelve-hour day when necessary," the native New Yorker told us proudly. "When former clients around the country are calling for advice and want me to consult with their present accountants, this is something that is very important to me."

For Warren Anderson, the best way to maintain continuity and purpose in his life was to go on with his career in a slightly altered form. Others, though, want complete retirement from their former line of work—and this does not mean the sort of purposeless existence which Mr. Anderson feared. They are devoting their energies to new, different activities which have always held special appeal for them, but which had to wait until the freedom of retirement years for fulfillment.

Sarah Kaye Rhodes recently began her retirement in the same rural southern community where she grew up, married, raised a family, and taught school. She spent twenty-one years as a teacher, carefully building up her educational credentials and experience credits so that she could "retire at the top of the scale." At age sixty-four she did exactly as she had planned.

"I wanted to leave while they still wanted me," she explained, "while I was still doing a good job. And anyway, I wanted to do something else!"

Not that she totally dismissed her former experience—she has made her expertise on Florida's history available on a part-time basis as a resource person for the school system and as a consultant to the Florida Pioneer Museum. Now she is busy branching out into other appealing fields of endeavor.

Sarah's additional free time has rekindled her interest in canning and in furniture refinishing. Her next project is the oak bed, dresser, and washstand which have been in her family since her parents' marriage. Another of her consuming passions is gardening. The camellias, hibiscus, and other thriving flowers and green plants in her home give testimony to her success.

"I even bought a bicycle," Sarah said with a laugh, "and I don't know how to ride a bike. But I'm going to try it. I always felt kind of cheated that I had never learned."

Sarah is planning to go to see the Passion play in Oberammergau, which is presented once every ten years. And she is planning to relax—and enjoy relaxation for its own sake. "It's such a wonderful feeling to be in bed in the morning and know that I don't have to get right up," she said. "I don't have to do anything if I don't want to. I enjoy reading, and if I want to take the whole day and read, I do. Now I can."

Sarah Kaye Rhodes's personal retirement planning decisions, to continue to live in her comfortable, familiar home and build up the activities which would sustain her interests in the future, have done a great deal to keep her feeling young. A poorly planned decision, though, which is not thoroughly researched or considered, can really knock the wind out of your sails.

Betty Carlson and her husband Charles moved to a major American retirement community immediately after Charles left his business career. They had vacationed in the area in the past, so they felt it was "kind of natural for us to come here." But now she wonders whether they would have been better off to have stayed at home, in Denver.

Charles Carlson declined rapidly upon retirement. "When he retired, he just retired," Betty told us. She could not get him to participate in any of the recreational activities offered in the bustling retirement community or get him motivated to choose some of his own activities. After two or three years of a very sedentary existence he took a turn for the worse. He had a major illness, nearly losing his life on the operating table, and though he has regained his health, he has never really been the same.

"My husband is frail," Betty sighed. "His mental capacity is gone. He probably did not have the fortitude to make this kind of change. We should have tried out this style of living before coming here—tried it and thought it over—before making a total commitment."

The Carlsons, who had previously been highly involved in local politics, changed their entire life pattern without adequately considering whether the country club atmosphere they were moving to would fulfill their needs as politically active, non-leisure-oriented individuals. The plan they chose was not right for them—but they did actively make a choice.

Clarence Herlitz did not. When he was busy with an exciting career on the San Francisco police force, and subsequently in the private security field, the notion of preretirement planning was all but unheard of. He simply left work one day and settled into the quiet home he had bought in 1932 to live a tranquil existence with his wife. He lost a crucial part of his life when his wife died suddenly of cancer, four years ago. Now, at eighty-four, Mr. Herlitz has nothing to do but watch television and read the papers. He is healthy enough to be active outside his house but has no interests to pursue and few friends with whom to share his time. He is not restricted by financial worries. "I have more than a thousand dollars a month now," he told us. "That's a lot more than I had when I was working. But what good is it?" he asked soberly.

Probably the most dramatic cautionary tale is that of Thomas Johnson and his wife Catherine. "I suppose I have adjusted to retirement," the fifty-seven-year-old military dentist, Thomas Johnson, began hesitantly. "Maybe more accepting now, but not really adjusted," he added, reconsidering, as he reviewed his state of mind since he was forced to leave the military service four years ago.

"I would go back in a second to being a colonel in the army. Then I got up in the morning with a job to do and a place to go." The former military man, who continues to seek, and not find, a replacement lifestyle, repeatedly stressed the phrase "being in charge."

When Johnson's private dental practice had proved to be less than thriving, he had closed his office and moved his young family into the military establishment. He rose from captain to full colonel, enjoying the perquisites, authority, and income that accompanied the eagle on his shoulder.

As a reservist, Johnson could remain in the military only until age fifty-three. With regret but no real apprehension, the colonel left the bustling dental clinic which had been under his command and immediately enrolled at a major university nearby, receiving a master's degree in public health the following year.

Honoring an earlier commitment to his wife, Johnson moved with her to Washington, D.C. Catherine entered art school to fulfill her long-frustrated artistic aspirations, and Thomas began looking for a job.

Middle-management types more than twenty years his junior were condescending, and junior personnel officers looked askance at his military credentials. Johnson's characteristic enthusiasm and his polished appearance deteriorated.

His sense of displacement became so severe that with great reluctance he finally sought psychiatric assistance at Walter Reade Hospital in Washington. He was placed in group therapy, but none of his fellow participants were familiar with his problem. The retirement issue was never confronted directly, and after six months Johnson quit the group, still restless and troubled.

Dropping both his professional and military titles, anonymous private citizen Johnson sought meaningful occupation in a totally different arena. He joined Forty Plus, an organization for displaced older executives seeking reentry into the job market. For a short time the camaraderie there soothed his wounded pride, but the same faces never turned up at the Monday meetings. Membership provided only some temporary jobs.

Ready or not, Johnson was destined to be retired, and once he had accepted the inevitable, a more realistic appraisal of his employment prospects began to take shape. A tip from a former professor resulted in another temporary job working on a nationwide dental survey being conducted by a Washington consulting firm. The pay was commensurate with the professional level of the activity, and although the work required continuous travel for a year, participation in the team effort helped to elevate the dentist's self-respect. It was sometimes difficult for him to see his wife's success in her newfound career. Catherine's work was accepted for a number of competitive art shows, and she won several awards. The growth of her enthusiasm was matched by the decline of Thomas's sense of self-worth.

A move from a small crowded apartment to a four-bedroom town house helped to restore a sense of balance and normality to the couple's life. There was space for all the furniture collected over the years of foreign travel, a place for an art studio for Catherine and a study for Thomas, and a guest room for the children and grandchildren to use on visits.

Johnson has finally decided to abandon the idea of a second career. If the dental study is renewed for another year, he will continue with the project. When this appointment ends, Johnson has resolved to create a new lifestyle for himself, and to try to enjoy the fruits of his past labor—through travel and the variety of leisure activities available to him.

"If I had been aware that this kind of depression could occur," Johnson says now, "there are a number of things I would have done to avoid it. I would have read every available book on retirement—I had never read anything on the subject before. Maybe even gone to a psychiatrist. Certainly I would have talked to other retired people. It would be great if groups of retired people could get together with preretirees to say, 'Look, this is what is going to happen.'

"I never did any of that," the Colonel said rather wistfully. "I was so sure it wasn't going to happen to me."

THE POWER OF POSITIVE PLANNING

The experience of planning in a comprehensive way may be unfamiliar to you, and you may feel intimidated by the idea of calculating a long-term path for the future. The only real life-planning many people have done is financial, and even there you may feel you've been *reacting* to the forces at work upon you rather than *acting* positively to shape these forces. Yet the kind of life management in which decisions are made crisis by crisis is not only stressful and potentially hazardous, it can also leave one with an unsettled, threatened feeling even when nothing in particular is going wrong.

Retirement is not an unpredictable crisis. You may even know years in advance the precise day on which you will leave your job. If you plan accordingly, you can gain a wonderfully satisfying, calming, positive sense that you are in the driver's seat, perhaps for the first time in your life. Your mastery of the situation will enable you not only to face the expected developments in your life with poise but to cope more smoothly with the twists and turns along the path, since you will react to unexpected conditions by making adjustments to a sound basic plan rather than by trying to piece together responses to sudden threats.

It takes time to find a home which will exactly fit your future needs, to gain proficiency in a sport or hobby you would like to pursue, or to develop the skills needed to run a small business in retirement, if that's what appeals to you. You'll also need time to discover and evaluate the options available to you. Begin your planning early, and you will widen the range of possible choices when you do retire.

If you are married, a major advantage of thinking about retirement long before the day arrives is that it helps you and your spouse to reconcile and realign your individual expectations for the future. During the work years, when the job and family priorities are dominant, a marriage can move along quite nicely. When responsibilities start to shift, though, time commitments change, and personal abilities and desires reshape themselves to fit the new realities of retirement living. This can place tremendous strain on a marriage. If you plan together, you can use retirement to strengthen your bonds, to make your marriage an element of stability and pleasure in the face of change and uncertainty. If you are single, advance planning for retirement will help you create goals and a program of activities to help replace the structure and companionship now provided by work.

Planning for Tomorrow Helps You Today

The feeling of security which arises from planning for the future will make you calmer and more confident right now. By eliminating some of your fears and uncertainties about tomorrow, you can deal more effectively with the present, enjoying its pleasures and solving its problems. Everyday disasters which plague us all can recede somewhat in importance when viewed from a broader perspective. If you have achieved a sense of flow within your life and are able to distance yourself somewhat from current problems and see them in their proper magnitude, you will find your retirement years that much more rewarding.

By making a conscious effort to expand your leisure interests now, you can make time in your present schedule for hobbies and other personal interests which tend to be overlooked in the rush to get through the week. By considering the future state of your health, you will reap immediate benefits as well—you will be in more vigorous shape for life today. And you may find yourself growing closer to your spouse, as you discuss the future together, sharing decisions, solving problems, and exploring options as a couple.

Last but certainly not least, you can enjoy your retirement twice— once in planning for it and once in living it. Planning itself can be an enjoyable part of your current activities. There are dozens of major and minor items to pick up along the way, and the field of possibilities is wide and inviting. Discovering new options, discussing them with your spouse, family, and friends, and finally making your selections is a tremendously invigorating, challenging, and rewarding activity.

Take your time about making a comprehensive retirement plan, and be flexible in your thinking. Planning should be a broadening activity, not a restrictive one. One of my problems is that I tend to plan meticulously, and I can't stand it when quirks of fate change things around. I admire my wife's flexibility—she can say, "All right, so we won't do that, we'll do this." I'll say, "But we planned to do this other thing," and it's difficult for me to alter my expectations.

You don't have to set down ironclad rules and regulations which you are obliged to follow to the letter. At its best, preretirement planning is designed to open up the potential for future happiness in each of us, by channeling our energies in promising directions set by our own desires, and by creating a smooth, pleasant sense of progression from middle to later years.

Your Personal Equation for Retirement Happiness

Retirement planning is a way of balancing your needs and desires against your resources to produce the greatest possible personal happiness. You will have to arrive at a pretty good estimate of each element in this equation before you can make reasonable decisions for your future.

- Your *needs* in retirement take in not only the physical necessities of food, shelter, clothing, and medical care, but also your psychological requirements as a human being who needs purpose, interest, and satisfaction in life. You will have to base your judgment of future needs on the way you live today, with an added understanding of what new requirements growing older will impose on you in your efforts to remain comfortable, healthy, and happy.

When I retired, my wife perceived correctly (and I did not) that it was bad for me to be away from the power centers. Phoenix, Arizona, is a very nice place, but it's not a power center. I had the idea that I could just sit out there and the major networks would be burning up the long distance lines with offers. And for the first two or three years, it happened that way—my speaking schedule was full, and I was asked by NBC to do some important specials. But Ruth was right—they eventually stopped coming after me. She made me realize that in my early fifties maybe I shouldn't be sitting around expecting the world to beat a path to my door. Because by waiting, I was neglecting some important needs.

- Your *desires* for the future may include the fulfillment of life-long dreams, or simply a continuation of present pleasures. Whether your plans are modest or grand, it is essential that you give your imagination its full rein during the planning process. If you envision yourself as a crotchety old coot in retirement, your standards for happiness will fall far short of your potential. With an optimistic self-image fixed in your mind, you can explore the ways in which you want to use your time on two fronts—by learning more about what is available to you and by learning more about your own personal preferences.

There are people who can retire from a lifetime of work, do nothing, and thrive. They're the exception. Other people will just be compulsively busy—I'm that type.

I've retired three times. Every time I have sought to end some routine and turn to something else, I've become busier, because I tend to take on more than I should. I think, "I'm free to do all these things now," and suddenly I'm doing them. If someone came to me today and said, "How'd you like to go to India and film a piece on such and such?" I'd *have* to say no because the ABC schedule wouldn't permit me to do it. But as soon as I retired all of a sudden I was saying yes all over the place and I was up to my hips in activities that I wouldn't have committed myself to otherwise. So I've decided to give up on retirement for now.

Actually, I've never retired with the idea of sitting on the front porch with a fishing pole, but I surprised even myself when I came back to regular broadcasting to do *two* shows simultaneously. Since both shows (*Over Easy* and *20/20*) fulfilled true longtime desires, I simply couldn't turn down either one of them.

- Your *resources* are not arbitrarily fixed. You can shape the future resources at your disposal to best meet your needs and desires, if you give yourself some maneuvering room by planning ahead. When I left the *Today* show, I voluntarily reduced my income to a little over a fifth of what it had been. I still had a decent living standard, but in the ensuing three years I divested myself of a racing car, an airplane, and a trawler yacht. I found that I was not diminished a whit by getting rid of these things. If anything, my life was enhanced. No matter how lucky you are financially, you can only sit in one chair and wear one suit of clothes at a time. If you're not hungry or unclothed or in need of medical attention, wealth has no direct proportional meaning to the quality of your life. The key is to provide for those things that are really most important to you. And you can do that by planning ahead.

You may discover that your financial situation consists of a single large windfall or perhaps a steady continuing trickle of money. Your home can be merely a place to hang your hat between trips or a base in a community which offers you support and active involvement. Your family can be a source of joy or just a set of names on envelopes at Christmas time. By actively building, nurturing, and managing all your future resources, you will be able to maximize the physical and emotional assets which will sustain you for the rest of your life.

This book requires work on your part—I don't want you to simply sit back and read passively. I'll be asking you to write letters, explore places, maybe even get out a hammer and nails and make some alterations on your home to make it a safer place to retire in.

The major effort on your part, though, is thinking. Organized, lively, exploratory, and intensely creative thinking. Solving the problems of retirement is work, sometimes hard work, requiring concentration and the devotion of a substantial chunk of time. At the same time, the mental effort you put into planning for the future can be stimulating and enjoyable, and it is certainly well worth the trouble. I hope you will enjoy the process of planning, with its many challenges and rewards, and that the materials presented here will help to enrich, enliven, and perhaps even lengthen the best years of your life.

RETIREMENT PLANNING SOURCES AND RESOURCES

Numerous opportunities, privileges, and sources of information are available especially for older Americans, and you can and should begin taking advantage of them now in planning for your retirement. A good place to start is to join one of the national associations actively serving the needs of the adult community.

The American Association of Retired Persons (AARP) and its companion organization, the National Retired Teachers Association (NRTA), make up a large and worthwhile body. To join AARP you must be fifty-five or older, but you need not have retired yet to be eligible. NRTA requires that you have worked in the field of education, without age limitations. Dues as of this writing are $4 a year or $10 for three years.

There are many benefits and services available to members, including:

- A bimonthly magazine. *Modern Maturity* is a glossy magazine sent to AARP members; NRTA members receive *NRTA Journal*. Both are filled with articles and features of importance to older Americans. The associations also publish monthly news bulletins to relay current developments of interest to members, as well as a series of retirement booklets on such subjects as housing, health, safety, and psychology, which are available free of charge.
- Purchase plans offering members discounts on group health insurance, medicines and medical supplies, travel, and various other services.
- Assistance in tax preparation, consumer affairs, employment service, health education, and crime prevention.

For further information and membership applications, write to American Association of Retired Persons, Membership Processing Department, P.O. Box 199, Long Beach, CA 90801.

Action for Independent Maturity (AIM) is a division of AARP which concentrates on the needs of people between fifty and sixty-five. Full membership is open to this age group only, but associate membership carries most of the same privileges for those older or younger. Membership dues include a subscription to the bimonthly magazine *Dynamic Years,* which addresses questions of health, career, housing, travel, and preretirement planning in middle age. AIM's free guidebooks also provide valuable in-depth coverage of major midlife issues, including physical fitness, money management, and legal affairs. The other privileges, such as insurance, pharmacy discounts, and travel service, are similar to those offered to AARP members.

Dues for AIM members are $5 a year, and membership information can be obtained by writing to AIM Membership Processing Department, P.O. Box 199, Long Beach, CA 90801.

The National Association of Mature People (NAMP) is a non-profit educational membership organization offering retirement planning services, a bimonthly magazine, local chapters, discount-purchasing programs, and a variety of booklets designed to assist members in preparing for and enjoying the best years. Membership costs $4.00 per year ($10.00 for 3 years), and further information may be obtained by writing NAMP at 2000 Classen Center, P.O. Box 26792, Oklahoma City, OK 73126.

FOR FURTHER READING

Resource Books

The following are valuable guides to services and resources for older Americans:

Tenenbaum, Frances, *Over 55 Is Not Illegal;* Houghton Mifflin paperback, 1979. Includes detailed, state-by-state coverage of educational programs, volunteer opportunities, community programs for older people, jobs and employment agencies, institutions, organizations, and agencies which serve retirees and preretirees.

Norback, Craig and Peter, *The Older American's Handbook;* Van Nostrand Reinhold paperback, 1977. Comprehensive listings, complete with local names and addresses of offices and agencies, providing practical information and assistance in medical and nursing care, housing, recreation, legal services, employment, in-home services, food, transportation, mental health, and counseling for older and retired Americans.

Periodicals

In addition to the AARP and AIM membership magazines, *50 Plus* does an admirable job of informing adult readers about topics essential to their greater enjoyment of life. The monthly publication calls on the services of such well-known columnists as Jack Anderson (politics), Lawrence Galton (medicine), Judith Crist (film reviews), and Sam Shulsky (investments) to provide reliable advice and interesting points of view. *50 Plus* is available by subscription for $10.95 for one year, from *50 Plus,* 99 Garden Street, Marion, OH 43302.

A more recent entry in the field of magazines for mature readers is *Prime Time,* which describes itself as "for people in their prime." The monthly publication aims at people between forty-five and sixty-five who enjoy the finer things in life, particularly in travel, food, leisure activities, culture, and financial affairs. *Prime Time* is available at many newsstands, or by subscription from *Prime Time,* P.O. Box 8600, Greenwich, CT 06835, for $12 a year.

United Retirement Bulletin is a monthly newsletter offering preretirement planning tips and financial advice. It is available at $18 per year, with a money-back guarantee, from United Business Service, 210 Newbury Street, Boston, MA 02116. The newsletter editors have compiled a 48-page booklet, "Where to Live When You Retire," which is available free with a one-year subscription.

2

RETIREMENT—
TOGETHER
AND ALONE

The supreme happiness of life is the conviction that we are loved.

VICTOR HUGO

FOR richer and for poorer, in sickness and in health, yes—but what about in retirement?

Over the years since you made your marriage vows you've shared the pleasures and responsibilities of life together. There were children to raise, money to be made, and an endless stream of neighbors, friends, doctors, lawyers, relatives, teachers, newspaper boys, and auto mechanics to deal with. You developed a system for coping with all this. Each of you staked out areas of authority and expertise, and you established a decision-making process to handle all the choices which were likely to arise.

Retirement will shake up some of the basic structures of your marital system. The demands on your time will change, so the daily chores may have to be allocated in a different manner. Can the interests you have shared in your free time be expanded to fill three or four times as many hours together? How will your marriage respond to the changing roles in your lives as the importance of being a breadwinner, a homemaker, a father or mother is altered? And what if one of you is ready to retire while the other wants to keep working?

My relationship with Ruth went through some changes while we were in Arizona, but if anything the bonds were cemented more tightly—not just because the kids were grown and off on their own, but because of the added time we had together. I could include her in many of my projects, which I had been unable to do in my broadcast career. To cite just two examples, she helped me put together the course in communications I taught at Arizona State University and participated with me in sessions of the Center for the Study of Democratic Institutions in Santa Barbara. We were closer than ever before.

Many of the marital stresses of retirement can be dealt with in advance, while others will come up unexpectedly. By establishing a sense of cooperation you can go a long way toward making all the adjustments easier.

Use the preretirement planning questions you *know* you will face to set a pattern for the rest of your decision making. Where will the money come from? Where will you live? What leisure activities will you pursue? Work out the answers together, as a couple, and you will have built a strong foundation for your future marital happiness.

FACING NEW BARRIERS TO COMMUNICATION AND COMPROMISE

How effectively do you communicate with your spouse? I'm not asking how often you have probing heart-to-heart discussions or lively intellectual debates. Often the way two people look at and act toward each other speaks more eloquently of their mutual love and respect than a volume of words. A marriage in which affection is both understood and expressed, information is exchanged easily, and decisions are calmly shared is likely to function well when faced with the changing circumstances of retirement.

Special problems can impede communications, even if your relationship has worked well for years. By spotting these potential difficulties early on, confronting them together, and if necessary getting help from a friend or a professional, you can avoid marital stress and strain in your transition to retirement.

One common problem centers on the fear of retirement and, with it, the fear of growing old. People who dread the appearance of a wrinkle and feel obliged to apologize for or to lie about their age will not welcome a discussion about retirement; they may even regard it as a form of personal attack. The result: Retirement becomes an off-limits subject, a mutually avoided danger zone. The risk of not planning is that you may transform what might otherwise be a gentle emotional bump at retirement into a towering precipice.

It may take a subtle but diligent effort to change such a spouse's attitude toward retirement. Perhaps you can convince him or her to read some of the positive, up-to-date books and publications which show what aging can really mean, or to talk to a retired person who is genuinely happy. These strategies will help your partner see that the future is not as bleak as some of the traditional beliefs about aging and retiring have made it seem.

In the long run, even if the subject remains a delicate one, you should *gently* insist on beginning preretirement planning right away. Focus your attention on the specific future possibilities which are particularly appealing to both of you. Perhaps you would both like to go out dancing more often, or be able to travel without strict back-to-work deadlines. Organize your discussion around the items which please you both, and then you can start to deal with retirement decisions as they relate to these key concerns. You will develop a set of priorities in financial planning, deciding where to live, and incorporating other leisure activities as your discussion branches out, until you have a fairly comprehensive retirement plan and can move in the directions you have outlined for the future. Orient yourselves toward the positive. By taking this approach you can avoid focusing your discussion on a negatively charged question like "What will we do when we grow old?" and decide instead "How can we have the life we would like in the future?"

You may face another problem: finding a compromise when you disagree. This can be more difficult than it has ever been in the past, since a decision made about retirement life is often seen as the final word on a particular topic. While you may have given in in previous years on the subject of a place to live or a major purchase, assuming that "someday we'll do it my way," it's hard to be so understanding about retirement decisions. You may have the feeling that if you don't get your way now, you probably never will. So what results is a hardening of positions and rapidly fraying nerves.

The underlying give-and-take of your marital decision-making system will have a great deal to do with your ability to reach compromises about your retirement plans. So will your creativity when it comes to finding solutions which at least partially answer all of your needs. How can you reach creative solutions together? We interviewed one husband who was eager to travel a great deal after retirement but whose wife hated sterile motels, the constant packing and unpacking, and the varying quality of the mattresses—which was a real issue for her because of her bad back. Their solution? They saved up enough to buy a comfortable motor home and equipped it with a bed which met the wife's specifications. In the past five years they have visited most of the continental United States in a state of matrimonial harmony.

In addition to the soothing effects of loving concession and problem-solving ingenuity, you can defuse some of your more potentially explosive arguments by looking for temporary solutions. There is no reason that you cannot change your mind if you make a conscious effort to leave yourself a way out. If a husband insists on living in Omaha near the children and a wife has always dreamed of living in a retirement community in Florida, there is probably no compromise location that will satisfy both of them. However, by *renting* instead of *buying* a home in one place or the other, and agreeing to try both possibilities for limited periods of time, some of the pressure is taken off. Don't be misled into thinking that you will be too old to pick up and start over if your initial decision doesn't suit you. You can expect to continue to change in situation and desires after sixty-five just as you did when you were younger, and to a large extent you will be able to adapt your lifestyle to your wishes.

Your Marital Roles in Retirement

A husband and wife serve many vital functions for each other throughout their life together. As you grow older, these roles remain basically the same but are subtly affected by changing circumstances and living conditions. If you are conscious of what you expect from your spouse in retirement and, equally important, of what your spouse expects from you, then you will be able to anticipate the areas where one of you may tend to disappoint the other, and you can work together to prevent this from occurring.

Your spouse has always shared with you—the good times and the bad. And with all the extra time available after you retire, the two of you will be able to enjoy many more hours together, building a better, stronger marriage. Right?

Well, yes and no. A radical change in the amount of time you spend together can upset the rather delicate balance between togetherness and privacy. And if yours is a marriage in which absence had really made the heart grow fonder, suddenly becoming twenty-four-hour-a-day *companions* could be the death knell to a stable relationship.

Some retired couples find it impossible to see too much of each other. Karl and Doris Hoff, for example, are quite content with the change in their forty-six-year marriage since Karl left his job three years ago. "We enjoy each other's company, and we go everywhere together," he told us. "We even coordinate the colors of our outfits. Doris gets dressed first; then I check on her outfit and select my own."

Many others did not feel like the Hoffs. Harry Mann said, "The problem is where a man and a woman don't like the same things, and yet they are always tagging along after one another. One woman I know follows her husband when he goes to play pool. He's busy playing, and she's sitting over there on a chair in the poolroom knitting away. I'm sure he would like to have her go somewhere else, but he can't tell her to go.''

The most frequent complaint we heard from married retirees was that one spouse had no life of his or her own. Instead of lively interplay and interdependence there was a constant demand made on one of the marital partners to provide entertainment for the other.

There *can* be too much togetherness, but there certainly doesn't have to be. The key in planning is to have separate activities available, as well as activities you pursue as a couple. You can't tell exactly how much time you will want to spend together. Most likely the only times you've been together day and night for more than a few days in the past have been vacations, and that is certainly not enough to judge the effect of having one another's company on a full-time basis.

You should therefore go into retirement with a fairly clear idea of what you would like to do with your time alone, and what activities you can share with your spouse. You should develop an understanding that there will be a balance between your private lives and your life together. Only by testing and experiencing will you discover the actual proportions in that balance.

There are going to be people other than your spouse in your life, of course, and it's wise to plan your leisure activities and living arrangements accordingly. In all your retirement planning, the question is not just *what* you will do, but *who* you will do it with. There is no reason not to have a wonderful assortment of fascinating people with whom to share your life, but they won't appear like magic. You will have to consider which clubs and organizations, volunteer or paid-employment projects and activities will bring you in contact with the type of people whose company you enjoy. Retirement seems to bring out the friendly streak in many people. As Harry Mann, who lives with his wife in a large retirement community, told us, ''There's more affection now between friends. It seems we got to know more people the first year we were here, and became pretty close to them, than we did in all those years in Chicago.''

Sharing companionship desires openly becomes particularly important when you are planning to retire and your spouse will keep on working. Be sure you know what your spouse intends in this direction—many a man has been unpleasantly surprised in recent years to learn that his wife's late-blooming career is more appealing to her than a housebound existence with a newly retired hubby. Lay your cards on the table early on, and you will be able to make your individual plans without undue friction or disappointment.

After years of firsthand observation, your husband or wife has a more intimate knowledge of your past history, your personal strengths and your weaknesses than anyone else—in some cases a better understanding of your personality than you have. In planning for retirement, your spouse can be the most valuable and caring *adviser* you could ever hope for. He or she can offer another point of view, seasoned with genuine concern and love.

Listen to your spouse's opinion. And try to be a constructive adviser when it comes to your spouse's proposed plans as well. If you have succeeded in establishing open lines of communication, you should be able to point out potential problems and offer reasonable alternatives without treading on toes. It may tax your powers of diplomacy, but in the long run the effort and caring involved will be appreciated.

Of course, sometimes the best course is *not* being tactful. Sometimes you just have to keep after a spouse to make sure that unpleasant or troublesome tasks are accomplished.

The point is not to nag in order to get your own way, but rather to have agreed beforehand on a course of action, and then make sure that the decision is put into effect. Helen Dickey told us about her own experience immediately following her husband Ralph's retirement. "For two years he had been making plans for a little woodworking business of his own when he retired.

"The thing was, when he finally left his job, he never set foot in the workshop. It got to the point where I thought I would kill him. He did nothing but watch TV, demanded that his meals be served right on time, like he was a king, and never lifted a finger to help out in the house. I tried talking to him, but it always turned into an argument very quickly.

"So I started bringing his meals downstairs, and his mail, leaving them on his workbench, and telling him that's where he'd find them. A few days after I started this I heard the sound of his power saw starting up for the first time since he'd left his job. By the end of the month he was filling orders. I guess he appreciated my nagging in the long run.''

You have had years to discover the best way of dealing with your own spouse and can judge the degree of gentleness or firmness needed to get the job done. A loving spouse can provide that necessary push, and by doing so can make the difference between self-defeating procrastination and rewarding activity.

There are times in every marriage when you must become your spouse's *helper*. It may be as a confidant, giving your time and a sympathetic ear. It may be on a more mundane level, doing a job, running an errand, making a few phone calls, or taking over some chores temporarily. The spirit of mutual cooperation and self-sacrifice is central to a healthy relationship, and will continue to be for as long as you live.

What will happen, though, if there are substantial changes in your spouse's life as you grow older—how can you best help then? If you are faced with a situation in which one of you is not able to keep up physically with the other, the only solution is to accept the facts, without dwelling on "what if's" and "if only's," and to try to build a lifestyle that offers the greatest possible enjoyment for each of you, within the limitations involved. As Hershel McManus, a recently remarried sixty-nine-year-old who has had his own health setbacks in recent years, told us, "At this age you have to make a lot of adjustments. Younger, you wouldn't make them, you would just say, 'the hell with it.' But you have more tolerance at this stage in life because you've been through more.''

Responsibilities: New Ways to Share

In many ways a marriage is like a business. There are a number of jobs and responsibilities which must be undertaken. There is money and property to be managed, legal affairs, public relations with friends and relatives, and a fair amount of manual labor in cooking, cleaning, and home maintenance.

Over the years a couple sets up a division of labor. Whether you have lived the traditional roles of husband who works and supervises financial affairs and wife who raises children and runs the home, or have shared the money-earning responsibilities in a two-career home and rearranged the other family jobs as well, there are certain areas which each of you oversees. Within your individual areas of responsibility you have substantial independence making decisions on how the task is to be handled, taking a certain amount of pride in the successful completion of even rather mundane chores.

Then one or both of you retire, and the division of labor is suddenly shifted. There are a great many free hours which used to be spent earning a living, and those available hours can be a blessing or a burden.

Suppose one of you is suddenly out of a job, and in order to fill up time starts taking over the responsibilities of the other. Traditionally it is the husband who appoints himself home maintenance supervisor upon his retirement. He starts explaining to his wife how much more efficiently she could be doing the housework, doing the shopping, even rearranging the furniture. She is very likely put out; after all, her system has worked for years—and worked just fine, thank you.

At this point, with the couples we spoke to, simply discussing the question of who would do what was usually enough to solve the problem. Some of the wives had held on tightly to the reins of the home, insisting that this was their work. Far more frequently, though, some equitable new division of household chores was agreed upon. Herb Rudolph, for instance, does the dishes and cooks breakfast every morning, even though he had never cooked before in his life. "Ann used to fix breakfast even when I had to get up for work at 4:30 in the morning. I never went without breakfast, and now I've turned the tables on her."

Deal with a Troubled Marriage Now

As you can see, there is a great deal of joint effort involved in entering retirement together. It is unavoidable that some of the adjustments will be difficult to make, and you may find your patience pushed to the limit if your partner has extreme personal difficulties in dealing with the transition.

Retirement can be the last straw in a troubled relationship. One man we met in Sun City, Arizona, was eagerly awaiting his forthcoming third marriage. His second marriage had lasted for sixteen years but collapsed just nine months after he and his wife arrived in the retirement community. "It wasn't a very loving relationship. We didn't fight. She just went her way and I went mine. I raised her two kids, sent them to college and all that, and then suddenly I'm sitting there with no one when I retired." It took him quite a while to climb "out of the pits" after his divorce, but happily he found a new, more loving relationship after the joint traumas of divorce and retirement had subsided. Not everyone is so lucky.

Under no circumstances should you expect retirement to solve your problems if your marriage is not working well now. It is easy to blame your marital difficulties on job tensions and time spent apart. But if the time you now spend together is tense and uncomfortable, it is likely to be more so when you retire and have even more time together.

When you remove a major element in your lifestyle, the others look much more important. With daily work activities gone, and with them a great deal of social and intellectual interaction with other people, your marriage will stand in the spotlight, with its flaws mercilessly exposed. If you know those flaws are going to give you trouble, try to deal with them now, either through your own efforts or with the help of a professional counselor.

PREPARING TO BE ALONE

There is, of course, more than just housework to keeping the businesslike functions of your marriage running smoothly, and financial and social responsibilities can also be shared in a more equal fashion in retirement. But what if you never married or are widowed or divorced? Then the entire burden falls to you—and you must prepare to shoulder it.

Taking on the Planning Yourself

Most of the jobs which you shared in the past will continue when only one remains. The financial affairs of the family are particularly urgent matters, of course, and these are all too frequently the exclusive domain of the husband. By dealing frankly and openly with the question of what will happen if one of you passes away, you can effectively prevent the additional burden of financial pressures at a time when emotional tensions are at their highest. Planning together for widowhood serves another purpose as well—it demonstrates the depth of your love for your partner.

The wives need the most protection for two good reasons. First, husbands have traditionally assumed the role of financial director of the family. This is unfortunate because the financially ignorant widow is a sad figure, an easy target for major mistakes and assorted con artists.

Second, the woman is more likely to be left alone. Census statistics show that 63 percent of the women over sixty-five are single, versus only 22 percent of the men.

What should *both* of you know about your family business affairs?

- You should each know exactly what your assets are and where they are. This includes all bank accounts, insurance policies, investments, and property. See the Personal Affairs Checklist, a useful guideline to follow, on page 147.
- Be careful to avoid the potential pitfalls of joint ownership. After the death of a spouse, assets owned in both your names can be frozen until after the will is probated, leaving the survivor without access to needed funds. Discuss the matter with

your lawyer. Be sure to keep copies of important papers accessible.

- Be sure that you each understand the provisions of any pension plans through which you are receiving benefits. See pages 175–83 for details.

- Understand your retirement budget. Go over your past financial records, including your income tax reports, the major bills, and the checkbook, together. And as you continue to spend money and make financial decisions in retirement, share your choices with your partner.

- Be sure that *each* of you has a will that is up-to-date and valid. See Chapter 9 for details.

- Each of you should be acquainted with the family financial and legal advisers, including your lawyer, your accountant, your broker, your insurance agent, and any other important professional counselors with whom you deal.

- Make sure that each of you has the knowledge needed to continue to manage your financial affairs in the manner you have decided on. If your retirement plan calls for substantial investments in the stock market, it is crucial that you both understand how to play the market according to the strategy you have developed.

- It is a good idea to make funeral arrangements ahead of time. No one finds contacting a funeral director and discussing the options available a pleasant task, but as soon as you leave him with instructions regarding your wishes, you can forget the matter. By doing so you make that inescapably traumatic period after the death of a spouse a little bit less difficult.

Retiring Alone

Whether you have always been single or have lost a spouse through death or divorce, approaching retirement as an unmarried person can pose special problems. It can also offer distinctive rewards. There is a great freedom in retiring alone, in the ability to direct your time and money to pursuits which fill your personal needs, without feeling constrained by the demands of a spouse.

The single retiree may have a larger challenge when it comes to finding rewarding activities to fill the time formerly devoted to a job. As Judy Salwen, a New York-based preretirement consultant, points out, "There are many more hours that a single person has to think about, because he or she has to take total responsibility for the shaping of time—there is no one else to take over some of the initiative." Of course, single people have already developed strengths and capabilities from previous experience in independent living. "You've learned to come and go as you please, make your own decisions, make friends on your own, and have a certain freedom which comes from not being directly accountable to someone else," explains Ms. Salwen. So the single person can rely on inner resources which may be more highly developed than those of a married individual suddenly entering retirement.

Adult singles often report that they appreciate the advantages of their situation and are reluctant to give them up. Lila Weir, a sixty-five-year-old retiree who has been divorced since 1947, told us, "When you've been alone this long, it's pretty difficult to adjust to another person. My friends and I have talked about getting married again, and we have all decided against it. I wouldn't want to get married now. I treasure my privacy."

Privacy does not mean isolation, and living alone does not mean being lonely—not by a long shot. The single retiree needs friends, family, neighbors, and acquaintances, and will get the most out of his or her retirement years by arranging to have frequent contact with these stimulating, interesting individuals. You should surround yourself with people you enjoy—a smorgasbord of humanity. Working, learning, and playing with others will allow you to find out more about them, and them about you, and the possibilities for closer relationships will grow. Judging from some close personal observation, I deeply believe that romance and new friendships can be as fresh, exciting, and attainable at eighty as at eighteen, as long as you are open to them and there isn't something seriously wrong with you. Fred Astaire, Averell Harriman, and Lowell Thomas are among those I know who have enjoyed romance after eighty.

Assert Your Single Self

You may find that creating a retirement lifestyle that suits you means saying no to other people's plans for you—plans which may be persistently, annoyingly thrust upon you. Your children may feel inclined to try to run your life because of a misguided sense of responsibility, a notion that you are too old to be left alone to take care of yourself. Don't be talked into a state of dependency as a result of their fears. Measure your own capabilities and stand up for your individuality wherever possible. If you *do* need help from your children, accept it graciously, but hold onto your privacy for dear life.

On the other side of the picture are the family members who think, since you are not working and don't have a spouse to care for, you are available to take care of babysitting, housesitting, or waiting all day for a delivery man to arrive. You may even find yourself pressured to move in with some other single relative, in order to free your family from the burden of looking after both of you! The answer to all this meddling is obvious, but instead of just getting angry, get at the root of the problem. Teach your children some respect for the rights of older people, and make them understand the stereotypes and half-truths which may control their thinking. You will be doing them a favor by keeping them from underestimating their own future abilities. Someday they'll be retiring too.

3

VARIETY
IN RETIREMENT
LIFESTYLES

Age is opportunity no less than youth itself, though in another dress.

HENRY WADSWORTH LONGFELLOW

I F you were given a ten dollar bill to spend as you like, what would you do with it? Buy a book? A delicacy for dinner? Would you add some of your other money to it and buy something big, or use the ten dollars a few cents at a time for a few small purchases?

Given the diversity of human tastes, there is clearly no one answer—it's only right if it's the one for you. You can delight in a wide, inviting set of circumstances from which to choose. And above and beyond what you might *do* with the money, you can derive pleasure from the fact that you received it in the first place.

What's the best way to spend your time and money in retirement? There is no single answer, any more than there is a single best way to spend a ten dollar bill. But you can be sure the odds of your coming to a satisfying decision are much slimmer if you don't know what possibilities are available to you and the important point to remember about enjoying your money in retirement is not how much you start out with but how much is left to spend *at your discretion* after paying the bills, the taxes, and other necessary expenses. Remove from your budget the costs of supporting your children, the hefty mortgage payments, work expenses like business clothes and commuting costs, and a substantial portion of your tax bill, and you may well find there's more money than ever left over for you to put to good use.

Your skills as a shopper have been tested many times in the past. But when you set out to invest your time and money in building a new lifestyle, your feeling for the alternatives may be somewhat lacking, and you might not even realize the gaps in your knowledge.

Do you feel you have a pretty complete, accurate sense of what's out there for you to choose from? If, like most Americans, you are not learning about the types of retirement lifestyles through firsthand observation—i.e., older people you really admire—how do you get this information? It is, after all, vital to your personal planning. We acquire much of what we know today through the mass media, by watching television, listening to radio, or reading newspapers, magazines, and books. Yet the media have had a tendency to shortchange the concerns of older people. Television, which is now *the* major source of information for the American public, has tended to ignore old people entirely or slant the material to conform with the hallowed stereotypes of old fogeys—people we may pity, perhaps even fear, but certainly not admire or emulate. Most people, then, have no positive role model of what life can be like in retirement, and one goal of this book is to provide such a model, to use the experience of others as a basis for pointing out the exciting new opportunities open to those who are aware and prepared.

*   *   *

YOUR GROWING OPTIONS

You'd be cheating yourself if you based your retirement on what your father did twenty years ago, or what the neighbor across the street did ten years ago. Changes are taking place in society, in medical knowledge, and in attitudes and opportunities, and they are opening doors to a new kind of retirement.

- You can live longer by adopting better lifelong habits. The earlier you start, the better your chances for an active old age blessed with continued health.
- You can stay on the job longer if that's what you want. Legislation passed in 1978 guarantees most workers freedom from mandatory retirement until age seventy (see page 307 for the exceptions to this rule).
- You can earn money throughout your life through part-time work or a business of your own. You will, of course, have to prepare during your regular working career for the employment you will want in the future.
- You can keep on learning and growing. Learning is a lifelong activity, and learning institutions, from trade and correspondence schools to colleges and universities, are making it easier for older people to further their education, by changing the admissions processes, providing financial assistance where needed, and even bringing classes from the isolated campus to more convenient locations.
- Marriage, remarriage, and living together are undergoing major upheavals in our society, and are not at all limited to the young and the restless. Growing numbers of people are establishing new loving relationships in their sixties, seventies, and eighties. And the facts about senior sex are finally coming into the open, revealing the truth that sexual pleasure and intimacy are welcome, important, and (barring disease,

injury, or psychological disorder) physically feasible as long as you are breathing.

- People are living in retirement all over the country—not only in the Sunbelt—and communities all over are adapting to the needs of an older population. Retirement communities, if they are your preference, are growing and changing as well.

- Retirees are healthier, more capable, and more active than ever before, and they are finding meaningful ways to put their substantial talents to use. In every community there are organizations courting retirees as volunteers in programs which make a considerable difference to the well-being of society as a whole.

- The political and financial clout of older Americans is now being recognized, and the first results are coming in. By becoming active, demanding proper attention to your continuing rights and desires, you can help assure that the resources for a happy retirement will be there when you need them.

THE FACE OF RETIREMENT TODAY

How are these changes and others affecting the way people retire today? To find out, we spent some time with retirees across the country, to ask them how they are finding life as we enter this new decade. The individuals we spoke with were all making ends meet, and most reported that they are happy in their retirement.

Some retirees we interviewed seemed content with a lifestyle of peace and quiet, similar to the working people I know who appear satisfied with simply making it through the day. However, the people who were making the most of their retirement years, whose enthusiasm and energy would be impressive at any age, were those who had found meaningful activities to involve and stimulate their thoughts and emotions. The activities which sparked their dedication varied widely, but there are certain common denominators for all of them:

- *Schedule.* Whether it's a matter of keeping an appointment or simply a routine set by the individual to keep his or her life in order, they all have a time scheme for the day or the week.
- *Goal.* Sometimes this is a definite completion point for a project, sometimes simply a feeling of progress or of making an ongoing contribution.
- *Other people.* All of them have some involvement beyond casual acquaintance through what they are doing. The relationships they have developed might be teacher-pupil, customer-client, worker-to-worker, or friend-to-friend, but they all required an effort in building up personal bonds and reaping the rewards of interacting with endlessly stimulating, amazingly diverse individuals.
- *Sense of challenge.* Instead of choosing the easiest possible activities, the retirees who seem to be living life to the fullest are seeking out more difficult tasks, both for the pure enjoyment of succeeding at them and for the feeling of self-assertion and pride they have while doing them.

For some of the people we interviewed, a change in lifestyle meant new involvement in business, or educational achievement, or finding romantic happiness in a second or third marriage. All have one strength in common: They have enough faith in themselves and their abilities to take a chance on getting involved. No one could tell them they were "past their prime."

What can we hope to do with our retirement years? The answer is different for each of us, based not only on our differing talents and ambitions, but on the opportunities open to us as well. Some people find the right opening just presents itself to them, in a happy coincidence. Others have to work a little harder to find the lifestyle that will make retirement work well. In either case, you have to recognize your opportunity and give it your best shot, without holding back.

Some Successful Choices

In the business world, experience and know-how are often the most valuable assets a company can have, and generally these resources come only with age. Many chief executives maintain control of huge enterprises well into their seventies and eighties, and this is increasingly true in lower-level positions as well. Daniel Grayson had never intended to be part of this growing trend—he had planned to sit back and enjoy the leisurely lifestyle of retirement living. But he changed his mind—and his plans.

Grayson has retired twice now—the first time in 1958, when he sold a prosperous small department store in Burlington, Vermont, and moved down to Florida to soak up the sun, and again in 1971, from a second career which gave him even more power, satisfaction, and financial reward than the first. That first retirement just didn't stick—some perceptive person in a local drugstore chain couldn't let all that business experience and talent go to waste and convinced Grayson to join the firm.

He brought with him a special understanding of the soft-goods market and increased the sale of nondrug items by inventing new ways of displaying, pricing, and packaging them to encourage impulse buying. His picture recently appeared beside that of the president and chairman of the board in the annual report of the nationally known retail chain, in recognition of his vital contribution to the firm's growth.

In 1971 Grayson became a reluctant retiree at the age of sixty-two, when his back began giving him trouble. From time to time he still misses being in the business world, despite a current lifestyle which includes a pleasant assortment of entertainment opportunities and a lot of travel.

"I get that passing fancy," he admitted, "but I get over it fast. Because of my back, I wouldn't be able to return, though I enjoyed it very much. I couldn't wait to get up in the morning and go to work. It was a challenge and they were good people to work with—a very hard combination to find as a rule. It's been fine—both the retirement and looking back at the job I did. I'm very pleased with both."

*   *   *

Your past accomplishments can form the basis for your future success, but it doesn't always work out that way. Wanita Allen was delighted to retire from her long career at the Ford Motor Company plant in Detroit. Her work had been a limiting factor in her life, making little use of her substantial talents.

She was just sixteen when she quit school to get married, and the children came soon after, so she had been obliged to earn a living from a very early age. It was not until fifty years later that she achieved one of her lifetime goals: She was awarded an associate degree from the local community college at sixty-six, and now plans to complete the requirements for her bachelor's degree and go on to a career in gerontology.

Ms. Allen has become a woman of some importance in her community. She is a member of the mayor's Commission on Aging in Detroit, and is a member of the Michigan Society of Gerontology. She has directed the operations of a community center for senior citizens, written a resource book for seniors, and been an active force in the battle against housing discrimination. When we met her she was looking forward to attending an upcoming assembly of the Consumer Federation in Washington, D.C. But it has taken a great deal of change and growth for her to attain her present position of prominence and personal satisfaction.

Divorced several years after her teenage marriage, Ms. Allen accepted what she believed a black woman would have to in that day and age—she took a job on the assembly line at the Ford Motor plant and stayed there for twenty-eight years. "When I first started out," she recalled, "men didn't work with women. You were always put on the hardest jobs because they were hoping if it was hard enough, maybe you'd quit." Despite the obstacles she faced, Ms. Allen worked her way up to a position as senior inspector on the line. She was assigned to the piston section, where there were grinding machines and the air quality was particularly poor. Two years before she was eligible for full retirement benefits, her lungs were in such bad shape that she was forced to quit, losing over half her pension, and it took four years for her to recover her health.

Then she began looking around for something to do with her new-found energy. "I was really at a loss when I first came home. When you've been working every day for twenty-eight years, it's hard to adjust. I had so much time on my hands.''

Finally she heard about the UAW retirement center, and one of the directors convinced her to take on the job of site director at the UAW Southwest Activities Center for senior citizens. She accepted the four-hour-a-day salaried position with reluctance, but thrived in her new responsibility. Despite a schedule that may be a bit too hectic, Wanita Allen has found health, success, and pride in her retirement years, which she sincerely believes are the best years of her life. In a very real sense, she began her true life's work in her sixties, and is now further from retirement than ever.

Jack Scussel is another individual who has taken advantage of a second career after retirement. He left a full-time, successful position in advertising and design after twenty-nine years to create a new lifestyle for his wife and himself and cringes at the word *retirement*—he prefers the word *change*. By carefully planning their choices for the future together, Jack and Mary Lou Scussel have made a major transition smoothly and happily, with a new home and new job interests for both of them. They set out on this adventurous new path on Jack's fiftieth birthday.

After twenty years as a commercial artist with a thriving design studio of his own, he became restless. With the youngest of his seven children nearing the end of his education, a large financial burden was gone. "I finally realized I wasn't going to become one of the top ten designers in the city of Chicago," he recalls. "I think I was in the top hundred, maybe in the top fifty, but I saw that my capabilities were only going to take me so far and I was reaching that plateau. And I asked myself, 'Why continue to do it and not achieve any more? Now strike out on something else. There's got to be another avenue. Why don't you go and search for it?' "

For the next four years he worked as an account executive for a former client, then did free-lance design work for another three years. By this time Jack and Mary Lou had established their "five-year plan."

"In the five-year plan, the idea of change was threefold," Jack explained. "Change geographically, change professionally, and change psychologically—the elimination of job-related pressures and worries.'' They had purchased a place on Marco Island in Florida with the idea that they might retire there. Eventually they settled in Clearwater because it had a larger population and would provide better job opportunities for Mary Lou and a bigger market for Jack's artwork.

When we met the Scussels, they had been installed in their new home only about six months, and some of the pieces of their new lifestyle were still falling into place. Mary Lou had not yet found a job she wanted, but she was actively exploring the possibilities and using her energies in the meantime to manage the real estate they had purchased several years earlier at their son's insistence. Jack had given himself a year to experiment with his painting.

There are many unanswered questions about precisely what lies ahead for the Scussels. Mary Lou expects to devote several years to building a career she can be proud of. Jack expects to set up his own studio, and certainly to travel—maybe even buy a sailboat or build one himself. He is taking over most of the housekeeping chores to free Mary Lou for a job, and savoring his newfound leisure time. ''I take longer walks; I do a lot more thinking; I help around the house; I write letters, which I never did before. I probably waste 30 percent of every day. But that's okay, because we are trying to break the pattern of pressure.''

Jack speculates that 50 percent of the people who have a reasonable income could do what he has done. It doesn't take that much in resources, he insisted. ''It takes something in your life to say 'I want a change.' And secondly, you have to be able to say to yourself 'Just because I'm changing, it doesn't mean I'm running away. I'm not escaping, or quitting.' ''

For Jack Scussel, a solid awareness of his own abilities gave him the confidence to move on from a situation which offered security without new challenges to a more stimulating, less familiar way of life.

For Bill Freeman, at age sixty-nine, it was a new marriage that helped establish a new way of life. He and Jan Wheeler, a forty-two-year-old school administrator, had met about six months before we visited them, had been living together for two months, and were to be married in a formal church ceremony in just three weeks.

Mr. Freeman retired in 1976 of his own choice from a position as an administrative judge. He loved what he was doing, but the climate back East was getting to him. Once he relocated to Arizona, he never wanted to leave. "I came out here to retire. I might write a book; I want to play golf; I don't want someone telling me when I have to get out of bed in the morning."

Jan Wheeler, who has spent thirty-three years in Phoenix, still goes to work every day, as food service director for the largest elementary school district in the state of Arizona. Like Bill, she has been married twice before; the first marriage ended in divorce, the second in the death of her husband from cancer. She spoke a little about the difference in age between Bill and herself, obviously a subject of some discussion in their community. "Age can be a barrier," she admitted, "but age is the way you live. I'm like forty-three going on fifty-eight, because I went through a lot of different experiences at a young age. But Bill no more acts his age than the man in the moon!" She laughed affectionately.

The former judge added, "Six months ago I met Jan, and life has changed for me. Jan likes the home life which she hasn't had for a while, and I'm living again. It's beautiful."

Retirement as a married person, whether in a long-standing relationship or a new and unexpected romance later in life, can deepen and expand your appreciation of the varied experiences that await you in your later years. But a large number of people entering retirement find themselves single and destined to remain so, particularly women, who far outnumber men in the older age brackets. Many of the single retirees we met are using their increased personal freedom of choice to create an exciting new lifestyle.

Christine MacKennon, a soft-spoken, self-sufficient native of Boston, has never married. She enjoyed an extremely interesting position as an administrator at Massachusetts General Hospital for many years, and work was the major focus of her life. "Where am I going to go?" she asked herself when it came time to retire. "What am I going to do?"

Chris had no close living relatives, and most of her friends were still employed, so she worked out her retirement pattern on her own. She decided on a total change—"a new environment, a new part of the world to look out on, new customs, totally new people.'' She chose Arizona because it was so different from Boston and had impressed her on a winter vacation. She had previously lived in a high-rise apartment house, so as part of her "total change" she decided to buy a home of her own.

Her substantial volunteer activities keep her in touch with a variety of interesting and involved people. "I think we should deemphasize this arts-and-crafts-for-senior-citizens business and stress what we can do for others as we grow older," she says. "The people who are running around to clubs and so on, giving nothing of themselves to the world. That's not the way to live. You are old, but you can still contribute. You have more time to do it."

Retirement is much better than Chris MacKennon thought it would be. "When I was young, I thought old age was a horrible thing. I connected it with bad health. Of course, I have marvelous health. I am fairly alert. I don't have any financial problems; it's just a great life.

"Every day I am excited by something new out here." After eight years of retirement, she adds cautiously, "I think it just may work."

Learning from Your Elders

The experiences of recent retirees can teach us an enormous amount. Their experiences aren't necessarily going to be a blueprint for your own retirement, but they can serve as a guide to your decision-making process. The conditions which affect retirement life are constantly changing, though, and if you are ten or fifteen years away from retirement now, the economic and social scene when you stop working full-time will undoubtedly differ substantially from present conditions.

One of the aims of this book is to bring you up to date on the latest facts about retirement living and point out the trends that appear to be shaping future living conditions. The most important lesson of retirement is the one that Christine MacKennon learned. She had her own mistaken impression of what growing older would mean, but found to her surprise and delight that she and most of her friends over sixty-five are capable, energetic, and very much alive—far more so than their own parents or grandparents were likely to have been at the same age.

When you retire, you can plan to feel good, plan to take advantage of the burgeoning opportunities available to you, plan to make the most of what is essentially a new development in the social structure of American life. Our forebears could not even contemplate a phase of life after their working years ended, nor the freedom from physical or financial handicap which can be yours in retirement. Those of us in our middle years today are at the cutting edge of an entirely new social phenomenon, a class of older individuals who bring talent, energy, and experience to their later years and demand a meaningful, enjoyable, rewarding lifestyle. By understanding the pleasures of aging, perceiving the advantages that await you as well as the potential pitfalls, you can make decisions today which will build a promising future for yourself.

You are living at a point in history when the rules for growing older are changing. By actively involving yourself in the trends of our times, you can prepare to make this stage of your life the best you've ever known.

4

KEEPING HEALTHY,
STARTING NOW

Ill-health, of body or mind, is defeat. . . . Health alone is victory. Let all men, if they can manage it, contrive to be healthy!

THOMAS CARLYLE

THERE'S a joke about a New York City cabdriver who went to see a doctor. He pulled up outside a very fancy Park Avenue office and rushed in. He told the nurse it was an emergency and she got him to see the cardiologist before any of the other patients in the waiting room.

"Doctor, please," the cabby said. "You've got to do something. I got a terrible pain in my chest."

The doctor saw that the man was really frightened and gave him a thorough examination. He ran several tests on him, checked him inside and out, and was able to report that there was nothing seriously wrong. The cabby was relieved but visibly jolted when he was told that the fee would come to two hundred dollars.

"Two hundred dollars!" he cried. "Do you realize what I do for a living? I can't afford two hundred dollars. My family would starve!"

The doctor, somewhat embarrassed, gave a slight shrug. "All right. *One* hundred dollars."

"One hundred dollars!" the cabby practically yelled. "There's no way I could pay one hundred dollars. Do you know how long it takes me to clear one hundred dollars driving that lousy cab?"

The doctor sighed. "Look, I won't charge you anything for the visit. But would you mind telling me why you came here? You saw the bronze nameplate on the door. You knew what kind of place you were walking into, and that my fee would be considerable. So tell me, why did you come to me?"

"Because, Doctor," said the cabdriver, "when it comes to my health, money is no object!"

FITNESS—THE BEST DEFENSE AGAINST DISEASE

How important is your health? That seems like an easy enough question to answer. Just about anyone will tell you that if you have your health, everything else falls into place.

And yet, how much thought do we give to the state of our health? When something is bothering us physically, we take care of it, but when nothing hurts, we assume everything is fine and go on with our daily business. Thanks to the amazing resilience of the human body, this lack of concern doesn't cause major problems in the first thirty or forty years of life, when our bodies will take just about anything we can dish out. You can smoke, drink, or eat an awful lot before the results are unpleasant enough to convince you to cut back. And there's always someone who is in worse shape than you.

But is not being in *bad* shape good enough? Will it be good enough in a few more years?

Good health and a healthy lifestyle have become more important to me as I've gotten older, and the truth is I feel better now than I did at twenty-five. I haven't smoked a cigarette in twenty-one years. It was a habit I didn't need. I've almost totally given up hard liquor, although I enjoy wine and beer in moderation. I try to get enough sleep, although with my schedule it's not always easy. When I was doing the *Today* show I was averaging about four and a half hours of sleep a night, which is a little too little for me. The result was that for about nine years I was chronically lacking sleep, and I feared that if I continued for another ten or fifteen years I might seriously bend my health. This was one of the reasons I left the show. When necessary I can do without a night's sleep without any serious effects, and it's nice to know the reserve is still there to be called on. There might come a time when it isn't there, and then I'll have to tailor my life accordingly. The key is that if you have limitations, you live within them, and there's still a lot of room to maneuver.

Have you let your "relatively" good health rob you of opportunities for enjoying life? A twenty-five-year-old who lacks the energy to walk around and enjoy a beautiful autumn day is a victim of failing health, as is the thirty-five-year-old father who feels winded after a few minutes of playing ball with his child, or the forty-five-year-old tennis spectator who says he would rather be out on the court himself but just doesn't feel up to it.

The fatigue of poor fitness follows us from home to work, where it cuts down our abilities and our potential for success. A fitter person is more physically attractive and usually has the kind of self-confidence that is a valuable asset in dealing with other people. And no artificial coverups, from clothing to cosmetics to plastic surgery, can give a person the attractiveness that the natural appeal of good health can give.

There is much more to be gained by keeping healthy than just making your life more enjoyable and active. The more we learn about the way the human body works, the more clearly we see that *most of the disease and disability which afflicts modern Americans could be prevented or postponed through taking positive steps to stay fit and healthy throughout our lives*. Good health is valuable at any age, but as we grow older, it becomes absolutely crucial; maintaining a sound body is the key to combating life-threatening diseases and prolonging your life.

Fears of illness increase as we grow older, and with good reason. When you hear about the forty-eight-year-old sales manager in your office who suddenly died of a heart attack, or the forty-five-year-old woman two doors down from you who lost a breast to cancer, the realization that you are in the same age—and risk—bracket may be difficult to deal with. Facing your own mortality can leave you feeling helpless and depressed.

You are *not* helpless, though; you can do a great deal to avoid illness if you start maintaining your body now, *before* you get sick. Illness in later life is not a sudden occurrence for most Americans. It is brought on by a lifetime of poor health practices which leave them open to serious disease. Improve your habits in the following six areas, and you will greatly increase your chances of living a long, healthy life:

- *Personal habits*—eliminate or moderate those habitual activities, such as smoking, drinking, and drug abuse, which are known to wear down the human body.
- *Safety*—eliminate anything in your environment that poses a hazard to your continued well-being.
- *Nutrition*—control your weight and provide your body with the foods that maximize potential.
- *Exercise*—maintain your strength and flexibility and keep your entire body moving smoothly longer, including your heart and lungs.
- *Stress management*—deal with the hidden killer which scientists are discovering is a prime factor in aggravating most modern medical problems.
- *Medical care*—make the most of current medical science, and learn how to get the best possible care from your doctor.

The best antidote to feeling old is feeling good. Your planning and efforts today to establish a healthful lifestyle will be repaid with many happier, livelier years to come.

A PROGRAM FOR LONGER LIFE

By continually renewing the promise to treat our bodies well and wisely, we can add many years to our lives. A ten-year study conducted by Dr. N. Belloc of the California Department of Health and Human Population Laboratory concluded that by eating healthy, regular meals, maintaining moderate weight, exercising regularly, getting enough rest, refraining from smoking, and drinking only in moderation, men would live an average of eleven years longer than their contemporaries who were lax about following these basic health practices. Women would gain an average of seven additional years of life expectancy (at present, women already enjoy a six-year advantage over men).

A similar study isolated seven key health habits:

1. three regular meals a day with no snacks
2. breakfast every day
3. moderate exercise two or three times a week
4. no smoking
5. sleeping seven to eight hours every night
6. no alcohol or moderate consumption
7. moderate body weight.

The forty-five-year-old man who followed this program to the letter could expect to live to be nearly seventy-nine, whereas if he kept up with only two or three of the rules, he would probably die by age sixty-seven. The men who practiced all these simple regulations had a life expectancy thirty years greater than those who broke them!

To celebrate his sixty-fifth birthday, bodybuilder Jack La Lanne swam over a mile in the chilly waters of Lake Ashinoko in Japan, towing behind him sixty-five boats loaded with over 6,500 pounds of wood pulp. "These things I do show that as you get older, you can still get thrills out of life," he said. "People don't die of old age, they die of neglect. . . . I'm going to live to be at least a hundred and fifty.''

While experience shows that Jack La Lanne will probably fall short of his goal, he has given himself the best chance possible to reach his century-and-a-half objective by pursuing an active lifestyle, exercising regularly, following a fat-free diet, refraining from smoking and drinking, and maintaining a positive, eager attitude toward the future.

Shouldn't you give yourself a chance, too?

What About Limits to Longevity?

No matter how you improve your bad habits, or what steps you take toward better health, there are limits to the degree of influence you have over your lifespan. You have inherited genetic patterns which determine not just the shape of your nose and the color of your hair but your susceptibility to certain diseases and your potential longevity as well. As the body ages, its defenses against infection and illness become weaker. And there are always accidents which cannot be prevented. Remember the classic case of the man who gives up smoking and drinking, cuts his calories, and exercises until he's a perfect physical specimen, and then is killed in a car crash.

Neither genetic factors nor the hand of fate are reasonable excuses for neglecting your body's needs, though. You can often circumvent your genetic legacy. In most cases, what you inherit is a *tendency* toward a disease rather than the disease itself. Say you have a family history of high blood pressure. If you take the proper steps to minimize aggravating conditions, you can avoid turning this tendency into a dangerous medical problem, or at least control it with medication. So you can modify your risk of serious illness through preventive controls.

What about infections and accidents? If you are in good shape, your resistance is better at any age, making you a less likely target for disease. In an emergency situation, a fire or flood, for instance, you will be better able to defend yourself and recover from any injuries you might sustain, if you are physically fit. A person in top condition is less likely to become a victim of a traffic accident since reaction time, alertness, and agility all improve as health improves. The multitude of benefits to be gained from physical fitness are well worth the extra effort required.

Preventive Medicine Versus the Modern Killers

If the first words that come to mind when you hear the word *health* are *doctor* and *medicine,* you have fallen into a common trap. Continued research to find cures for disease has produced astounding results, which are widely publicized and acclaimed. As a result, people tend to think of their health in terms of *treatment* rather than prevention, and that's dangerous. It is unreasonable to expect a physician to step in and instantly cure conditions which arise from years of physical neglect and abuse. And it is neglect and abuse that cause most of the deaths from disease in America today. Table 1 will give you a profile of the leading killers in America today.

Six of the ten leading causes of death in the United States—heart disease, cancer, stroke, diabetes, cirrhosis of the liver, and arteriosclerosis—are diseases brought on or aggravated by the modern American lifestyle. Modern—let me stress the word—*modern* killers.

In 1800, influenza and pneumonia were the nation's leading killers. In 1976 the death rate from these diseases was one tenth of what it had been at the turn of the nineteenth century. On the other hand, the death rate from heart disease has climbed to more than two and a half times its rate in 1900. In the mid-1800s, it was so rare that it took a highly qualified specialist to diagnose it. Today it has reached epidemic proportions, as has cancer. One out of every four Americans now living can expect to suffer from some form of the disease in his lifetime.

As scientists explore the causes of the deterioration which leads to heart attacks, strokes, and cancer, their findings point consistently to those elements in our lifestyle which are radically different from those in our ancestors'. The high-technology environment that makes us so dependent on machines affects the way we eat, the way we

Table 1. Leading Causes of Death in the United States in 1976

Rank	Cause of Death	Number of Deaths	Rate per 100,000 Population
	All causes	1,909,440	889.6
1	Heart disease	723,876	337.2
2	Cancer	377,312	175.8
3	Stroke	188,623	87.9
4	Accidents	100,761	46.9
5	Influenza and pneumonia	61,866	28.8
6	Diabetes mellitus	34,508	16.1
7	Cirrhosis of liver	31,453	14.7
8	Arteriosclerosis	29,366	13.7
9	Suicide	26,832	12.5
10	Infant mortality	24,809	11.6

SOURCE: United States Public Health Service

move our bodies, the way we breathe, and the way we sleep—virtually every aspect of our lives. Now it's time to explore whatever means we have at our disposal to bring our cultural and physical needs back into alignment.

A Brief History Lesson

If we attempt to get a historical perspective on preventive medicine, we find that the most effective steps taken to improve the health of the general population have always been the preventive measures taken to control the spread of illness—cleaning up living conditions and improving dietary habits, for example.

In mid-nineteenth-century England and Wales, infectious diseases were the killers. Tuberculosis was the leading cause of death, with bronchitis, pneumonia, influenza, whooping cough, and measles all high on the list. The major factors in the decline of these diseases were environmental, not medical; improvements in sanitary conditions, alleviation of overcrowded housing and unsafe working conditions, and improvements in nutrition all helped to ease the stranglehold of infectious diseases long before vaccinations, sulfa drugs, or antibiotics were ever dreamed of.

The enemies of health are different today. Instead of contaminating food with bacteria, we strip it of its nutritional value and pump it full of chemical additives. Our water and air carry industrial pollution instead of virulent microbes. Instead of a shortage of food, we have an abundance of foods that make us fat and weak. Instead of working ourselves to the point of exhaustion and physical deterioration in sweatshops, we lead sedentary lives and bring on physical deterioration through lack of exercise. Our affluent, leisured culture tacitly approves social smoking, drinking, and drug use.

The difference between the preventive medicine of the past and today's disease-fighting health practices is that you no longer have to wait for major public health projects to improve your chances of continued health; most of the factors in your environment that could cause you trouble are under your control.

There is a new accent on healthier eating, more exercise, and less smoking. There has been a boom in the active-sports industry, highlighted by the popularity of health spas, jogging, racquetball, and other sports. There is good evidence that consumption of high-fat, high-cholesterol foods declined in the seventies. Per capita tobacco consumption in the United States has decreased every year since 1971 and hit a 46-year low in 1978. The "health nut" of twenty years ago is the responsible citizen of today.

The problem is far from being solved, though. Although the death rate from coronary heart disease has decreased considerably in the past decade, an American is still ten times more likely to die from a heart attack than a Japanese. Many experts feel that we have barely scratched the surface when it comes to preventive medicine. In *The American Way of Life Need Not Be Hazardous to Your Health,* Dr. John W. Farquhar, founder and director of the Stanford Heart Disease Prevention Program, states, "At least ninety percent of the fatal and near-fatal episodes of premature strokes and heart attacks before age 65 are preventable."

We still have a long way to go, but the figures indicate that we are finally on the right track—that we know enough now to eliminate many of the probable causes of heart attack, stroke, cancer, and diabetes from our lives.

Risk Factors

The basic aim of preventive medicine is to isolate risk factors in our lifestyle and discover ways to eliminate them. A risk factor is a specific personal characteristic believed to *contribute to causing* a particular health problem. We could say, for instance, that drinking liquor is a risk factor in automobile accidents. That does not mean that if you drink you will necessarily be involved in a car crash. However, statistics indicate that if you drink you are *more likely* to be involved in an accident than the person who doesn't drink.

Table 2 indicates some of the areas of risk in our lives. Locate your own patterns in each of the categories and check to see how great a risk you may be taking.

Table 2. How Healthy Is Your Lifestyle?

Risk Category	No Risk	Slight Risk	Substantial Risk	Heavy Risk	Dangerous Risk
Smoking	No smoking or stopped for at least 10 years	Less than 10 cigarettes, 5 pipes or cigars a day	Half pack a day	1 pack a day	2 or more packs a day
Alcohol	Nondrinker	Stopped drinker	Less than 6 drinks per week	More than 6 drinks per week	More than 2 drinks per day
Trimness	Lean	Slightly plump	Moderately obese	Considerably obese	Grossly obese
Physical activity	Walk more than 2 miles a day or climb 20 or more flights of stairs a day	Walk 1.5–2 miles a day or climb 15–20 flights of stairs a day	Walk only 0.5 to 1.5 miles a day or climb only 5–15 flights of stairs a day	Walk only 2–5 blocks a day or climb 2–4 flights of stairs a day	Walk less than 2 blocks a day or climb less than 2 flights of stairs a day
Prescription drugs	With doctor's consent following orders carefully	Take medication daily without side effects	Take medication when needed with few side effects	Use sleeping and nerve pills regularly without doctor's supervision	Without doctor's consent, mix with other drugs or alcohol
Nonprescription drugs	Use occasionally only for short periods. Label warnings heeded.				Continuing use, alcohol used or auto driven despite label warnings
Alcohol and driving —boats, cars, motorcycles, snowmobiles	Never drink. Drive only with safety aids—seat belt, helmet, life jacket	Never drive after drinking without safety aids	Drive after 2 drinks with safety aids	Drive after 2 drinks without safety aids	Drive after more than 2 drinks without safety aids

	Always wear seat belt	Wear seat belt more than half of the time	Wear seat belt as a driver half of the time	Wear seat belt as a passenger half of the time	Wear seat belt less than half of the time
Motor vehicle safety					
Water safety—swimming and boating	Qualified expert	Know how to swim and the safety rules	Know how to swim and may swim after 1 drink or nerve drug	Do not know how to swim but use life jacket half of the time	Do not know how to swim; never use life jacket
Blood cholesterol	Less than 180	180–220	220–280	280–320	320 and up
Blood pressure	120/80 or less	120/80–140/90	140/90–160/100	160/100–180/105	Above 180/105
Blood sugar	Less than 120, 2 hours after a meal of syrup and pancakes	Between 110 and 130, 2 hours after meals; checked each 3 months	Blood sugar more than 150 without diet control	Blood sugar more than 150 without diet control, doctor's care	Diabetes without doctor's care at less than 45 years of age
FOR WOMEN ONLY					
Breast check for lumps	Monthly self-exam and yearly check by physician	Monthly self-exam but no doctor exam	Self-exam 2–3 times a year but no doctor's exam	1 time a year by a doctor	Never
Pap smear	Every year	Every 3 years	Every 4 years	Never	Never; nonmenstrual bleeding

NOTE: Some risk factors are more important than others, and so it is not possible to score the results of this self-analysis accurately. But for a longer and healthier than average life, try to change your health habits so you will be in the categories on this page rather than the opposite one.

SOURCE: Methodist Hospital, Indianapolis. Prepared by Pamela Hall under the supervision of Drs. Lewis C. Robbins and Jack H. Hall, developers of the Health Hazard Appraisal System.

The risk factors in the table are based on studies which relate causes of death to elements in the victim's lifestyle. The underlying risk factors, the root causes of dangerous conditions, which can bring on disease or death, are not always easy to determine.

High blood pressure, blood cholesterol, and blood sugar are all identified as risk factors, since it has been conclusively shown that people with high readings in these areas will die earlier than people who are free of these hazards. The underlying risk factors, though, are the behavior patterns which *bring on* those high readings. Because we lead such complicated lives, the search for the specific factors in our lifestyles is difficult detective work. As the clues in the risk factor puzzle are painstakingly put together by scientists around the world, we can look forward to gaining a greater understanding of how we get sick, and how we can stay well.

TAKE CHARGE OF YOUR HEALTH

A well-informed, cooperative physician is an important person in your plans for a long, healthy life. Your doctor is a professional who has years of training and access to up-to-date information on advances in medical science. But he is not the key to maintaining your health throughout life—*you* are. He can advise, but you must act.

A perfect example is the case of my father. He was put on a blood pressure medicine that is obsolete but still on the market and still being prescribed by some doctors. The side effects were so severe they were giving him tranquilizers and Ritalin to overcome the depression. The result was that between ten and two each day he'd be on such a high it was as if he were intoxicated, and by the afternoon, when the effects wore off, he'd be so down I worried whether he might want to do himself in. He showed evidence of senility, but it wasn't senility, it was pseudosenility. He finally changed the medicine (by changing doctors) to a modern one that seemed to work, lowering the blood pressure without the awful side effects.

The conventional wisdom was that he would have to be on this medicine for the rest of his life. But he decided he didn't want to be on any medicine for the rest of his life. He changed his diet and kept monitoring his blood pressure every month at the local fire station, where they have a paramedic unit. He comes from the Midwest and was in the habit of eating such things as fried steaks and pan gravy, but he started eating vegetables that were only lightly cooked, fruit, and no salt or refined sugar. As his blood pressure came down, he started reducing the medication, until finally he went for months with no medication and his blood pressure was that of a forty-five-year-old man. And it has stayed there. When he got off that medication he turned around completely, and at eighty-one he's younger than he was fifteen years ago.

When I mentioned this to a top gerontologist, that the change of diet combined with the will to get off medication produced these results, contrary to conventional medical wisdom, he said, "We are beginning to find that out." So sometimes a change of habits can reverse this type of condition. But by far the best approach is the preventive one.

As long as you are "relatively healthy," your doctor is not going to spend very much time coaching you on preventive medicine—he's too busy dealing with sick people. So it's up to you to gain some understanding of the current state of knowledge in the field of preventive medicine. Chapters 5 and 6 will give you a rundown of the basics and some positive steps to take right now, and the books listed at the end of each of these chapters will offer further explanations and advice. If you have questions, by all means ask your doctor for his opinion. But do your homework first. Choose a nutritional plan which you can live with, both in terms of keeping you healthier longer and fitting your personal tastes in foods (pages 94–101). Map out a general exercise plan, perhaps based on the program recommended in this book (pages 112–18). Understand the facts about stress and the ways to combat it (pages 118–29).

Then, as an informed layman, you can deal with your doctor on a far more meaningful level. By establishing a partnership between doctor and patient, you *can* take charge of your health, and in virtually every case, improve it tremendously.

The field of preventive medicine is booming. More and more attention is being focused on finding the *causes* of disease and stopping illness before it starts, instead of simply treating it once it occurs. This continuing research has produced some extremely interesting findings which offer great hope for improving health care techniques in the near future. Scientists are probing the inner workings of individual cells, the complex interrelationships between lifestyle and health, the functioning of the body's immune system, and the effect of different levels of vitamins and minerals on all the body systems, in an attempt to control the development of disease, and possibly the aging process itself. But this is all in the experimental stage. Right now we have to concentrate on specifics for better health. It is important for you, as an informed and concerned health consumer, to know where to turn for further reliable information. There is a tremendous amount of information and misinformation coming to us from books, magazines, television shows, and conversations with friends, so how are we to sort out the valuable lessons from the distortions and outright lies?

The best way is to learn some basic facts about health care and then rely on responsible sources of information to help us evaluate the current state of preventive medicine.

The federal government, for one, has a sincere commitment to public health, as well as the resources to analyze complex scientific data and come up with reliable recommendations. It generally takes a while to get through all the red tape, but at least when the government *does* take a stand, it is usually carefully considered and thoroughly researched.

Other good sources of up-to-date information are the nonprofit organizations that have taken up the fight against particular diseases. Experts working with the American Heart Association, the American Cancer Society, and similar groups not only conduct research but provide the public and the medical profession itself with sound information about the state of prevention and treatment in their specialties. Several other nonprofit groups also provide reliable advice, including the American Association of Retired Persons and the Center for

Science in the Public Interest. Recently Blue Cross/Blue Shield has expanded its commitment to preventive medicine, and publishes a number of brochures containing advice from top health care professionals. The organization has a health education center in New York City that conducts public workshops on timely health topics.

When it comes to books, magazines, and newspapers, you will have to be an intelligent shopper. It is essential in *any* of your reading to carefully evaluate the source of the information. Read an author's credentials before accepting his opinions. Is he associated with a respected organization or medical center? Is he an established writer in his field? More important, is he offering miracles? If so, think very carefully before adopting his plan.

By all means, speak to your personal physician when contemplating major changes in your pattern of living. Just remember, he is the source of approval—*you* are the source of initiative and action for better health for today and tomorrow.

Making the Most of Medical Care

So far we have emphasized the importance of taking charge of your own health care in order to prevent disease. It is equally important for you to understand what to do when something goes wrong with your body, since you will be not capable of curing all your ailments yourself or second-guessing your doctor's advice. Each of us can benefit from becoming an informed consumer of medical care.

- Understand when your condition is serious enough to call a doctor and when it is *not*. Some people postpone necessary medical treatment through fear or ignorance, while others rush to the phone and bother their physicians for every ache and pain. If you learn to recognize changes in your body and react appropriately, you will be at a tremendous personal advantage.
- Gain the ability to communicate with your doctor about your condition, so that you can understand what is happening to

you and what the prescribed treatment is supposed to do. When you can describe your condition accurately, you make it easier for your doctor to diagnose the problem.

- Feel secure in your ability to cope with emergency situations, and try to take the right actions at the right time should anything go wrong. Illness is stressful in and of itself, but if you are knowledgeable about your physical makeup you can strip away the air of mystery which makes illness so much more frightening, and deal only with the real problems.

If the partnership between you and your doctor is going to work, you will have to give yourself some medical education. Luckily, there is probably no subject under the sun which is as fascinating to read about as our own bodies. This is particularly true today, with the trend toward greater patient involvement in the health care process.

Your next responsibility as a patient is choosing the medical professionals who will care for you and dealing with them effectively. It is particularly important that you feel confident about the abilities and services of your family physician, since you will be relying on his trusted recommendations for specialists, testing procedures, and health care facilities.

You can choose either a family practitioner (f.p.) or an internist as a general family doctor; the two differ somewhat in training. An f.p. is essentially what we used to call a g.p.—general practitioner—but has done postgraduate work and should be certified by the American Board of Family Practice.

An internist has trained extensively in all areas of medicine except surgery, obstetrics, and pediatrics, and diagnoses the common ailments of adult patients. The internist you choose should be certified by the American Board of Internal Medicine.

Who can recommend a good doctor? Your local hospital administrator can recommend hospital staff members who practice in your area. A hospital prides itself on the quality of its staff and strictly screens any physician who wishes to practice there before granting affiliation.

You can also call your county medical society for recommendations and for specific information such as a doctor's hospital affiliations, board certifications, and alma mater.

The professional organizations will not be as unhesitating in their recommendations as personal contacts, who may like their doctors and wish to pass on the good news. Ask your dentist, lawyer, or other professionals with whom you deal. These people are likely to know which physicians enjoy good reputations in the community. You can speak to friends in the neighborhood and ask about their experiences as well, but do try to get an idea of the doctor's reputation from a number of sources.

If you are looking for a new physician because you are moving to a new area, ask your present doctor for recommendations before you leave.

But you need more than just a name—you need a doctor with whom you can establish a rapport, a personal relationship which is open, trusting, and mutually respectful.

Essentially you are looking for someone who is compatible in the following areas:

1. *Availability.* Your personal physician must have an office near your home with convenient hours. Find out who covers for your doctor when he is not available, and check into the credentials and reputation of this doctor as well.

2. *Willingness to explain.* Your doctor is a busy professional, but it is essential that he be willing to take the time to explain what is wrong to you. He should let you know what he is doing about it by prescribing a given medication or treatment, what you should expect, and what your options are. And a brief burst of medical jargon won't do—you need the information in layman's terms.

3. *Willingness to accept consultations and second opinions.* Doctors are fallible. While you should certainly have enough confidence in your physician to accept his diagnosis of a routine ailment, you should also know that he can send you to an appropriate specialist when there is reason. If he is sensible, he will not object if you suggest that you would like to seek a second opinion in instances where you feel that treatment has not progressed satisfactorily, or when the treatment suggested is significant.

4. *Reasonable fees.* Don't be ashamed to ask the doctor what he

charges for his services. Doctors' fees do vary considerably. It is also worth investigating the availability of a health maintenance organization (see page 218), which charges one overall fee for all of your medical services.

5. *Compatible attitude.* There are many areas in which the doctor's personal opinions will substantially affect his medical decisions, so it is a good idea to find out where your doctor stands. Ask him how he feels about preventive medicine, and prepare a few specific questions on some aspect of nutrition or stress, to gauge his reaction.

Ask your doctor what he feels is possible for you as you grow older. If he is enthusiastic about your future health possibilities, that's fine. If not, you may find that he will ignore or shrug off conditions which he would treat in a younger individual. You know that there is no reason for you to set low expectations for your future health, but not every doctor recognizes this fact. Gerontology, the medical study of aging, was not widely taught in medical schools until the last decade, so it is the younger physicians who are likely to be the most informed and the most open-minded.

It is not easy to size up a doctor at your first encounter. However, by questioning his attitudes and certain aspects of his practice, and by observing the way you are handled when you do require treatment, you will soon have a good idea of whether or not a particular physician will be able to serve your total needs as a patient.

You have a part to play in this relationship, of course. You should be sure to ask your doctor the right questions and describe your symptoms adequately if you expect satisfactory answers.

You are responsible for following your doctor's advice faithfully and for dealing with him openly and honestly. Give him all the facts, including the psychological and personal circumstances which might be affecting your condition. And this cooperative spirit should extend to paying the bills as well; if you know you are going to have difficulties paying for treatment, at least let the doctor know, and try to make some mutually acceptable arrangement beforehand.

Your doctor may be a competent, intelligent professional, but he is not a miracle worker. The patient has rights and a say in his or her own health. Remember that it is only through a partnership with your physician that you will achieve the best medical care.

You *Can* Grow Older and Be More Active Than Ever

Your own attitude toward aging can help to ensure your continued health. If you believe that growing older means getting sick, you will be defeated before you even start. Despite what you may have been led to believe, the odds strongly favor your continued freedom from the kinds of health problems which would limit your activities. We found dozens of vital, happy retirees across the country whose admirable physical fitness was a key element in their busy lifestyles. Their activities—swimming, golf, vigorous walking, working out at a spa—provide, as they put it, relaxation, and renew their sense of freedom in retirement. These people in their sixties, seventies, and eighties certainly don't fulfill one of our most deeply ingrained definitions of old age—they are active. They enjoy their bodies and what they can do with them, and thrive on a busy lifestyle which would be impossible without vibrant good health. Being in shape lets them establish a way of life which in turn helps them keep in shape so they can continue that active lifestyle.

Retirement for many busy people has meant more time to get back to enjoying physical recreation. In a recent study of retired business managers, 77 percent reported that they took part in active sports on a regular basis, and that participation remained at a solid 57 percent even after age seventy-six.

The majority of the retirees we spoke with were pleasantly surprised at how good they felt. Perhaps many had planned on *not* feeling well, and are now finding ways to make the most of their unexpected asset. You can enjoy your health even longer if you begin to realize your possibilities in middle age. Take the time to build a lifestyle based on healthful habits, and maximize your physical fitness while enjoying yourself by learning new sports and games and preparing for active forms of recreation which you can continue in retirement.

One of the activities I've taken up recently is skiing. I got on skis for the first time two years ago, when my ten-year-old grandson dragooned me into it. He opened the door to a whole new sport, and I'm enjoying it, although I don't have the time to make a passion of it.

I also became a balloon pilot a few years ago, and I've engaged in hobbies such as flying, gliding, and diving with people of very advanced years. If my health became impaired in some way, and that can happen at any age, I might have to slack off on some of my hobbies. But some people just go on and on, like Lowell Thomas, an avid skier who'll be eighty-eight this year. He went skiing during his recent honeymoon, in fact.

Don't plan to be unhealthy when you retire. If you fail to keep up with your nutritional needs, or to keep physically active, or to seek adequate medical attention, because you think that physical deterioration is inevitable, you are only hurting yourself. It is not age that will cut you down. It is the cumulative effect of treating your body badly for years. An enlightening look at the facts will show that you can feel good, perhaps better than you've ever felt, as you grow older.

Several studies on aging done in recent years have found that, despite the popular image of older people as decrepit and sickly, most of those polled don't feel sick. General good health is the rule rather than the exception at age sixty-five plus. And your heightened health awareness can bring you a sound mind and body and a happier way of life into your seventies, eighties, and beyond.

Some Facts About the Aging Process

Physical aging is operative throughout life. In the early stages it is responsible for the body's growth and maturity. There are changes in the circulatory system during the mid teens. Shortly after puberty, certain gland activity slows to a stop (or we would grow to be thirty feet tall). The brain and central nervous system reach a peak of computer efficiency in the late twenties. Skin elasticity begins to fade in the thirties; most people require reading glasses in the early forties, and hair follicles stop putting out pigment (and sometimes hair) at different times for different individuals (some people get gray in their twenties—others much later).

The eventual result of these and other changes is a decline in physical capabilities and a decrease in the amount of abuse your body will accept. However, there is as yet no definitive information about what changes actually take place, to what degree, at what rate, and how long they can be postponed through our own constructive efforts.

We can define physical aging as the increasing inability of the body to adapt to the demands of its external environment and to adjust its own internal functions. But age itself is not fatal; no one ever "died of old age." The weakening of the body's systems with advancing years can allow disease to gain control and end life. Someone may die of heart disease, cancer, pneumonia, or any number of diseases, but not of age itself.

New studies have produced some startling revelations about the effects of aging. The prejudices about physical and mental abilities which have long influenced the treatment of older Americans are now being challenged and refuted.

One of the major ongoing studies attracting enthusiastic attention is the Baltimore Longitudinal Study of Aging, a federally funded program that is examining the aging process in eight hundred men and women over several decades. The study, launched in the 1950s, includes volunteers ranging in age from 20 to 103 who report each year or two for a three-day series of exhaustive tests. The results for each person are then compared with his or her own test performances in previous years, so that scientists can see a continuing pattern of aging as it affects individuals over the course of time.

Some big changes in the common wisdom have been indicated already. While all the standard graphs indicate that kidney function declines steadily with age, some subjects in the Baltimore study have revealed *improved* kidney function with the passing of time. Who knows what other misconceptions will be corrected under this careful scrutiny?

There are gains made with age in skill and experience which don't show up in laboratory experiments but which do add immeasurably to personal capabilities. As for the aging process itself, there is no firm timetable. Many physical functions will change so slightly during a lifetime that they will have little or no practical effect on daily affairs. The effects of other changes can frequently be offset by modern medicine and technology—and by personal determination to overcome whatever obstacles might arise.

Young and *old* are simply words to describe the length of time we have lived. You may well have been "old" at forty, but that doesn't mean you can't grow "younger" now. After all, how many of us feel as good as we *could* feel? You are far better off being a fifty-five-year-old in top condition than a thirty-five-year-old who has let himself fall apart. A loss of physical and mental abilities can occur at any time of life, not just in the retirement years. Nor is failing fitness irreversible—increasing age can mean rejuvenation rather than decay if you change your lifestyle.

In the following two chapters, I'm going to concentrate on two crucial health factors—nutrition and fitness—that can influence the course of your life. Before you can decide what you are going to do with your retirement, you have to commit yourself to a program which will help you to enjoy it, and that's exactly what good eating and good exercise will do for you.

FOR FURTHER READING

Books

Alvarez, Walter C., M.D., *Help Your Doctor Help You;* Celestial Arts paperback, 1976.

Belsky, Marvin S., M.D., and Gross, Leonard, *How to Choose and Use Your Doctor;* Arbor House, 1975.

Miller, Lewis, *The Life You Save: A Guide to Getting the Best*

Possible Care from Doctors, Hospitals and Nursing Homes; William Morrow, 1979.

Farquhar, John W., M.D., *The American Way of Life Need Not Be Hazardous to Your Health;* W. W. Norton paperback, 1978.

Ubell, Earl, *How to Save Your Life;* Harcourt Brace Jovanovich hardcover, 1973; Penguin paperback, 1976.

The Farquhar and Ubell books each provide a full rundown on the proper patterns of nutrition, exercise, stress avoidance, and personal habits for long life and health; they also give you tips on *how* to change your habits to fit a healthier lifestyle. They show you how to use behavior modification techniques and action programs to acquire the motivation and the mechanisms needed to keep fit and healthy.

There are several well researched, readable, and reliable consumer-oriented guides to medical care. Two that rate special attention are *How to Be Your Own Doctor—Sometimes* by Keith W. Sehnert, M.D., with Howard Eisenberg (Grosset and Dunlap, 1975), and *Take Care of Yourself* by Drs. Donald M. Vickery and James Fries (Addison-Wesley, 1976). Each contains sound advice for choosing a doctor and dealing with the medical community, as well as sound preventive medicine techniques. They give simple, clear-cut advice on when to call the doctor and when to treat an illness or injury yourself. They take the mystery out of a wide range of common complaints, explain when home remedies will be adequate, and provide detailed instructions on how to treat the problem for best results. The goal of these books is to make you an "activated patient"—an informed, capable individual who can handle medical problems calmly, rationally, and successfully, through command of some basic knowledge about your body.

Magazine

An excellent source of continuing information on preventive medicine and the health care field in general is *Family Health* magazine. It combines sound research and high editorial standards with sprightly writing and eye-catching illustrations. The full subscription price is $10 a year (the magazine is published ten times annually), but there are often special new subscriber rates available. For current information contact *Family Health,* Subscription Department, Portland Place, Boulder, CO 80302.

5

NUTRITION FOR BETTER HEALTH

Now learn what and how great benefits a temperate diet will bring along with it. In the first place you will enjoy good health.
HORACE

AS you grow older, it becomes more important than ever to reduce the dietary risk factors in your daily life. By making a few simple changes in nutritional habits you can improve your health now and help to ward off illness in the future. Armed with this information, and the specific suggestions in the Action Plan (page 94), you will also be able to discard all the garbled advice you may have picked up in the past, and safely modify your diet to fit your nutritional needs.

It's hard for some people to believe that simply eating whatever tastes good can jeopardize their health. But many foods which have become staples in our busy, commercialized way of life are in fact bad for you. It is sad but true that Americans prefer foods which are overprocessed, high in fat and calories, and low in nutritional value.

My wife and I are eating more healthfully than we did in our early years together, and we're both feeling a lot better as a result. It started when we were experimenting with different diets to lose a little weight, and we found that the nutrition programs recommended for weight control were being recommended also for better health. We started eating more fruits and lightly cooked vegetables, and we're still doing it. And twenty years ago I didn't feel I'd eaten right if I didn't have steak for lunch *and* dinner.

Which made me wonder, where did our ideas of what tastes good come from? The research on this question points to a natural preference, even in newborn babies, for sweet and salty foods, and a natural dislike for sour or bitter ones. In the distant past, this preference helped us survive, since naturally sweet foods provided needed nutrition, salt is essential to help retain moisture in the body (sodium is necessary to sustain life), and foods that are spoiled or poisonous will generally have a bitter, unpleasant taste. From infancy on we are subjected to environmental influences which teach us our lifelong eating habits.

We learn to eat the way we do to stay healthy, but eating is a primary social activity as well. Offering food is a sign of a parent's love for a child, or friendship toward a guest. Elaborate preparation of large quantities of food is an important element in celebration and ritual around the world and is a sign of prosperity. Food is something we work for, something which fulfills a basic need, something which helps give us personal and ethnic identity. Certain foods have prestige value: sirloin steak gets higher points than a peanut butter and jelly sandwich. And, as so many of us are aware, there are psychological rewards in abundant quantities of foods.

Food is a major business. In fact, food production and processing is the largest industry in America today. It may not be entirely a coincidence that medical care ranks as number three. More than 50 percent of the current American diet goes through some form of processing before we consume it; the more processing done to a food, the higher the profit margin, since many processed foods are loaded with water, sugar, and other less expensive "fillers."

In 1975 about *$1.15 billion* was spent in the United States to advertise food products on television, and an equally large amount was spent in other media. Advertising is regulated by the government to protect us from hazardous sustances, but anyone who listens to the news has undoubtedly had the depressing experience of learning that some chemical previously thought harmless has been unmasked as a potential killer. It's easy to feel that "there's nothing left that's safe to eat," and for this reason many people give up on the attempt to maintain good eating habits. Others have been partially awakened to the need for improved nutrition but haven't figured out how to go about it.

In recent years food manufacturers have realized that there's money to be made by supporting the cause of better nutrition—or by convincing the public that they are doing so. The movement to put more healthful commercial brands of food on the market is certainly a step in the right direction, but it takes an informed consumer to wade through the jingles and slogans and set a nutritionally beneficial table. You can and should be that informed consumer.

With the facts we're about to give you, you'll be able to come up with a plan for eating which will not just restrict your intake of certain foods but will replace them with new, interesting, and enjoyable foods you may not have tried.

BASIC RULES FOR IMPROVING YOUR NUTRITION

● *Eat and Enjoy Eating*

Much of the resistance to diet change comes from the feeling that, in order to improve your health, you must give up the pleasures of eating. We have come to think of diet strictly as sacrifice, but the truth is that merely cutting foods out is a poor answer to the weight-loss-for-health question. However, you can cut down on fattening foods and get equal enjoyment from more nutritious, equally delicious foods which will satisfy your hunger *and* keep you healthy. Don't think of food as an enemy. Good food is necessary to good health, and if you cut back on all your eating, you are looking for new problems brought on by undernutrition.

There is a brief dialogue between Carl Reiner and Mel Brooks on their comedy album *2000 and Thirteen* that neatly sums up the importance of enjoying eating. On the album, Mel Brooks is the world's oldest living man, at the age of 2013, and Carl Reiner is interviewing him to discover the secret of his longevity.

Interviewer: What does your diet consist of today?

2000 Year Old Man: Very strict—a very strict diet. Almost nothing. No starches, because starches turn to sugar, sugar turns to diabetes, diabetes turns to the grave. No meats, because meats are fat and fat has cholesterol.

Interviewer: And fowl?

2000 Year Old Man: No fowl. Fowl is foul.

Interviewer: There are no starches, no fowl and no meats. What about fish?

2000 Year Old Man: No fish. Fish has iodine. Too much iodine and you'll get a goiter, your eyes will spring out of your head.

Interviewer: Well then, naturally, you live on vegetables.

2000 Year Old Man: No, fruit and vegetables are very bad. They have roughage and they make tons and tons of gas. And I have to be very careful, because if I make bloozer I could blow myself right out of this world.

Interviewer: At your age you're very brittle, I understand that. But you've left yourself nothing to eat.

2000 Year Old Man: Very little. Cool mountain water, ten degrees below room temperature. Just cool mountain water.

Interviewer: And that's all you eat?

2000 Year Old Man: Just that . . . and a stuffed cabbage, that's all.

Interviewer: Is stuffed cabbage allowable on your diet?

2000 Year Old Man: Who the hell cares if it's allowable? I love it! What am I gonna live for? For a little mountain water you think I'm gonna stay alive? Are you crazy?

The medical information from this ancient sage may be off target, but the moral is simple—any new diet pattern you adopt must still give you the satisfaction derived from eating or you won't stick with it, and the best diet plan in the world won't do you any good if it's tucked away in the back of a drawer.

For every high-calorie, high-fat dish you remove from your diet, substitute a tasty, healthful dish. Make your nutritional improvement campaign a plan for food discovery, not an exercise in self-deprivation. There are plenty of good-nutrition recipes available in magazines and cookbooks. Try any one and you will find that eating "better" can mean eating better-tasting food and better health.

● *Follow Your Doctor's Advice Regarding Special Diets*

If your physician has placed you on a special diet to combat ulcers, diabetes, or whatever, there is a good reason. Under no circumstances should you decide that you can prescribe a better diet for yourself. If you feel there is room for improvement within the limitations of the program your doctor has ordered, discuss it with him before making any changes.

For the healthy individual, though, it is not only safe, but beneficial to alter the present balance between the food groups we eat, as long as we don't cut out a major class of foods entirely. If you have any doubts about the dietary changes you propose to make, by all means ask your doctor for his approval. But nutrition is preventive medicine, and *you* will have to take the leading role in that aspect of your life.

● *Understand the Basics of Nutrition*

Most people have some vague recollection of the food groups from their schooldays and know simply that it is important to eat a balanced diet. In recent years there has been a wave of diet books and plans on the market, each with a different memorable word or phrase which makes the diet distinctive. In the face of high-protein low-fat, high-fat low-carbohydrate, low-protein low-fat, high this low that, we can easily forget what each of these words means. Here's a brief refresher course.

The Basics of Nutrition

Nutrients, Macro and Micro. We eat and drink to provide our bodies with nutrients, which are needed to provide energy, to grow and repair living tissue, and to regulate certain body functions. There are six categories of nutrients: the macronutrients—carbohydrates, fats, and proteins—which supply us with energy; and the micronutrients—vitamins, minerals, and water.

Carbohydrates. Carbohydrates are chemical compounds manufactured by green plants. Their primary function in our bodies is to provide energy. They are found in our diets in starches, fiber, dairy products, grains and baked goods, sugars and syrups, fruits, and vegetables.

There are two classes of carbohydrates. The simple carbohydrates are the simple sugars like refined sugar or honey, which the body can use directly. The complex carbohydrates are the starches, which must first be broken down into sugars before the body can use them. Simple carbohydrates do tend to make us fat without providing much in the way of nutrition, but the complex carbohydrate foods are not fattening foods. They provide the body with necessary vitamins and minerals, as well as the fiber which we need for good digestion.

Fats. Fats provide a concentrated source of energy to the body. They are needed to carry the fat-soluble vitamins A, D, E, and K to the cells. Major sources of fat in our diets include butter, shortening, cooking and salad oils, milk, meat, eggs, and nuts. The quantity of fat actually required by the body, though, is extremely small, and fat is, well, fattening. Just remember that proteins and carbohydrates each contain four calories per gram, whereas fat contains nine calories per gram.

The difference between saturated and polyunsaturated fats involves the molecular composition of the fat. Saturated fats, which are found in meat, milk and milk products, certain oils—such as coconut oil and palm oil often used in store-bought baked goods—and processed foods, are usually hard at room temperature. Polyunsaturates are soft or liquid and are found in fish, corn oil, safflower oil, most other vegetable oils, and some margarines.

Our bodies handle saturated and polyunsaturated fats differently, particularly in regard to the relationship of fat consumption to heart disease. However, simply adding more polyunsaturated fats to your diet is hardly the miracle cure to today's heart attack epidemic.

Proteins. The source of the body's basic building materials are the proteins. There are millions of different types of proteins, but they are all composed of only twenty different component parts, called amino acids, arranged differently in different proteins. In the body the proteins are broken down into their component amino acids, which the cells then reassemble into new compounds. These can be used as parts of the structural composition of the body or to perform various functions, such as aiding in digestion or fighting off infection.

Meat is a primary source of protein, but we also get substantial supplies of protein from dairy products, eggs, cereals, peas and beans, and some vegetables.

Micronutrients. Water is an essential component of our diets—actually, the human body is two-thirds water. We can survive without food far longer than we can without water.

Vitamins are a group of organic chemicals which in small amounts are essential to human life. Vitamins perform different functions in the body and are important in that a *lack* of any one can cause deficiency diseases such as scurvy or rickets. Neither of these diseases has been very troublesome in recent years.

The situation is similar with the *minerals*. Their effects both individually and in combination are only dimly understood, and the speculation which has convinced some people to dose themselves with large quantities of a wide array of vitamins and minerals is potentially dangerous.

The Food Groups. A traditional way of assuring that we get enough of each nutrient we require is by organizing the foods we eat into categories, called food groups. Each of the foods in the different groups provides basically the same nutritional elements, so if we make sure to eat the recommended number of servings of foods from each food group, we will have a balanced diet.

The traditional food group concept sets minimum requirements on consumption of healthful foods. It does not cover all the foods we eat, nor does it deal with the question of weight control or the quantities of particular food components, like salt, sugar, fat, or cholesterol. It does, however, give us a rough picture of the nutritional diversions within our diet, and allows us to "shop around" within these groups to find the foods which will do us the most good. Table 3 (pages 96–99) provides a basis for developing an up-to-date, healthful, personal eating plan.

Dietary Goals

In response to growing public confusion over the role of diet in preventive medicine, the United States Senate Select Committee on Nutrition and Human Needs evaluated the scientific evidence to date and arrived at a series of guidelines for healthy nutritional practices. The committee considered the recommendations of various professional panels in the United States and other countries, and in December 1977 published *Dietary Goals for the United States*. While there are still reservations regarding the goals among some scientists and members of the committee itself, they provide a reasonable response to the current state of scientific knowledge and will serve as a useful framework for planning your own dietary program.

Surveys of this kind are not to be considered scientific proof, certainly, but they do indicate the overwhelming nature of scientific opinion. They also represent a reassuring agreement on the safety of changing eating patterns which have taken on the comfort of familiarity despite their hidden dangers. Most scientists agree that there is a connection between diet and the development of coronary heart disease, for example, and that a modified diet of less fat, sugar, salt, and cholesterol, fewer calories, and more fiber and starchy foods will be beneficial for each of us. Following is a list of the goals, a look at some of the supporting evidence, the kind of change they require in our diets, and the potential overall benefits offered.

● *Goal 1: To avoid overweight, consume only as much energy (calories) as is expended;* if overweight, decrease energy intake and increase energy expenditure.

Dr. Beverly Winikoff of the Rockefeller Foundation presented some disturbing statistics on the effects of American obesity to the Senate nutrition committee. One-third of the American population is overweight to a degree that can diminish life expectancy. Over 30 percent of all men in their fifties are 20 percent overweight, and 60 percent are more than 10 percent overweight. Nearly 700,000 people die of coronary heart disease each year in the United States, so we should heed the results of a 1973 study which shows that each 10 percent weight reduction by men from thirty-five to fifty-five years old reduces the chance of coronary heart disease by 20 percent.

There is clearly far more to being overweight than fitting society's notions of physical attractiveness. In the past you may have thought of watching your weight as just a matter of good looks, but overweight is now a threat to your life, because overweight individuals are more likely to suffer from heart disease, atherosclerosis, hernia, thyroid disease, colitis, ulcer, and cancer. You owe it to yourself and those you love to make an effort to stay alive and healthy by slimming down.

• *Goal 2: Increase the consumption of complex carbohydrates* and "naturally occurring" sugars from about 28 percent of calorie intake to about 48 percent of calorie intake.

Carbohydrates have acquired a bad name in recent years, but nutritious high-carbohydrate food can be the cornerstone of a healthy diet. The grain products and fruits and vegetables of this group accomplish many goals. They can help reduce fats and cholesterol in the diet, which is a primary goal of good nutrition. Research indicates that fat and cholesterol levels are lower among southern Italians than among Britons, Swedes, or Swiss, and of course the Italian diet derives 55 to 60 percent of its calories from carbohydrates.

There are other advantages. The carbohydrate group, particularly fruits and vegetables, is very high in both vitamins and minerals. Frozen or canned fruits and vegetables are good, economical substitutes for more highly processed, high-calorie foods. And fresh produce is even better. These are "rich" foods as well—low in calories, high in nutrition, and extremely flavorful, with a naturally strong, delicious taste that cannot be duplicated by artificial flavorings.

The recent emphasis on fiber as a magic ingredient to good health has been overdone, but it is based on sound nutritional evidence, and the complex carbohydrate foods are the ones which give us our dietary fiber. Natural fiber is essential to keep the food we eat moving through our digestive system. Lack of fiber has been strongly linked to cancer of the colon, which is the most common form of cancer in the total population, and to diverticulitis, which is one of those hidden diseases that catches up with us in our later years. Diverticulitis is an inflammation of small pockets which develop in the lower bowel, causing severe discomfort. There is no need to go out and buy fancy dietary supplements, or even highly advertised high-fiber foods, though some of them are worthwhile. Just eat your fruits, vegetables, and whole grain foods.

Further advantages of the complex carbohydrates are their benefits in weight control and in balancing the food budget. You can buy the finest fruits and vegetables on the market and still not spend what you would on a steak. If you concentrate on complex carbohydrate foods, you will have no trouble controlling your weight, as long as you stick with relatively unsweetened baked goods, and vegetables and fruits, and avoid large helpings of heavy sauces on your pasta and rice.

● *Goal 3: Reduce the consumption of refined and processed sugars* by about 45 percent of total calories to account for about 10 percent of total calorie intake

We consume an extraordinary amount of sugar, most of it in processed foods. Americans eat over a hundred pounds of sugar per person per year—that comes to more than five hundred calories a day in sugar alone! You may protest that you never touch candy, cake, ice cream, or breakfast cereals. But what about all of the sauces and syrups, the canned fruits, the gallons of sodas we drink? All are full of sugar.

Processed sugar has no nutrient value at all, so by taking a large part of your daily calorie intake in this form you are robbing yourself of the foods that provide substantial nutrition. We caution children to avoid sugar because it is bad for their teeth, but forget that tooth decay—and with it gum disease—leads to loss of teeth in adults. This is a disease that catches up with you over the course of time, and one which complicates your nutritional picture by making eating good foods difficult.

What about sugar and diabetes? The balance of evidence seems to be that if you are not genetically inclined toward diabetes, you will not get it from eating great quantities of sugar. However, current estimates indicate that one out of five Americans will suffer from the disease during their lifetime, so decreasing your sugar consumption and keeping your weight down may reduce your tendency. And age is a definite factor in increasing your susceptibility to diabetes. Experts suggest that the likelihood of developing diabetes doubles with each decade of life.

- *Goal 4: Reduce overall fat consumption* from approximately 40 percent of total calories to about 30 percent of calorie intake.

- *Goal 5: Reduce saturated fat consumption* to account for about 10 percent of total calorie intake; and balance that with polyunsaturated and monounsaturated fats, which should account for about 10 percent of calorie intake each.

- *Goal 6: Reduce cholesterol consumption* to about 300 milligrams a day.

Let's deal with goals 4, 5, and 6 together, since they are closely related. All are based on the assumption that excess cholesterol in the bloodstream can cause heart disease and other related diseases. The solution to the problem is lowering the levels of fat and cholesterol in the blood. The primary villain is atherosclerosis. If the body's arteries become clogged with cholesterol, the efficiency of the circulatory system is greatly diminished. The vital arteries may eventually close entirely, causing heart attack.

Dietary studies have shown dramatic correlations between intake of fats and cholesterol and the incidence of heart disease. In nonindustrial, "primitive" nations, where the intake of meat and processed foods high in saturated fat is far lower than in the United States, heart disease is a minor problem. And even within the

United States, heart disease has risen sharply since the turn of the century as American diets have changed for the worse.

What is the best way to reduce blood cholesterol? It's hard to say. Fat and cholesterol are often found in the same foods, so it is difficult to assess their individual effects. Current clinical evidence indicates that reducing cholesterol intake lowers the blood cholesterol level in many individuals, but this effect has been disputed. Even if there were no such effect, though, the connection between increased fat consumption and elevated blood cholesterol is clearly proven.

The dietary guidelines suggest a daily maximum of 300 milligrams of cholesterol, so you should exercise moderation when it comes to shellfish, liver, and eggs—each egg contains 250 milligrams! Considering the amount of cholesterol you eat in the rest of your food, and the hidden eggs in much of the baked food we eat, it is certainly wise to consider cutting down on your consumption of eggs, especially if your other risk factors are high, or if you have a family history of heart disease. Ask your doctor about your own blood cholesterol level at your next checkup, and ask his or her advice on lowering it if it is elevated.

The committee made a specific recommendation on the effect of polyunsaturated and saturated fats. The best course is to *cut back on the total fat in your diet,* rather than adding polyunsaturates to balance saturated fat intake, especially since there is already a widely held belief among researchers that high fat intake is a major cause of cancer. Emphasize polyunsaturated fats only as a substitute for some saturated fat. It is by no means a cure-all, and you should not try to use it as a dietary balancing act.

A hopeful sign in recent research is the discovery of a difference between two types of *lipoproteins,* substances which transport the cholesterol and other fatty substances throughout the bloodstream. Scientists have identified low density lipoproteins (LDL) and high density lipoproteins (HDL). The level of LDL, which carries a great deal of cholesterol, is very responsive to the dietary intake level of fat and cholesterol. HDL carries less cholesterol and appears to help prevent heart disease, possibly by removing some of the cholesterol from the walls of the arteries. For as yet unknown reasons, people with high levels of HDL have been shown to have less risk of heart disease, and HDL levels have been experimentally increased through exercise, nicotinic acid, and estrogens. Continued research in this area may lead to a greater understanding of the workings of heart disease, particularly the importance of female hormones (estrogens). Premenopausal women are far less likely to suffer from heart disease than men. While research is still going on in this area, the best procedure is to keep your fat and cholesterol consumption low and your exercise level higher.

- *Goal 7: Reduce the intake of sodium* by reducing the intake of salt to about five grams a day.

The primary villain here is hypertension, which is not some sort of psychological disturbance resulting from too much stress; *hypertension* is another word for high blood pressure, a disease which increases the likelihood of atherosclerosis and stroke. Sodium intake has been conclusively shown to raise the blood pressure of hypertensive individuals, and has been implicated as a cause of hypertension as well, but only in certain individuals. The substance won't cause the disease unless you have a hereditary weakness, but in large amounts it appears to bring on the disease if the tendency is present in your genetic makeup.

Estimates indicate that 20 percent of the total population is susceptible to hypertension, with the figure rising to 40 percent in older people. More than ten million Americans are known to suffer from the disease, and there are an unknown number of additional undiagnosed cases. This all points to one suggestion: Cut back on your salt intake.

Salt has crept into virtually every processed food on the shelf. You can make a point of checking labels as you shop and choosing those products with the least salt (remember, ingredients are listed on the label in order, according to the quantities in which they appear in the product), but a better suggestion is to cut back on your consumption of processed foods.

By leaning heavily on fresh foods, you will cut back on your intake of salt and other chemical additives. If you are an average American, you are currently eating between 27 and 75 times as much salt as your body requires. Follow the advice of Dr. Jean Mayer, formerly professor of nutrition at Harvard University and now president of Tufts University. When asked for the single simplest recommendation he could make for people who wanted to avoid heart diease, Dr. Mayer answered, "Take the salt shaker off the dinner table. And cut down on salt in cooking."

There are many holes in the present state of nutritional knowledge, and they allow critics to question the advantages of dietary change. But the real question is, why *not* change our diet? Dr. D. M. Hegsted of Harvard University asked the Senate committee, "What are the risks associated with eating less meat, less fat, less saturated fat, less cholesterol, less sugar, less salt, and more fruits, vegetables, unsaturated fat, and cereal products—especially whole grain cereals? There are none that can be identified, and important benefits can be expected."

And surely, the program suggested is going to be better for you than the processed or fast foods you may have been consuming. The New American Eating Guide (Table 3, pages 96–99) can be one of your most useful tools in retirement, since it will help you feel right to live the life you have chosen.

ACTION PLAN FOR NUTRITION

The dietary goals of the committee are quite explicit about how to improve your health. By changing your general eating pattern toward more healthful groups of foods, you can meet the committee's standards for a well-balanced diet. The Center for Science in the Public Interest, a nonprofit consumer advocacy group, has prepared the New American Eating Guide, based on widely accepted nutritional principles of preventive medicine (see Table 3). By organizing commonly eaten foods into categories of relative value, taking less-valuable foods into consideration, you can balance your diet without keeping a calculator on the table. And this is a program the whole family can follow—setting good eating patterns is just as crucial to grandchildren as it is to grandparents.

Eating can be a real joy, especially when you know that your diet is keeping you healthy.

Eat foods from each of the four food groups every day. Each food group contains different nutrients that your body needs. But each group has some foods that are better than others. These indications of plus foods and minus foods will help you select the best plan for good health.

A good diet consists of vegetables, fruits, whole wheat bread and grains, potatoes, beans, lean meat, fish, poultry, and lowfat dairy products. This diet is high in nutrients and low in fat, sugar, salt, and cholesterol.

Pick plenty of "anytime" foods—they should be the backbone of your diet. They are low in fat (less than 30 percent of a food's calories) and low in sugar and salt. Grain foods are mostly unrefined whole grains, and therefore high in fiber and trace minerals.

Next best are the "in moderation" foods. They contain moderate amounts of either saturated fats or unsaturated fats. Some items contain large amounts of fat, but mostly monounsaturated or polyunsaturated. Footnotes in the table indicate the drawbacks of the foods listed.

Eat small portions of "now and then" foods and eat them less often than the other foods. They are usually high in fat, with large amounts of saturated fats, or they are very high in added sugar, salt, or cholesterol.

Foods that contain low to moderate amounts of fat but are high in sugar, salt, cholesterol, or refined grains are listed as "In Moderation" or as "Now and Then" foods.

You can make a game out of rating your diet by keeping track of the foods you eat for one or several days. "Anytime" foods get one point, "in moderation" foods do not get any points, and "now and then" foods lose one point. If you have a plus score, congratulations! If you have a minus score, shape up!

Bon appetit!

Table 3. New American Eating Guide

Group 1. Beans, Grains, and Nuts
(four or more servings per day)

Any Time	In Moderation	Now and Then
bread and rolls (whole grain)	cornbread[8] flour tortilla[8] granola cereals[1 or 2] hominy grits[8] macaroni and cheese[1,(6),8] matzoh[8] nuts[3] pasta (other than whole wheat)[8] peanut butter[3] pizza[6,8] refined, unsweetened cereals[8] refried beans, commercial[1] or homemade in oil[2] seeds[3] soybeans[2] tofu[2] waffles or pancakes with syrup[5,(6),8] white bread and rolls[8] white rice[8]	croissant[4,8] doughnut (yeast-leavened)[3 or 4,5,8] presweetened breakfast cereals[5,8] sticky buns[1 or 2,5,8] stuffing (made with butter)[4,(6),8]

Group 2. Fruits and Vegetables
(four or more servings per day)

Any Time	In Moderation	Now and Then
all fruits and vegetables except those listed at right applesauce (unsweetened) unsweetened fruit juices	avocado[3] cole slaw[3] cranberry sauce (canned)[5] dried fruit french fries, homemade in vegetable	coconut[4] pickles[6]

Group 2. Fruits and Vegetables (continued)
(four or more servings per day)

Any Time	In Moderation	Now and Then
unsalted vegetable juices potatoes, white or sweet	oil[2] or commercial[1] fried eggplant (vegetable oil)[2] fruits canned in syrup[5] gazpacho[2,(6)] guacamole[3] potatoes au gratin[1,(6)] salted vegetable juices[6] sweetened fruit juices[5] vegetable canned with salt[6]	

Group 3. Milk Products
(children: three to four servings per day; adults: two servings per day)

Any Time	In Moderation	Now and Then
buttermilk made from skim milk lassi (lowfat yogurt and fruit juice drink) lowfat cottage cheese lowfat milk, one percent milkfat lowfat yogurt nonfat dry milk skim milk skim milk cheeses skim milk and banana shake	cocoa made with skim milk[5] cottage cheese, regular, 4 percent milkfat[1] frozen lowfat yogurt[5] ice milk[5] lowfat milk, 2 percent milkfat[1] lowfat yogurt, sweetened[5] mozzarella cheese, part-skim type only[1,(6)]	cheesecake[4,5] cheese fondue[4,(6)] cheese soufflé[4,(6),7] eggnog[1,5,7] hard cheeses: bleu, brick, Camembert, cheddar, Muenster, Swiss[4,(6)] ice cream[4,5] processed cheeses[4,6] whole milk[4] whole milk yogurt[4]

Table 3. New American Eating Guide (*Continued*)

Group 4. Poultry, Fish, Meat, and Eggs
(two servings per day)

Any Time	In Moderation	Now and Then
Poultry: chicken or turkey, boiled, baked, or roasted (no skin)	**Poultry:** chicken liver, baked or broiled[7] (just one!) fried chicken, home-made in vegetable oil[3] chicken or turkey, boiled, baked, or roasted (with skin)[2]	**Poultry:** fried chicken, com-mercially pre-pared[4]
Fish: cod flounder gefilte fish[(6)] haddock halibut perch pollack rockfish shellfish other than shrimp sole tuna, water-packed[(6)]	**Fish** (drained well, if canned): fried fish[1 or 2] herring[3,6] mackerel, canned[2,(6)] salmon, pink, canned[2,(6)] sardines[2] shrimp[7] tuna, oil-packed[2,(6)]	
	Red meats (trimmed of all outside fat!): leg or loin of lamb[1] pork shoulder or loin, lean[1] round steak or ground round rump roast[1] sirloin steak, lean[1] veal[1]	**Red meats:** bacon[4,(6)] beef liver, fried[1,7] bologna[4,6] corned beef[4,6] ground beef[4,6] ham, trimmed well[1,6] hot dogs[4,6] liverwurst[4,6] pig's feet[4] salami[4,6] sausage[4,6] spareribs[4] untrimmed red meats[4]

Group 4. Poultry, Fish, Meat, and Eggs (continued) *(two servings per day)*		
Any Time	**In Moderation**	**Now and Then**
Egg products: egg whites *only*		**Eggs:** cheese omelet[4,7] egg yolk or whole egg (about three per week)[3,7]

SOURCE: Center for Science in the Public Interest
NOTES: The small numbers after items in the chart denote a food's drawbacks.

[1] moderate fat, saturated
[2] moderate fat, unsaturated
[3] high fat, unsaturated
[4] high fat, saturated
[5] high in added sugar
[6] high in salt or sodium
([6]) may be high in salt or sodium, depending on manufacturer or recipe
[7] high in cholesterol
[8] refined grains

SWEETS

Adding a teaspoon of sugar to your food or eating occasional sweets will not cause any problems. Sugar becomes a problem when you eat high-sugar foods frequently, particularly between meals. Refined sugars now make up almost one-fifth of the average diet, three times as much as a hundred years ago. This sugar promotes tooth decay and obesity. Also, sugar's "empty calories" squeeze more nutritious food out of the diet.

FATS ADDED TO FOOD

Fats, oils, and shortening—like the fat that occurs in meat, dairy products, and other foods—add calories to the diet and can help make *you* fat. Even more importantly, eating too much *saturated* fat greatly increases the risk of heart disease. Use as little fat as you can. The better fats are mayonnaise, margarine, and vegetable oils (except coconut and palm), but even these can be overdone. The fats to avoid are those richest in saturated fat: butter, sour cream, cream cheese, lard, and coconut and palm oils. Fats used commercially (in restaurants, bakeries, etc.) often are high in saturated fat.

SNACKS

Snacking is fine, as long as the snacks are healthful and do not spoil your appetite for meals. Fruit, plain popcorn, raw vegetables, skim milk and banana shakes, and some of the foods in the "anytime" column all make fine snacks. Chocolate, doughnuts, ice cream, pies, and pastries are among the worst snacks, because they are high in both sugar and fat. When a sweet tooth strikes, and you are out of fruit, choose blueberry muffins, gingerbread, ice milk, sherbet, animal crackers, and graham crackers, which are high in sugar, but at least low in fat. Drink water, fruit or vegetable juice, or lowfat milk instead of soda pop and imitation fruit drinks. Good snacks usually lead to good health.

FAT AND CHOLESTEROL

Foods rich in saturated fat (meat, hard cheese, coconut and palm oils, etc.) and cholesterol (especially egg and liver) increase one's blood cholesterol level and the risk of heart disease. In some lucky people, however, this does not happen. Unless you know your cholesterol level and it is low (below 160 for young adults and 200 for middle-aged people), play it safe by eating fewer foods high in saturated fat and cholesterol.

All fats—saturated and unsaturated—may increase the risk of bowel and breast cancers.

SALT

Too much salt increases the risk of severity of high blood pressure. Instead of salt or soy sauce, try lemon juice, sour salt (citric acid), onions, curry powder, herbs, spices, or nothing, depending on the food. Use less salt, and let the real taste come through.

ADDITIVES

If you avoid foods with artificial colorings and sodium nitrite, not only do you avoid the most questionable additives, but also many foods that are high in sugar and fat. Also avoid foods artificially sweetened with saccharin.

ALCOHOL

A bottle of beer, a glass of wine,
  Now and then, they are just fine;
But much too much can cause liver disease,
  And don't forget the calories!

Beer (12 ounces, regular)	150 calories
Beer (12 ounces, lite)	75–100 calories
Wine (4 ounces)	100 calories
Gin, rum, vodka, whiskey (90 proof, 1 jigger)	110 calories

COOKING TIPS

Trim excess fat before and after cooking. Boil, broil, and bake, rather than fry. Try lowfat yogurt or applesauce on baked potatoes and bread, or use just a bit of margarine or other spread. Use less salt, shortening, or sugar than recipes call for. Substitute skim milk, lowfat milk, or buttermilk for whole milk; lowfat yogurt for sour cream and mayonnaise; and egg whites for eggs.

"New American Eating Guide": The preceding nutritional program was prepared by the Center for Science in the Public Interest, and is available in colorful poster form for $2 from C.S.P.I., 1755 S Street NW, Washington, D.C. © 1979 by Center for Science in the Public Interest. Reprinted by permission.

FOR FURTHER READING

Books

Deutsch, Ronald, *Realities of Nutrition;* Bull Publishing paperback, 1976.

Mayer, Jean, *A Diet for Living;* David McKay, hardcover, 1975; Pocket Books, paperback, 1976.

These two books provide solid answers to your nutritional questions and do not advocate the fads and fantasies of the "miracle cure" diet books now available. Dr. Mayer, who was a professor of nutrition at Harvard University for over twenty-five years before becoming president of Tufts University, is always worth reading. He is a frequent contributor to *Family Health* magazine, and writes a syndicated newspaper column (with Johanna Dwyer) which is an entertaining way to keep up to date on the latest findings and opinions on food and fitness.

Jacobson, Michael F., *Eater's Digest: The Consumer's Factbook of Food Additives;* Anchor Doubleday paperback, updated 1976.

This easy-to-understand guidebook describes over one hundred commonly used additives, assessing their relative safety and the degree to which each has been thoroughly tested.

Jacobson, Michael F., *Nutrition Scoreboard;* Avon paperback, 1975.

Along with an in-depth discussion of nutrition and its relationship to the development of disease, this volume features a simple rating system which makes it possible to compare the relative nutritional value of each food.

Cookbooks

American Heart Association Cookbook; McKay hardcover, 1975; Ballantine paperback, 1977.

Heiss, Gordon, and Heiss, Kay, *Eat to Your Heart's Content: The Low Cholesterol Gourmet Cookbook;* Chronicle Books, 1972 (out of print, but widely available in libraries).

Keys, Dr. Ancel, and Keys, Margaret, *How to Eat Well and Stay Well the Mediterranean Way;* Doubleday, 1975 (out of print, but widely available in libraries).

Lappe, Frances Moore, *Diet for a Small Planet;* Ballantine paperback, 1975 (vegetarian cuisine).

Ringrose, Helen, *The Anti-Coronary Cookbook;* Chartwell Books, 1978.

Roberts, Leviton, *The Jewish Low-Cholesterol Cookbook;* P. S. Eriksson, 1978.

Robertson, Laurel, et al., *Laurel's Kitchen: A Handbook for Vegetarian Cookery and Nutrition;* Nilgiri Press hardcover, 1976; Bantam paperback, 1978.

Booklets

Center for Science in the Public Interest Publications:

Midget Encyclopedia. The five volumes in this "encyclopedia" are each eight-panel brochures, amusingly written and illustrated but with serious messages about "newtrition," the movement away from high-cholesterol, high-fat, high-salt-and-sugar, additive-ridden foods, and why this change is important to each of us. $1.00 for the set of five.

Posters. "The New American Eating Guide" presented here on pages 96–99 is available in the form of a colorful poster for $2.00.

"Chemical Cuisine" is an 18-by-24-inch poster which dramatically illustrates the relative safety of the additives found in our food. Based on Michael Jacobson's book, *Eater's Digest* (see above), available for $2.00.

Based on another of Dr. Jacobson's books (he is the president and founder of CSPI), "Nutrition Scoreboard" will tell you at a glance the relative nutritional value of over two hundred foods, along with valuable nutritional tips. The "Nutrition Scoreboard" poster is available for $1.75.

Note: All indicated prices are subject to change.

Magazine. CSPI publishes a monthly magazine called *Nutrition Action,* which is often controversial in the way it takes on the food industry; it is certainly interesting and thought-provoking for the concerned consumer. Subscriptions cost $10 for one year, $18 for two years, $7.50 a year for full-time students or people over age sixty-five.

All CSPI publications can be ordered from CSPI Reports, P.O. Box 7226, Washington, DC 20044.

United States Government Publications:

Food. Prepared by the Department of Agriculture, this colorful booklet concentrates on selecting healthful, nutritious foods in the light of current medical information, with special attention to the question of what to eat for breakfast, given the poor traditional choices of bacon, eggs, and highly sweetened cereals. Available for $3.25 from the Consumer Information Center, U.S. Government Printing Office, Washington, DC 20402.

Nutrition: Food at Work for You. Explains functions and sources of major nutrients; how to estimate your daily food needs; tips on buying and storing food. Available free from the Consumer Information Center, Pueblo, CO 81009.

Mazola Nutrition Library. The Mazola Margarine Company is offering a set of four free booklets about the benefits of proper low-cholesterol diet and exercise. You can receive "The Fitness Connection," "Eating Well (Nutrition Facts You Should Know)," "Four Keys to a Healthy Heart," and "Shaping Up for the Long Run" by sending your request to Mazola Nutrition Library, Dept. BYB Box 307, Coventry, CT 06238.

6

EXERCISE
AND FITNESS

Better to hunt in fields, for health unbought,
Than fee the doctor for a nauseous draught.
The wise, for cure, on exercise depend;
God never made his work for man to mend.
                                        JOHN DRYDEN

If we can honestly be said to have a national pastime today, it may very well be sitting. Technology has removed the need to walk from place to place, to exert yourself in keeping up your home, heating it, or providing it with water. Most of us earn our living at jobs which require very little physical labor. The body, unfortunately, hasn't changed to meet the new freedom from demands which all of our mechanical wonders have given us. Instead, it has deteriorated from disuse, leaving us not only more prone to disease but less able to enjoy the pleasures of life. As our bodies become burdens to us, we box ourselves in with our sedentary indoor amusements. But before your first day of retirement arrives, you *can* and *should* get in shape to participate actively in the rest of your life.

I must admit that it's a mystery to me how I keep in such good shape. Every time I get a physical examination a doctor or nurse will say, "Oh, you must be a jogger." I ask them why, and they tell me I have a very low pulse rate and a rapid pulse recovery rate. I don't jog—I used to, but I hurt my knee years ago and every time I run for a couple of weeks, the knee begins to give me a problem, and then it takes two months to heal. So I said, Why do that to my knee?

I get my workout now by walking up thirty-four flights of stairs once a day (going up to our apartment), and according to the "How Healthy Is Your Lifestyle" table on pages 66–67, this amount of physical activity is sufficient to put me in the "no risk" category. I don't really get as much exercise as I'd like, but the muscle tone seems to stay, so I must be lucky in this respect.

The word *exercise* is not a pleasant one. It conjures up images of physical fitness drills in high school gym class, or grunting overweight women struggling to shed a few pounds. In either case, someone else is the drill sergeant, submitting the unfit to exercises on command.

As an adult, *you* should be able to decide what sort of exercise program fits your needs and temperament, and then take pleasure in the activity. Certainly, exercise requires exertion, but you can enjoy exerting yourself if you do it right. There is nothing like the sensation of well-toned muscles moving at your will, or an improved self-image from your new feeling of accomplishment, attractiveness, self-control, and good health. Medical science tells us that a physically fit body:

- is less likely to develop heart disease or hypertension
- is more resistant to infection
- preserves a youthful metabolic rate
- maintains stronger, less brittle bones
- has greater muscular strength, endurance, coordination, flexibility, and balance
- is relatively free of minor aches, pains, and stiffness
- displays better posture
- has a more attractive general appearance

- adjusts to stress more easily
- shows better reaction time

All of the above can be true of your body if you participate in a regular exercise program. And you don't have to become an athlete or a bodybuilder. In fact, the latest findings indicate that there is very little gained through extremes of physical exertion. The key word is *moderation*. Twenty minutes a day at least three times a week, on nonconsecutive days, will produce benefits to the cardiovascular system and the body as a whole. And I'm not suggesting you throw yourself down to do push-ups or other calisthenics—one of the best exercises, particularly if you are just starting your physical fitness program, is brisk walking.

EXERCISE AND AGE

Perhaps you feel that you are too old to exercise? It just isn't true, although certainly you must use good sense in selecting a program appropriate to your present physical condition. Gerontologist Dr. Alex Comfort cites a 1968 study in which a group of seventy-year-old men took part in a regular supervised exercise program for one year and ended up with results equal to those accomplished by men thirty years younger. Exercise can even promote healing among patients who have suffered accidents or illness at advanced ages.

We met many people, in the course of researching this book, whose continued vitality and physical prowess later in life was extremely impressive. One of the most outstanding examples was Warren Anderson, a semiretired accountant.

The unwrinkled, energetic man we encountered in the locker room of a midtown Manhattan gym looked to be in his early sixties. "I am eighty-two years old by the calendar," said Anderson, who has been working out at the gym only a year and a half, "but physically I haven't reached that point yet." Genetic heritage is partially responsible for his good health (he delights in showing his most recent medical readout, which shows everything to be within normal range), but Anderson credits his exercise regimen as well. "It's the greatest thing I could have done. It's had a great physical and mental effect, and I would recommend it to anyone whose doctor approves."

After a year and a half of three-times-a-week exercise, Anderson's physical strength has improved dramatically. "I've developed muscles where I had flab for years," he says with obvious satisfaction. This increase in physical endurance has not only helped to maintain his health but has also had a salutary effect on his sense of emotional well-being.

Like good nutrition, the effects of exercise are cumulative throughout your lifetime. The earlier you start, the better off you will be. You can start your program of improved fitness today. If you are in reasonably good health, go outside and take a brisk walk. It will make your blood flow a little faster, put some fresh air in your lungs, increase your alertness, and whet your appetite for more. On the road to physical fitness, it is literally true that the journey begins with a single step.

What Kind of Exercise Program for You?

Exercise must become a regular part of your life, and the only way you will stick with it is to choose a program which fits your personality, your lifestyle, and your abilities. Your physical fitness program will have three goals:

- Cardio-respiratory fitness. The maintenance and improvement of your circulatory system and lung capacity is the key to lowering your chances of heart disease.
- Flexibility. When you are able to move smoothly and easily through exercise, your everyday movements will seem easier and you can fight the feeling of "creakiness" or stiffness.

- Strength. Increasing your muscular strength gives you the power you need to move and carry things yourself, to be self-sufficient, and to maintain an attractive appearance.

Forget about the exercises you hate, the ones which were probably inflicted on you as a child. You want to *avoid* push-ups—or any other exercise which involves locking your joints in place. You want to *avoid* sit-ups and toe touching with stiff knees—they're bad for your back and do little to build up your muscles.

The key to your exercise program is *movement*. The only kinds of exercise which can help to build your heart and lung capacity are aerobic exercises. Aerobics, a technique popularized by Kenneth Cooper, is not a gimmick or far-out system. Aerobic exercises are those which force your body to use more oxygen, to breathe more heavily and increase your pulse rate, for a prolonged period of time. These exercises include walking, running, jogging, rope skipping, swimming, bicycling, skating, rowing, cross-country skiing, and aerobic dance, among others. Any of these, combined with simple stretching movements, can get you into excellent physical shape.

I haven't included competitive sports in the list because competition tends to push people to overexert themselves in order to win, leading to strained muscles and often to a psychologically defeating experience. A constructive exercise program pushes you to personal limits, not those set by your adversary's abilities. Finally, you must have a partner to engage in a competitive sport, and if your partner isn't available, you'll lose the regular pattern of exertion which is essential for proper conditioning. This is not to say that sports should not play a part in your physical fitness. Competition adds spice to any endeavor, and a session on the basketball court or softball field is a wonderful way to enjoy the fitness your regular exercise provides.

Many people find that it helps them to make exercise a part of their regular routine if they belong to a group or organization which offers a fitness program. In almost every community there are YMCAs, adult education programs, or community centers which offer exercise classes, often organized by age groups and sex, which offer instruction, supervision, and the chance to meet other people in a friendly atmosphere.

Many companies, including Xerox, Chase Manhattan Bank, and

several smaller firms, are providing medically supervised exercise programs for their executives as a worthwhile investment in the health of the company. Many corporate fitness programs have been limited to executives in the past, but this is slowly changing, and we can look for a growing demand for this kind of preventive health care as an employee benefit. There are already several firms which supply fitness advisory services to companies which care about their employees' health.

Or you might join a commercial health spa or club. The drawbacks of these facilities include high prices and an accent on saunas, exercise machines, and weightlifting equipment rather than cardiovascular conditioning. However, these establishments do have the stationary bicycles, pools, and other equipment which can be tools to better fitness. The best spas have professional exercise specialists who can personalize a program for you. If this route appeals to you, try to get a short-term contract before making a high-priced lifetime commitment.

Make Your Life More Difficult

One of the easiest ways to work more exercise into your life is to do things the hard way for a change. For years you have used the least exertion to get from place to place, work in the house, do your job, and so on. Now is the time to look at your daily schedule and find the places where a little extra effort can be conveniently expended.

If you travel to work by bus or train, maybe you can walk to the next station away. The same is true of those quick hops in the car to go shopping. If you walk an extra mile in each direction (that's only a fifteen-minute walk at a brisk pace), you will have started on the road to aerobic conditioning.

Climbing stairs, even when you don't have to, is another convenient exercise opportunity. This is terrific exercise—with every step you take upward, you are lifting your entire body weight up a few inches and are strengthening your legs and your cardiovascular system. Challenge yourself to increase the number of flights you can walk without getting winded. Don't push yourself to the point of exhaustion—just feel the effects of your exertion and enjoy them, knowing that in just a few minutes you've done yourself some good.

You can work a little stretching exercise into your daily routine as well. At home or at the office, take a few moments off from what you're doing and just stretch. You'll find the brief break you take will do a lot more to perk you up than that extra cup of coffee.

Medical Care and Exercise

The first part of any physical fitness plan should be getting your doctor's okay. If you have had a physical examination in the past six months or year, it may be enough to call your doctor on the phone for his approval. An annual check-up is generally recommended for anyone over fifty, and it is even a good idea if you are over forty, especially if you have some chronic disorder in your personal, or even your family, history.

Again, remember to do your homework *before* you see the doctor. Have an exercise plan in hand that you would like to start, and explain why you think it fits your needs. Your doctor may know of a program that is more suited to your current physical condition, or even recommend a local group which will provide an organized framework for your workouts.

One of the best approaches to exercise is obtaining *an exercise evaluation profile* from one of the growing number of programs and clinics across the country. Under a doctor's supervision, these clinics thoroughly test your current level of exercise tolerance, using treadmill or stationary bicycle tests, and then provide a personalized exercise preparation for you to follow. Call your local YMCA, a community hospital, the local chapter of the American Heart Association, or a doctor who specializes in cardiology for further information about these evaluation programs. The testing is fairly expensive (about $150 through the YMCA, sometimes more with other organizations), but this could be the most valuable investment of time and money you've ever made. You'll be buying a tool to build yourself a better body.

ACTION PLAN FOR EXERCISE

The following is an easy-to-follow exercise program designed in cooperation with Sally J. Stewart, director of health and physical education at the McBurney Branch of the YMCA of Greater New York. It is aimed at increasing your cardiovascular fitness through aerobic exercise and improving your flexibility and strength. You should plan to set aside about an hour for exercise on at least three nonconsecutive days a week.

There are three parts to your conditioning exercise session:
1. Warm-up
2. Exercise
3. Cool-down

Warm-up (10 minutes)

Spend the first part of your session doing a few simple exercises to get your heart pumping a little faster than normal and to loosen up your muscles and joints.

FIRST 3–5 MINUTES

- Walk around at a relaxed, easy pace, with an occasional burst of quicker movement.

- Shrug your shoulders, rotating them forward and backward.
- Standing upright, raise first one knee, then the other, repeating several times.
- Standing upright with arms outstretched, twist slowly from side to side, letting arms swing freely, keeping knees bent and letting heels come off the floor as you swing.
- Sitting on the floor with your feet straight out in front of you, lean back slowly until you are resting on your elbows. Pedal with your legs as if you were riding a bicycle.
- Stand in front of a wall at arm's length (about 18 inches away). Place both hands against the wall, with your feet flat on the floor, and bend your elbows so you lean into the wall. Keep your heels on the floor throughout.

SECOND 5–7 MINUTES

- With hands on your hips, bend at the waist, first forward, then back upright, then from side to side.
- Lying on the floor, do sit-ups *with knees bent,* feet flat on the floor.
- Lying on the floor, keeping one knee bent, slowly raise and lower the unbent leg several times. Switch legs and repeat.
- Lie down on your stomach. Lift one leg up behind you until you can grab it with your hand. Pull the leg toward your head *gently,* stretching the muscles. If you have a good sense of balance, you can try this same exercise while standing on one foot.

Aerobic Exercise (20 minutes)

Your goal in this segment of the exercise session is to perform regular, rhythmic movements with your major muscles, increasing your heart rate (giving your respiratory and circulatory systems a workout) and improving your stamina.

How hard should your heart beat in order to provide the beneficial training effects of aerobic exercise? To determine your target heart rate, start by subtracting your age from 220. The result will give your *age-estimated maximum heart rate*. Your *target* heart rate is between 70 percent and 85 percent of this figure. For example, a fifty-year-old man or woman would subtract 50 from 220 to get a maximum heart rate of 170. This person's target zone is then between 119 (70% of 170) and 145 (85% of 170) beats per minute.

In your exercise session you should try to reach your target zone and sustain it for at least twenty minutes. During the first few weeks of your program, if you are starting out in fairly poor shape, you might settle for a target rate of only 60 percent of maximum, but try to progress quickly beyond that level. As you continue to gain in endurance and strength, you will find that it takes more strenuous effort to raise your heart rate and that you can comfortably maintain this level of exertion for longer periods of time.

When you start your program, you will have to determine your target zone by taking your pulse to determine your heart rate during your workout. As you continue to exercise regularly, you will come to recognize it by the way you feel—how hard you are breathing, how your heart is pounding, whether or not you are sweating. Initially, though, take the time to take your pulse, either by placing your fingers on your waist in line with your index finger, placing your hand over your heart, or placing two fingers on your temples. Count the beats you feel for *ten seconds*. Multiply this number by six to get your heart rate.

Take your pulse about halfway through the aerobic portion of your workout, keeping your arms and legs moving slightly. If your pulse while you are working out is lower than the 70 percent figure, increase the intensity of your exercise. If it is above 85 percent, take it a little easier.

In addition to monitoring your target heart rate, there are two other ways of telling whether you are overexerting yourself in performing your aerobic exercises. First, you should be able to talk while you exercise. If you are too winded to do this, slow down.

Second, you should not feel pain while exercising. You should feel like you are exerting yourself and a bit tired after working out for a while, but you should not experience physical discomfort. If you do feel pain while exercising, stop, cool down, and start again, more gently, another day. The key to success in exercising to condition your body is to work up gradually, *not* to place sudden burdens on your system.

There are many exercises that will build up your heart rate and keep it at a high enough level for a long enough period of time to do you some good. These include running, ice skating, jogging, roller skating, walking, bicycling, hiking, rowing, swimming, cross-country skiing, rope skipping, and folk or square dancing. There are certain sports that can fill the bill as well, such as tennis, table tennis, and volleyball, but the way sports are usually played, they do not provide the *continuous* effort needed for aerobic benefits.

For beginners, the best choices for the exercise segment of your workout are probably walking, running, jogging, or cycling. These activities are easy to pursue faster or slower at will, allowing you to maintain control over your exertions. They also require little in the way of equipment, and with a little preparation can be performed indoors as well as out.

Tables 4 and 5 show two training regimens which have worked for hundreds of beginning exercisers in the YMCA fitness programs. Whether you decide to try one of these or prefer to try your own combination of aerobic activities, your goals remain the same—to raise your heart rate until it falls within your target zone and to keep it there for between fifteen and sixty minutes. And to enjoy yourself.

Table 4 shows a thirty-minute walking program designed for those who are in fairly poor condition. It involves two walking paces—a stroll (covering a mile in about eighteen minutes, this is a fairly relaxed walk) and a brisk walk (covering a mile in about thirteen minutes). Of course, you are free to adjust the pace to fit the way you feel and the way your heart rate reacts. The program is broken up into two halves, the first somewhat more strenuous than the second. After the first fifteen-minute segment, take your pulse and make sure that you are on target. If not, increase or decrease your activity accordingly.

The second program (Table 5) is for those who are in somewhat better shape and feel a little more ambitious. It incorporates brisk walking and jogging, which should be done at a speed of about six miles per hour (covering a mile in about ten minutes). Since you will be moving faster, the workout will last only twenty minutes.

Table 4. Walking Program for Aerobic Conditioning

	First 15 Minutes	Second 15 Minutes
Week 1	30 minutes of continuous strolling	
Week 2		
Week 3	stroll 3 minutes, brisk walk 1 minute (repeat until 15 minutes expire)	stroll 5 minutes, brisk walk 1 minute (repeat until 15 minutes expire)
Week 4	stroll 2 minutes, brisk walk 2 minutes	stroll 4 minutes, brisk walk 2 minutes
Week 5	stroll 2 minutes, brisk walk 3 minutes	stroll 4 minutes, brisk walk 3 minutes
Week 6	stroll 1 minute, brisk walk 4 minutes	stroll 3 minutes, brisk walk 4 minutes
Week 7	stroll 1 minute, brisk walk 5 minutes	stroll 2 minutes, brisk walk 5 minutes
Week 8	stroll 1 minute, brisk walk 6 minutes	stroll 2 minutes, brisk walk 6 minutes
Week 9	stroll 1 minute, brisk walk 7 minutes	stroll 1 minute, brisk walk 7 minutes
Week 10	full 15 minutes brisk walking	full 15 minutes varied-pace walking

Table 5. Brisk Walking-Jogging Program for Aerobic Conditioning

	First 10 Minutes	Second 10 Minutes
Week 1 Week 2	20 minutes of continuous brisk walking	
Week 3	brisk walk 2½ minutes, jog ½ minute (repeat until 10 minutes expire)	brisk walk 2½ minutes, jog ½ minute (repeat until 10 minutes expire)
Week 4	brisk walk 1½ minutes, jog 1 minute	brisk walk 2½ minutes, jog 1 minute
Week 5	brisk walk 1 minute, jog 1 minute	brisk walk 2 minutes, jog 1 minute
Week 6	brisk walk 1 minute, jog 2 minutes	brisk walk 2 minutes, jog 2 minutes
Week 7	brisk walk 1 minute, jog 3 minutes	brisk walk 1 minute, jog 2 minutes
Week 8	brisk walk 1 minute, jog 4 minutes	brisk walk 1 minute, jog 3 minutes
Week 9	brisk walk 1 minute, jog 5 minutes	brisk walk 1 minute, jog 4 minutes
Week 10	jog 10 minutes	walk/jog 10 minutes

Cool-down (5–10 minutes)

When you have completed your aerobic exercise, *don't* stop immediately. Slow down gradually. Ease up on your exercise, and intersperse some more stretching and limbering exercises like the ones you did in the warm-up period with calisthenics.

Your heart rate should be no more than 120 beats per minute five minutes into the cool-down period, and below 100 within ten minutes. If it takes you longer than this to recover your normal heart rate, you have been working out too strenuously.

STRESS

Stress has been present ever since human beings first got up and walked on two legs. Whether it was an immediate need to catch an animal for food or an immediate need to escape an animal which was contemplating a human lunch, our primitive ancestors had the same reaction we do today in the face of stress: a rapid pulse, a rush of energy, maximum muscle strength, quickened reaction time, heightened senses, faster breathing. This is the "fight or flight" reaction: the body pours all its energy into those functions which would produce peak physical efficiency.

Although our lifestyle has made violent solutions to problems generally unacceptable, the human body reacts in more subtle ways to contemporary stress. When your boss attacks one of your pet ideas, your adrenaline pumps, your digestive system shuts down, and your physical state often interferes with your calm, rational abilities.

In today's world, we have a constant stream of relatively minor stimuli which keep our bodies at an almost-continuous low level of stress. The evening news, the broken appliance, pressure on the job, the persistent roar of traffic may not bother us on a conscious level, but our bodies still react.

Not all stressful incidents are negative. Sexual activity is certainly not passive—pleasurable as it is, it involves tension, and the tension is in direct proportion to the pleasure. But unlike other forms of stress, sex is not likely to leave a residue of harmful, unrelieved tension and may actually carry away other accumulated pressures of daily living.

Dealing with Stress

It was not until the 1950s that scientists began to recognize chronic stress as a significant factor in medical problems. Since that time, research has linked stress to high blood pressure, kidney disease, ulcers and other digestive problems, and the rheumatic diseases. It has been shown that stress wears down the body's immune system, leaving you more vulnerable to infection. It is also a strong risk factor in the development of heart disease and cancer. The psychological reactions to prolonged stress—in short tempers, inability to concentrate, and lack of sleep—have become so second nature to modern man that we rarely dig down to the cause of these complaints. The fact that the tranquilizer Valium is now the most widely prescribed drug on the market is ample proof of the epidemic proportions of stress in our society. It is possible, though, to deal with stress and minimize its harmful effects by carefully evaluating your personal situation and taking the steps necessary to gain control of the problem.

The realm of stress-provoking incidents is as wide as human personalities are diverse. You may have a strong emotional reaction to mice, or financial problems, or minor physical pain. Your neighbor doesn't worry if he's down to his last cent in the bank, but he becomes hysterical when his mother-in-law visits for the day. It is difficult to isolate universal factors here. Your personal history will determine to a large degree the events or conditions you find stressful and your degree of adaptability to stressful conditions. Dr. Jerome E.

Singer and Dr. David C. Glass, authors of *Urban Stress,* have identified three key characteristics which help to minimize the effects of stressful situations:

- *Predictability.* If the stressful element occurs on a regular, predictable basis, it is far easier to deal with. The classic example is the family who lives by the railroad tracks, so used to the trains passing in the night that they sleep right through the noise.
- *Social Context.* If a person perceives a benefit to himself derived from the stress-producing activity, he will accept it more readily and suffer fewer after effects. For instance, the hammering of a carpenter putting up shelves in your own apartment probably won't bother you at all; the same noise coming from your neighbor's apartment may drive you up the wall.
- *Control.* If you feel that you have control over a cause of stress, you will be less likely to suffer ill effects. In one of their experiments, Singer and Glass subjected two groups of volunteers to identical potentially annoying noises. One group had buttons which would cut off the noise if it became too bothersome; the other group did not. Even though most of the group with the control buttons did not use them, and so were subjected to the same noise as the second group, those who felt they had control dealt better with frustration and with other people.

By actively dealing with stress you are taking a major step toward an easier, happier, healthier life. If you can consciously eliminate stressful stimuli from your life and cope with those which are unavoidable, you will gain a feeling of control over your life. The positive reinforcement you will give yourself by conquering stress in one area will feed your feeling of control, which in turn will make it easier to confront other causes of stress.

Look at your reasons for reacting to people and events in certain ways. Don't make your self-appraisal more difficult than necessary, but give yourself an honest, thorough going-over. The first level of self-examination is external, identifying those elements in the world around you which cause you stress. As you identify them, you may see a pattern emerging, a personality profile which will give you some insight into the way you tick. Knowledge of your own personality patterns fulfills two of the goals for alleviating stress—it makes stressful incidents more predictable, and gives you more control in dealing with them.

ACTION PLAN FOR STRESS MANAGEMENT

1. Keep a stress diary. Carry a small notepad with you for one weekday and one weekend day. Jot down everything stressful that occurs. Be sensitive to all the incidents that trigger a stress response in you, not just the ones you would expect. Also take note of the ways in which you react. Do you rant and rave if the paperboy delivers the newspaper late? Does your stomach tense as you contemplate another day at the office?

    You may find that you are scribbling away furiously, but if you can't find the immediate *source* of your tension, just write down your stress *symptoms*—fast talking or eating, irritability, impatience, chain smoking—for later analysis.

2. Look for stressful factors you can eliminate. Give yourself some time alone to examine the results of your stress diary. How many simple annoyances could be easily eliminated? If the paperboy is always late with his delivery, why not make a point of picking up the newspaper yourself? Cut down on negative stress by ridding yourself of as many constant sources of annoyance as possible, and give yourself credit for every stress producer you conquer.

3. Look for stressful factors to which you overreact. Why does a particular incident have such a strong effect on you? Try to

get some perspective on the things that annoy you, and make an attempt to find some humor in the situation. Instead of holding in your annoyances and allowing them to simmer and stew, bring them out into the open and put them in their place. Try them out on a friend with a sympathetic ear, a positive attitude, and a hearty laugh.

4. Try to identify the basic problems. Let's say that your daily schedule is getting you down because it is not interesting or challenging enough, and you are bored. Living with that boredom and letting it eat away at you is allowing a poison to remain in your system. Take control of the situation through some positive action.

Add some new activities to your life or enroll in a course to improve some of your skills or pick up new ones. There is very rarely a situation in life which does not leave some room for improvement; think about your next move and pursue it with determination. Whether it's your daily routine, your friends and family, your material possessions, or your way of life that is bothering you, don't be a victim! As you arrange your finances, improve your health, and investigate your new opportunities, you will find that the act of planning itself is a primary stress prevention technique, since it effectively takes away much of the fearful uncertainty about the present and the future.

5. Cope with unavoidable stress. There are, of course, many types of stressful circumstances which cannot be avoided. There are varying levels of stress whenever there is pressure to perform, and that includes not only job situations but social gatherings, recreational activities, and sexual involvement as well. All major change in life brings stress, whether it is the joy of an anniversary party or the birth of a grandchild, or the pain of loss or suffering. Accept the fact that the cause of this tension cannot be eliminated, and then work toward moderating its effect.

If you feel that you are under too much stress, take frequent breaks, even if each is quite short. If you work in an office, make a point of getting up from your desk from time to time and stretching, or taking a short walk. Take a minute from any prolonged period of concentration, close your eyes, and let your mind wander to a peaceful, relaxed setting where you have had pleasant experiences. Plan full-scale vacations when you can manage them, but try to work some mini-vacations into your plans also. A few hours during an evening or a weekend for a stroll through an art gallery, or a movie, can make an enormous difference in the way you feel. Time off is sound preventive medicine.

6. Talk to someone. Many of us build up complex systems of emotional conflicts. These can often seem like just too much to handle. If you feel that you are losing your balance, that you are on your way to a nervous breakdown, don't suffer in silence. Seeking help is *not* a sign of weakness.

If you are having trouble dealing with a problem by yourself—whether it is big or small—find someone to talk to whom you feel you can trust. That might be your spouse or a friend, but if you have trouble being open with someone you are close to, try your clergyman or your family doctor. They may be able to help you sort through the pressures which are troubling you and focus on possible solutions. They might recommend that you speak to someone who specializes in mental health, such as a psychiatrist or psychologist. You may have mixed feelings about consulting a professional, but you might at least give it a try just once. A therapist can provide a sympathetic, concerned outlook free from any embarrassment or pressure. A professional's experienced guidance can help you understand your situation and gain control of it.

You may never need this sort of assistance, but don't write it off as a possibility. And don't think that you are too old to be helped. Even if you are "set in your ways," a constructive suggestion which could make your life more enjoyable is a powerful motivation for change.

There are specific techniques designed to help you combat stress, including traditional disciplines like yoga and modern innovations like biofeedback training. The following drills for bringing about muscle and mental relaxation are used in the Stanford Heart Disease Prevention Program. Try them out today, and take them seriously. Even though they don't come with a prescription, they can be powerful medicine for improving the state of your health.

Deep Muscle Relaxation

Though this simple relaxation method is by no means the only effective one, it is easy to learn and practice. (Two important points of caution: First, under no circumstances should anyone taking blood-pressure-lowering drugs stop using these medications—or any other medication—after starting relaxation training. You may find that your pill dosage can be reduced, but this should be done only in close cooperation with your physician. Second, if you have a history of serious mental illness, do not begin a program of stress management without consulting your doctor.) Take time to learn this drill and the mental relaxation drill that follows. Make them work for you. Do not skip them. With practice, they can enable you to reduce muscle tension, lower blood pressure, and decrease headaches, insomnia, and anxiety.

DEEP MUSCLE RELAXATION DRILL

1. Find as quiet an environment as possible. Lie on your back in a comfortable position or sit comfortably. Close your eyes.
2. Begin with your hand of preference (right hand if you are right-handed, left hand if you are left-handed). Physically tense it for an instant, then relax it and let it go loose. Tell your hand to feel heavy and warm. Continue with the rest of that side of the body, moving up to forearm, upper arm, shoulder, then down to the foot, lower leg, and upper leg. Next, follow the same procedure on the other side of the body. The hands, arms, and legs should feel relaxed, heavy, and warm. Wait for these feelings. After mastering the

technique, you will not need to tense your muscles before relaxing them.

3. Next, relax the muscles of the hips and let a wave of relaxation pass up from the abdomen to the chest. Do not tense these muscles. Tell them to feel heavy and warm. Your breathing will come more from the diaphragm than from the chest and will be slower. Wait for this breathing change.

4. Now let the wave of relaxation continue into the shoulders, neck, jaw, and the muscles of the face. Pay special attention to the muscles controlling the eyes and forehead. Finish the drill by telling your forehead to feel cool.

Practice this drill twice daily; fifteen to twenty minutes is ideal (but even three minutes is better than nothing when circumstances do not permit a longer session). Practice before meals or no sooner than one hour after meals. You can also practice before an anticipated stress experience but no more frequently than four times a day.

With practice you will learn to attain deep muscle relaxation—the feeling of heavy, warm, inert muscles and a cool forehead—in as short a time as two minutes.

If you are not sure whether or not you are relaxed during this drill, ask another person to raise your arm or leg about six inches and then let it go; if it drops as a dead weight, your muscles are relaxed. Resistance indicates that muscle tension is still present. The benefits of deep muscle relaxation are many: lowered pulse rate and blood pressure, lowered breathing rate, decreased oxygen consumption, and a general feeling of calmness and tranquility.

Mental Relaxation

When you have learned to achieve at least a partial state of deep muscle relaxation, you are ready for the next step: clearing your mind of stressful thoughts and worries through mastery of the mental relaxation drill.

MENTAL RELAXATION DRILL

After entering a state of deep muscle relaxation, you are ready to begin the mental process that deepens the relaxation state. Your eyes are closed and your forehead is cool.

1. Enter a passive state; let thoughts flow through your head.
2. If thoughts recur, respond by saying "no" under your breath.
3. Imagine a calm blue sky or sea or any blue area or object without detail (with your eyes closed). Try to see the color blue (which has been found to be a particularly relaxing color).
4. Become aware of your slow, natural breathing. Follow each breath as you inhale and exhale.
5. If you still do not feel calm and rested, you may find it helpful to repeat a soothing word or sound (such as "ah"). Think of the word or sound silently, preferably during exhalation. Always remind yourself to keep the muscles of the face, eyes, and forehead loose and to keep the forehead cool.

The deep muscle relaxation drill and the mental relaxation drill are interactive and should be done together. Once you have learned both, simply combine them and practice them whenever you have a moment—until these skills are mastered. It may take you a few weeks to lower your blood pressure and achieve the general feeling of relaxation and control that you gain from better stress management.

Imagery Training

Imagery training is a useful method to assist you in the deep muscle relaxation and mental relaxation drills. Imagery training breaks down mental blocks to the use of your imagination. For people who are out of touch with their bodies, deep muscle relaxation is sometimes difficult to learn. Test yourself. Think of your left ear and imagine it feeling warm; then imagine your right calf muscle as feeling warm and heavy. Next try two harder tests. Imagine that your left leg is heavier than the right leg; then reverse the feeling. If you can do these tests easily, you should find it relatively easy to achieve deep muscle relaxation. If you cannot, you will benefit from the muscle-finding drill.

DRILL FOR MUSCLE FINDING

1.   Lie comfortably on your back in a quiet room. Become passive.

2.   Tense all the muscles of your body for about five seconds; then let them go as limp as you can. Notice the difference in feeling.

3.   Repeat Step 2, but now exhale your breath slowly during the total body relaxation. This will help create a limp, relaxed state.

4.   Try tensing and "letting go" of individual sets of muscles: hand, foot, arm, lower leg, upper leg, buttocks, neck, jaws, mouth, face, and forehead.

After a few weeks' practice, almost everyone will be able to reduce muscle tension significantly. Relaxation tapes for home playing may be helpful for those who have difficulty; taping your own instructions for these drills may also be helpful.

Even when you achieve deep muscle relaxation, intrusive, racing thoughts may prevent you from reaching a stage of complete muscle *and* mental relaxation. You may find this stage of partial deep muscle relaxation and free association of ideas rather pleasant; it can be a time for surprisingly effective problem solving. To achieve complete mental relaxation, it is helpful to incorporate imagery training into your combined relaxation drill by following these steps.

IMAGERY DRILL FOR MENTAL RELAXATION

1.   Bring yourself as deeply into the deep muscle relaxation/mental relaxation state as possible. Assuming that intrusive or racing thoughts remain a problem, continue.

2. Use the following two methods of "thought stopping":

a. When a thought returns too frequently or persists, say "no" out loud. If it returns, say "no" again. Repeat this self-command over a five- to ten-minute period, while remaining in the deep muscle relaxation and mental relaxation states.

b. If the verbal commands to stop seem to decrease the frequency of the recurrent intrusions, then change to a silent "no" when an unwanted, recurrent, or persistent thought prevents your entry into complete mental relaxation. When a further reduction in active thinking occurs, you are ready to continue.

3. Imagine a pleasant scene, such as a mountain lake, a calm ocean, a blue sky with drifting white clouds. Focus on this scene to replace the previous intrusive, racing thoughts.

4. When this succeeds, let the pleasant scene fade and enter the final stages of the drill.

5. Let a gray or black "nothingness" be the image before your closed eyes. Ignore any visual detail.

6. Finally, let blue colors drift in, often as patches. When they come, hold on to the particular feeling that lets the blue colors in. When you are at this point, you have usually reached zero muscle tension and complete mental relaxation.

Instant Relaxation

After you have achieved a satisfactory degree of success in deep muscle relaxation and mental relaxation, you should be able to enter partially into deep muscle relaxation and mental relaxation states within thirty seconds to three minutes.

INSTANT RELAXATION DRILL

1. Sit comfortably. (You can also learn to do this while standing, such as waiting in line, or just prior to an anticipated stressful event.)

2. Draw in a deep breath and hold it for five seconds (count to

five slowly), exhale slowly, and tell all your muscles to relax. Repeat this two or three times to become more completely relaxed.

3. If circumstances permit, imagine a pleasant thought ("I am learning how to relax") or a pleasant scene (a calm lake, a mountain stream, etc.).

Develop cueing systems to remind yourself to use this drill (for example, whenever you become impatient over having to wait). The instant relaxation drill takes from thirty to sixty seconds. In most stress circumstances, you can benefit from using either the deep muscle relaxation and mental relaxation drills or the instant relaxation drill. Each can be used when you are consciously attacking a specific, recurrent stress that you have identified. Each can also be used effectively as a refresher interspersed in your daily routine.

PERSONAL HABITS

Smoking. You must already know that smoking will make you a candidate for an early grave. Smoking has been reliably linked to death from heart disease and circulatory ailments, cancer of the lungs and other forms of cancer, chronic bronchitis, and emphysema. The State Mutual Life Assurance Company of America found that total death rates for smokers were more than *twice* as great as those for nonsmokers at all ages. A healthy, nonsmoking thirty-two-year-old man can expect to live to be 78.9 years old, while the thirty-two-year-old smoker can expect only 71.6 years. That's a 7.3-year penalty for puffing on cigarettes. Smoking is nothing more than a form of self-poisoning.

If everything you have already heard has not convinced you to stop, another set of statistics won't do the job, but the fact that you haven't quit in the past doesn't mean that you can't. The commitment you're making right now to plan for the future is a commitment to making the most of the rest of your life, which may well provide the motivation you lacked in the past to beat your nicotine habit.

Alcohol. A little alcohol can make your life more pleasant. It helps you to relax, makes you feel more sociable, and may even aid your health, according to some studies. Moderate drinking is fine, but many people who consider their intake "moderate" are kidding themselves—and an addiction to alcohol is no joke. If you feel that you may be headed for trouble, take a few minutes to answer this questionnaire from the National Council on Alcoholism:

What Kind of Drinker Are You?

1	☐ ☐ YES NO	Do you occasionally drink heavily after a disappointment, a quarrel, or when the boss gives you a hard time?
2	☐ ☐ YES NO	When you have trouble or feel under pressure, do you always drink more heavily than usual?
3	☐ ☐ YES NO	Have you noticed that you are able to handle more liquor than you did when you were first drinking?
4	☐ ☐ YES NO	Did you ever wake up on the "morning after" and find that you could not remember part of the past evening, even though your friends say you did not "pass out?"

5 ☐ ☐ When drinking with other people, do you
YES NO try to have a few extra drinks when others
will not know it?

6 ☐ ☐ Are there certain occasions when you feel
YES NO uncomfortable if alcohol is not available?

7 ☐ ☐ Have you recently noticed that when you
YES NO begin drinking you are in more of a hurry to
get the first drink than you used to be?

8 ☐ ☐ Do you sometimes feel a little guilty about
YES NO your drinking?

9 ☐ ☐ Are you secretly irritated when your family
YES NO or friends discuss your drinking?

10 ☐ ☐ Have you recently noticed an increase in
YES NO frequency of your memory "blackouts"?

11 ☐ ☐ Do you often find that you wish to continue
YES NO drinking after friends say they have had
enough?

12 ☐ ☐ Do you usually have a reason for the occa-
YES NO sions when you drink heavily?

13 ☐ ☐ When sober, do you often regret things you
YES NO have done or said while drinking?

What Kind of Drinker Are You? (*Continued*)

14	☐ ☐ YES NO	Have you tried switching brands or follow-ing various plans to control your drinking?
15	☐ ☐ YES NO	Have you often failed to keep the promises you have made to yourself about control-ling or cutting down on your drinking?
16	☐ ☐ YES NO	Have you ever tried to control your drinking by changing jobs or moving?
17	☐ ☐ YES NO	Do you try to avoid family or close friends while you are drinking?
18	☐ ☐ YES NO	Are you having an increasing number of financial and work problems?
19	☐ ☐ YES NO	Do more people seem to be treating you unfairly without good reason?
20	☐ ☐ YES NO	Do you eat very little or irregularly when you are drinking?
21	☐ ☐ YES NO	Do you sometimes have the "shakes" in the morning and find that it helps to have a lit-tle drink?
22	☐ ☐ YES NO	Have you recently noticed that you cannot drink as much as you once did?

23	☐ ☐ YES NO	Do you sometimes stay drunk for several days at a time?
24	☐ ☐ YES NO	Do you sometimes feel very depressed and wonder whether life is worth living?
25	☐ ☐ YES NO	Sometimes after periods of drinking, do you see or hear things that aren't there?
26	☐ ☐ YES NO	Do you get terribly frightened after you have been drinking heavily?

If the answer is "yes" to **any** of the questions, possible symptoms of alcoholism are indicated. "Yes" answers to several questions indicate various stages of alcoholism. Several "yes" answers to the questions in group 1–8 may indicate an early stage. Several "yes" answers to the questions in group 9–21 may indicate the middle stage. Several "yes" answers to the questions in group 22–26 indicate a later stage.

If you do have a drinking problem, you are not alone. Recent estimates indicate that there are over ten million alcoholics in the United States today. If you are part of this group, you must deal with your problem now, and not a week or a year from now. Alcohol abuse will draw you away from involvement in the world around you and rob you of the pleasures of life. It can cause severe physical damage to your liver, your heart, and your brain, and psychological damage to yourself and those you love.

But don't give up, because there are programs and treatments which can help you quit. If you have a problem, admit it, first to yourself, and then to someone you trust who will help you find the expert counseling and guidance you need.

Drugs. Medicines prescribed by a good doctor, taken according to his instructions, can help to make you healthier. The moment you begin to decide for yourself how or when to take medication, you are abusing drugs and risking very serious consequences. Do you sometimes feel that you need a tranquilizer or a diet pill, and that it would be easier to ask your friend next door who has a prescription than go to a doctor? Do you ever double the dosage of your prescribed medication, hoping that twice as much will make you feel twice as good? If so, you are abusing drugs.

Modern medicines are powerful substances, capable of curing quickly, but also capable of causing permanent damage when taken in large doses or in combination with other substances in your system. Other than an occasional aspirin or cold tablet, take only those drugs specifically prescribed by your doctor, in the quantities he has indicated.

Do you find that a difficult piece of advice to follow? If so, you may have a problem which requires professional help. If you feel anxiety at the idea of discussing your drug use with your doctor, then try turning to a spouse, relative, or close friend. Think very carefully about why you are worried, and see if you can handle the problem. If you can't, there are drug-abuse programs in your community that can help.

Action Steps for Combating Smoking, Drinking, and Drug Abuse

Think about your future. Take some time by yourself and think about what you would like to do with the rest of your life. The exciting possibilities for your later years all depend on your continued good health. Think about your future plans in terms of individual moments. If you want to travel, picture yourself enjoying a trip to a place you've always wanted to visit. If you intend to spend a lot of time with your family, picture yourself playing with your grandchildren, or attending their high school graduation. Use your imagination to create vivid, believable pictures of each event. Linger on the details, the tastes and smells, the sounds and the textures.

Now think about losing them, about having them taken away from you. If you continue to follow a pattern of bad habits, *you* are the one who is stealing your future happiness. You can change, but you must want the change badly enough, and you should take action, immediately.

Get help. There are many places to go for help. First, read further on the subject. If there is any doubt in your mind about the dangers of continuing any of these practices, do enough reading to gain a clear picture of the problem. Try to relate the information you are reading to your own situation. These are not abstract problems—they are as specific and concrete as your next cigarette, drink, or pill. Books can help, but you will probably need more personal assistance if you are really going to succeed in breaking your habit.

Then get your family on your side. Make sure that you have someone who understands what you are going through and wants to see you succeed. Speak frankly to your spouse or your child, sharing your feelings and your hopes for the future. A close personal friend can also be a good source of support, but someone you live with will be a source of continual positive reinforcement.

Finally, call the appropriate organization. If you are trying to quit smoking, the best place to start is the American Cancer Society. There are many local chapters that distribute literature and sponsor antismoking programs. Call your chapter and explain your problem to the person who answers the phone. The immediacy of their response will help reinforce your determination. If you cannot find a local chapter of the Cancer Society, contact the national headquarters, at 777 Third Avenue, New York, NY 10017, and ask them for advice on a program in your area. The American Lung Association (headquartered at 1740 Broadway, New York, NY 10019) and the American Heart Association, which also has many local branches (headquarters at 6320 Greenville Avenue, Dallas, TX 75231) should be able to help you find assistance in kicking the habit. SmokEnders and the Schick program are two commercial groups with high success rates. They advertise frequently in local newspapers, or you can contact their main offices (New York City and Los Angeles, respectively), for the chapter nearest you.

Alcoholics Anonymous and Al-Anon Family Groups offer help in conquering a drinking problem. They are both national organizations with excellent reputations and a good record of success.

Your personal physician or clergyman can also assist you in locating a local alcohol or drug program. Hospitals, clinics, and community health organizations are also active in fighting alcohol and drug abuse. Many progressive companies have started their own programs, although if you are worried about confidentiality, you may be better off searching for help outside the job.

The problem is not finding someone to help—it is making the decision to accept the available help and making the personal commitment to follow through on whatever program you choose.

SAFETY

Accidents are a threat to our continued health at any age. As we grow older, the potential causes of accidents don't change much, but the injuries we sustain in a fall or a traffic accident can be more severe than they would have been when our bodies were younger and more flexible. In planning a retirement lifestyle, and especially in considering the home you will live in when you are older, preparing a safe environment is a key part of good preventive health care. The publications listed on page 138 will provide you with sound professional advice and helpful tips on reducing the accident risk factors in your lifestyle.

FOR FURTHER READING

Books

Cooper, Kenneth H., *The New Aerobics;* Evans hardcover, 1970; Bantam paperback, 1970.

Myers, Clayton R., *YMCA Physical Fitness Handbook;* Popular Library paperback, 1977.

Rosenberg, Magda, *Sixty-Plus and Fit Again; Exercises for Older Men and Women;* Evans paperback, 1977.

Booklets

Adult Physical Fitness: A Program for Men and Women. Prepared by the President's Council on Physical Fitness, this 64-page booklet with dozens of photographs presents step-by-step fitness programs for those at different condition levels, along with exercises in isometrics, water activities, and weight training. Available for $1.50 from the Superintendent of Documents, U.S. Government Printing Office, Washington, DC 20402.

The Fitness Challenge in the Later Years: An Exercise Program for Older Americans. This booklet was designed by the President's Council on Physical Fitness and the Administration on Aging with the goal of providing reassurance, careful guidelines, and a clear, step-by-step exercise program for those Americans who feel they are "too old" to exercise. The three graduated exercise regimens included here will take you from your first, totally out of shape workout to a state of substantial physical fitness. Available for $.75 from the Superintendent of Documents, U.S. Government Printing Office, Washington DC 20402.

Exercise Your Right to Live. Free on request from Occidental Life Insurance Company of California, this nicely illustrated guide was prepared in conjunction with the National Athletic Health Institute. Clear instructions for conditioning, flexibility, endurance, and strength exercises are included, with the stretching exercises particularly valuable. Write to Occidental Life Insurance Company of California, Advertising Department, Box 2101 Terminal Annex, Los Angeles, CA 90051.

Safety Guides

- *Your Retirement Safety Guide*. This 24-page booklet, published by the American Association of Retired Persons and National Retired Teachers Association, includes a roundup of the potential hazards in each room of your home, some advice on avoiding traffic accidents, and some basic first-aid pointers in case of emergency. Available free of charge from AARP-NRTA, P.O. Box 2400, 215 Long Beach Boulevard, Long Beach, CA 90801.

- *Guide to Home and Personal Security*. This booklet, published by Action for Independent Maturity, concentrates on home safety from the perspectives of accident, fire, and crime prevention, with step-by-step instructions. Available free of charge from Action for Independent Maturity, P.O. Box 2400, 215 Long Beach Boulevard, Long Beach, CA 90801.

- *Handle Yourself With Care: Accident Prevention for Older Americans*. This cheerful, cartoon-illustrated government pamphlet will alert you to the hazards in and outside the home which lead to accidents, and steps you can take to avoid them. Available for $.40 from the Superintendent of Documents, U.S. Government Printing Office, Washington, DC 20402.

- *Home Accidents Aren't Accidental*. This 8-page folder presents the American Medical Association's tips for making

your home a safe place to live. Available for $.25 by order-
ing publication #OP-359 from Order Handling Department,
American Medical Association, 535 North Dearborn Street,
Chicago, IL 60610.

- *National Fire Protection Association pamphlets.* This associ-
ation publishes a number of free informational booklets on
fire prevention and planning your actions should a fire occur.
For your copies send a self-addressed stamped envelope to
National Fire Protection Association, 470 Atlantic Avenue,
Boston, MA 02210.

- *Tips on Home Fire Protection.* This useful summary of the
fire prevention steps each of us should know is published by
the Council of Better Business Bureaus. You can obtain a
free copy by writing to the Council at 1150 17th Street
NW, Washington, DC 20036.

2

ACHIEVING
FINANCIAL
SECURITY

7

YOUR FINANCIAL
NEEDS AND
RESOURCES

*O money, money, money, I am not necessarily one of those who
   think thee holy,*
*But I often stop to wonder how thou canst go out so fast when
   thou comest in so slowly.*

OGDEN NASH

Money is a terrible master but an excellent servant.

P. T. BARNUM

FINANCIAL security is probably the single greatest requirement for happiness in the retirement years. If you are constantly beseiged by worry and doubts about money, you simply won't be able to take full advantage of the many opportunities
these years offer. While each person has his or her own attitude
toward money, one thing seems almost certain concerning money and
the retiree: More is better. The more money you can count on, the
greater freedom and peace of mind you will have to enjoy life as you
see fit.
A significant percentage of older citizens are living below the level

to which they had become accustomed while working. Fourteen percent of Americans over sixty-five are considered poor. But on a more positive note, four-fifths of those past sixty-five own their own homes, and 80 percent of these are mortgage-free. While double-digit inflation greatly harms those living on fixed incomes, Social Security payments are increased each year to help retirees keep up with the rising cost of living. So poverty is no longer a great threat for the majority of today's retirees. You *can* deal effectively with the challenge of providing for your financial future. There are sound retirement investments to make, tax shelters such as IRA and Keogh plans to help your savings program along, and the possibility of continuing to earn income after "retirement," among many other options. If you take the time to learn the basics of retirement financial planning, chances are good you will be able to assure yourself a comfortable lifestyle.

How much time and effort are you willing to devote now to achieving this goal of financial security? Let me put this question into perspective. If you retire at sixty-five, you may live another fifteen to twenty-five years—or longer. You will have between 130,000 and 220,000 *hours* of retirement, during which you can either sleep soundly and live each day without major financial worry, or be plagued by financial anxiety at every turn. An investment of only a couple of hundred hours over the next few years can make the difference.

When a group of retirees was surveyed recently by the Louis Harris Organization, 41 percent of those polled said their standard of living is less than adequate. However, of those who reported doing an adequate job of preretirement planning, only 10 percent complained that their standard of living is inadequate. The evidence is clear. Start early to develop your plan, take the time to learn the techniques of retirement financial planning, and you're going to feel a lot more comfortable.

Everyone can benefit from the hard-earned wisdom of the retirees in this poll. The majority of those questioned advised that retirement planning should start before age forty-five. Equally important, they instructed preretirees to create multiple sources of future income while still in the prime working years. "Don't rely solely on Social Security and pensions for retirement income," was their warning.

Formulate your own retirement financial plan now. It's the best

way to ensure confidence and independence during your retirement
years.

HOW TO USE THIS SECTION

I don't expect you to become a financial expert simply by reading
the material in this chapter. There are other sources (recommended at
the end of Chapter 8) you may want to refer to for more in-depth information on specific subjects. My intention here is simply to in-
troduce you to a new framework for thinking about the financial
aspects of retirement, and to guide you with a variety of step-by-step
exercises to help you plan along the way. The idea is to

- understand the different sources of income available to you
  after age sixty-five and how you can maximize them;
- learn how to get all you can out of your income and assets
  from now until you retire;
- estimate your retirement expense budget;
- develop a good, practical financial plan from which to
  operate, which will leave you with a greater sense of clarity
  and peace of mind about your financial future;
- understand the benefits of putting your will, estate plan, and
  other legal matters in up-to-date order.

You are not alone if you feel uncomfortable laying out lots of figures and making complex calculations. It seems like a formidable
task. In reality, though, the process of developing your plan boils
down to four basic steps:

  1. Decide at what age you will want to stop working in your cur-
      rent job or career, and what standard of living you would like

to have then as compared to now (most people would like to maintain a living standard similar to the one they have today).

2. Estimate the monthly expenses you will have after retirement, using today's expenses as a basis for comparison.

3. Determine what your approximate monthly income will be, based upon currently expected sources (pension, Social Security, investment income).

4. Figure out how large a gap there is between this income and your projected monthly expenses in retirement, and develop a plan of action using a variety of potential resources to fill this gap.

Don't worry if you have no idea at this point as to how to follow these four steps—that is the purpose of this part of the book. By filling in the worksheets provided throughout, you will painlessly pass from Step 1 to Step 4.

DEVELOPING YOUR PERSONAL FINANCIAL PLAN

Your Expenses in Retirement

As a general rule, a retired individual or couple can live on about 50 percent of gross preretirement pay or about 70 percent of the *take-home* pay they needed before retirement. One reason is that many work-related expenses are reduced or eliminated when you stop your regular work. Commuting (especially by car), lunches out, business clothing, contributions, gifts, and dues all take a chunk out of your monthly income today, but this money can be used for other things when you retire.

Certain other expenses will also be lower after retirement. If you have paid off your house, you will no longer have a monthly mortgage payment. Your taxes will be lower (see pages 187–90). You will no longer be paying the F.I.C.A. deduction (Social Security) on most of your income. This deduction eats up 6.65% (in 1981) of the first $29,700 of your salary earnings.

Many discounts are available to people over sixty-two or sixty-five, for transportation, movies and cultural events, educational programs, checking accounts, drugs, travel, and other goods and services. Membership in one of the national organizations for retired people (see pages 27–8) can give you access to more discounts. Another expense which can be reduced for many people is life insurance (pages 204–9). On the other hand, medical expenses will probably be higher, as will medical insurance (pages 209–19).

Go through all your current monthly expenses, item by item, and then estimate what you will spend for the same categories in retirement. It can be misleading to rely on figures for an "average couple," but we have provided these figures as a point of reference.

Use the following worksheet to estimate your expenses in retirement, using your current expenses as a standard of comparison. Where an expense is easier to figure on an annual basis, take the annual figure and divide by 12 to arrive at the monthly average. Don't worry for now about how inflation will increase each category's cost in the future. Later on, we will make adjustments to the retirement expenses total to take inflation into account.

Monthly Expenses	Today	In Retirement
Housing—		
Rent or mortgage	$ ____	$ ____
Utilities	____	____
Homeowner's insurance	____	____
Telephone	____	____
Repairs, maintenance, lawn and garden	____	____
Property taxes	____	____
Furniture and furnishings	____	____
Domestic help, household upkeep	____	____

Monthly Expenses	**Today**	**In Retirement**
Food— Include meals at home and away from home	$ _____	$ _____
Clothing	_____	_____
Laundry and dry cleaning	_____	_____
Transportation— Automobile expenses (Include gas, maintenance, and depreciation)	_____	_____
Other vehicle or boat expenses	_____	_____
Auto insurance	_____	_____
Train or bus travel	_____	_____
Medical care— Doctor bills (unreimbursed by insurance)	_____	_____
Health insurance premiums	_____	_____
Medicare payments*	_____	_____
Prescription drugs	_____	_____
Dental care	_____	_____
Life insurance and annuity payments	_____	_____
Installment loans	_____	_____
Vacation and travel	_____	_____
Education expenses	_____	_____
Newspapers, magazines, books	_____	_____
Personal care (including haircuts, beauty salon, cosmetics, sundries)	_____	_____
Gifts and contributions	_____	_____
Entertainment (cable TV, movies, theatre, music)	_____	_____

Monthly Expenses	Today	In Retirement
Hobbies, sports, club dues	$ _____	$ _____
Miscellaneous	_____	_____
TOTAL MONTHLY EXPENSES	$ _____	$ _____
TOTAL ANNUAL EXPENSES	$ _____	$ _____

*See page 209.

Table 6 was developed from figures provided by the U.S. Labor Department's Bureau of Labor Statistics. It gives a rough idea of relatively modest expenses for an "average retired couple" over 65, at three different standards of living. Use it as a base line for your own projected retirement expenses. How do they compare?

These budgets reflect 1980 prices, and apply to couples living in a metropolitan area (where costs are higher than in rural areas).

What Are the Sources of Retirement Income?

If you, like many people, have relied primarily on salary income to support your family, retirement financing may seem confusing at first. For the first time you will be figuring on as many as five or six major sources of income. The economic conditions of our country, the rate of inflation, changing legislation concerning Social Security and pensions, and the flux and flow of the investment markets all contribute to the risk and uncertainty of any one income source. The best retirement income plan is one in which there is considerable *diversification*—reliance on several different high-quality sources of funds.

A basic shopping list of possible sources would include the following fourteen, as well as such windfalls as inheritances and the sale of collections or other property. You are already in line for some of the following sources. Others may or may not come into play as you

Table 6. Annual Expense Budget for Retired Couples

	Higher Budget	%	Inter-mediate Budget	%	Lower Budget	%
Food	$3,217	24	$2,564	28	$1,934	31
Housing	4,958	37	3,172	35	2,198	35
Transportation	1,531	11	829	9	425	7
Clothing	699	5	454	5	270	4
Personal Care	394	3	270	3	184	3
Medical Care	802	6	796	9	791	12
Other Family Consumption (recreation, reading materials, etc.)	865	6	437	5	263	4
Other Items (gifts, contributions, insurance)	1,024	8	545	6	273	4
TOTALS	$13,490	100	$9,067	100	$6,338	100

determine how best to fill in the gap between expected retirement income and projected expenses.

1. Social Security
2. Company or government pension
3. Individual or supplemental pension (i.e., IRA, Keogh plans)
4. High-quality stocks (yielding dividends)
5. High-quality bonds
6. High-interest savings accounts, money market funds, or savings certificates

7. Annuities and endowments
8. Proceeds of sale or refinancing of your primary residence
9. Income property
10. Second-career income
11. Cash value of life insurance
12. Dividends of life insurance kept in force
13. Veteran's benefits
14. Disability payments

Let's start with the income sources about which you are reasonably certain. First calculate estimated Social Security benefits, using the information on pages 160–74. Do the same for company or government pension benefits, being careful to note possible restrictions and exclusions discussed in pages 175–83.

Next, include the monthly value of any annuities you have purchased, and do the same for Individual Retirement Accounts (pages 183–87) or other supplemental pension plans whose benefits are already known (based on your monthly contributions). Add a conservative estimate of monthly earnings you and your spouse expect in retirement, and monthly rental income from real estate properties you expect to hold, if any. Include interest from long-term bonds and dividends from stocks if you plan to retain them as income-producing investments after retirement.

For now, leave aside your cash savings, investments you expect to convert into cash before retirement, the cash value of life insurance, and the value of your home, all of which will be discussed separately.

	Monthly	*Yearly*
1. Estimated expenses in retirement (from the worksheet on page 147)	$____	$____
2. Retirement income already known	$____	$____
Social Security	____	____
Pension	____	____
Supplemental pensions	____	____
Annuities	____	____
Earnings	____	____

	Monthly	*Yearly*
Rental income	——	——
Investment income (stocks and bonds)	——	——
TOTAL INCOME	——	——

3. Subtract TOTAL INCOME (2) from EX-
PENSES (1). The result is your *retirement income gap,* amounting to: $—— $——

4. Now we will bring your other assets into the picture. Let's assume you convert these into cash, place the cash in a conservative fixed return investment (high-interest savings accounts or high quality bonds, for example), and withdraw interest and principal at a rate necessary to fill your retirement income gap in each year of retirement. You may not choose to do this, but for now we simply want to obtain a conservative estimate of how far your potential cash reserves can fill the income gap.

Estimate the future value of each asset listed below at the time of your retirement. If you plan to sell your home and move into a smaller one, estimate net proceeds of the sale after purchase of the new residence. If you plan to rent, use the total proceeds from the sale of the home (since a gain of up to $100,000 from this sale is tax-free after age fifty-five, we will assume for the moment that no taxes are due). If you have a consistent track record of annual saving, estimate the accumulated value of these savings when you retire. Finally, if you expect to cash in some or all of your life insurance upon retirement (see pages 204–9), estimate the cash proceeds of this transaction. If you are not sure, leave this blank for now.

	Total Value at Retirement
Cash in bank	$——
Stocks and bonds to be liquidated at retirement	——
Net proceeds from sale of home	——
Cash value of life insurance	——
TOTAL CASH RESERVES	——

5. Take the amount of your estimated *retirement income gap* (3), and calculate what percentage of your cash reserves this annual cash need represents. Example: Let's say the gap is $5,600 per year, and your re-

tirement cash reserves total $68,000. You will need to withdraw $ 5,600 / $68,000 each year, which is 8.24 percent of the cash reserve.

ANNUAL WITHDRAWAL PERCENTAGE_____%

6. The next step is to estimate the after-tax rate of return you could receive on your cash reserves over the long term. Let's use 8 percent for purposes of this example. Check Table 7 below to see how many years your cash reserve will last you if it is earning 8 percent, as you withdraw the percentage you need each year. In the example we used

Table 7. How Many Years Will Your Retirement Cash Reserves Last?

Annual Rate of Withdrawal	Annual Interest Rate or Return on Investments									
	5%	6%	7%	8%	9%	10%	11%	12%	13%	14%
5%										
6%	36	Years								
7%	25	33								
8%	20	23	30							
9%	16	18	22	28						
10%	14	15	17	20	26					
11%	12	13	14	16	19	25				
12%	11	11	12	14	15	18	23			
13%	9	10	11	12	13	15	17	21		
14%	9	9	10	11	11	13	14	17	21	
15%	8	8	9	9	10	11	12	14	16	20

EXAMPLE: A savings account earning 8 percent would last twenty years if 10 percent of it were withdrawn each year. Money invested at an overall return of 10 percent would last eleven years if 15 percent of the investments were cashed in each year. *Where there is no number of years indicated, the fund would last forever at the stated interest rate and rate of withdrawal.*

above, if you were to withdraw 8.25 percent of the reserve each year, and the reserve were earning 8 percent, your retirement cash reserves fund would last over thirty years. If you need to withdraw 10 percent annually ($6,800), the fund would last twenty years.

NUMBER OF YEARS FUND WILL LAST_____

7. Now estimate your life expectancy, or the combined life spans of you and your spouse. The average 65-year-old man today can expect to live to age 80; for a woman, the average is about 83. If your parents and grandparents lived beyond average expectancy, add another five years to be on the safe side. How many years of your expected life span are not provided for by your cash reserve?

NUMBER OF LIFE EXPECTANCY YEARS NOT PROVIDED FOR_____

Now we have to adjust for inflation. While nobody can accurately predict what the long-term rate of inflation will be, even a comparatively low average annual rate, such as 6 percent, would cause your annual income needs to increase by up to 2½ times in fifteen years. To compensate for this factor, *add ten years* to the number of life expectancy years not provided for if you expect to retire within ten years, and *add fifteen years* if you plan to retire more than ten years from now.

INFLATION-ADJUSTED NUMBER OF YEARS NOT PROVIDED FOR_____

Multiply the inflation-adjusted number of years not provided for by the annual *retirement income gap* (3). This additional amount is a reasonable estimate of what resources beyond those already provided for which you might need to achieve lasting financial security.

ADDITIONAL RETIREMENT FUNDS NEEDED TO ACHIEVE LASTING FINANCIAL SECURITY_____

Is It Safe to Withdraw Principal?

Increasingly, the idea that principal is sacred and that one should never "dip into capital" is being discarded for purposes of retirement planning. Inflation and increased life spans mean that you must provide a larger fund to insure financial support for a greater number of years. By using Table 7 you can gauge your annual withdrawals and be reasonably confident that your principal will never run out in your lifetime. You may want to set aside some assets or investments from which you will draw only interest or dividend income, preserving the principal for your heirs. But if you are the rare individual or couple who can support an adequate retirement lifestyle solely through the income provided by your investments, without needing to draw upon principal, more power to you!

Some people strongly desire to leave a significant inheritance to their children or other loved ones, and the plan outlined above does not exclude this possibility. If you can afford to do it, by all means do so, but don't jeopardize your retirement security needlessly. The long-range security of your spouse and yourself should be your first and foremost consideration.

COPING WITH INFLATION

Inflation seems to be with us to stay, and its effects make retirement planning all the more imperative. Of course, we can't accurately predict how rapidly the cost of goods and services will escalate, so it is difficult to feel confident that we have provided adequately for future conditions. As inflation erodes our purchasing power we find it harder to put extra dollars away for retirement. Remember this, though: While you are in the work force your salary or wages will generally rise over time to keep pace with inflation; much retirement income, however, is fixed at a specific annual amount and does not grow with inflation.

Social Security benefits are adjusted once a year for increases in the cost of living, and these adjustments are tied directly to changes in the Consumer Price Index. Company pension benefits are often not adjusted. According to a study by the Congressional Budget Office, private pension plans compensate on average for only 29 percent of Consumer Price Index increases. It was found that 37 percent of company pensions do not grant cost-of-living increases of any kind, and only some 3 percent grant explicit adjustments tied directly to the rising cost of living.

The traditional sorts of retirement investments, including bonds, savings accounts, and most annuities, have fixed returns. Unless you are able to lock into a high interest rate when the inflation rate is dropping, these investments will probably not keep pace with inflation. Regardless of this pessimistic picture, I want to assure you that we are not totally defenseless against inflation. There are some effective tactics you can employ in fighting it. First, let's take a look at the enemy. In Table 8, we took the 1980 expense budget figures for an "average retired couple" over sixty-five and projected them out to future years, at two different rates of inflation.

Table 8. Effect of Inflation on Retirement Budgets

1980 (current dollars)	Higher Budget $13,490		Intermediate Budget $9,067		Lower Budget $6,338	
Annual Inflation Rate	6%	8%	6%	8%	6%	8%
1985 Projection	$18,053	$19,821	$12,134	$13,322	$ 8,482	$ 9,313
1990 Projection	$24,159	$29,124	$16,238	$19,575	$11,350	$13,683
1995 Projection	$32,330	$42,793	$21,730	$28,762	$15,189	$20,105

These projections to the future are a dramatic illustration of two powerful economic forces that can work either for you or against you: *compound interest* and a long period of *time*. Where inflation is concerned, these forces work *against* you, and they work hard.

Take the higher budget projections, for instance. Notice that in 1985 a 2 percent difference in the rate of compounding (or the rate of inflation), which lasts for five years (1980 to 1985), will have produced a 10 percent difference in the two accumulated amounts by 1985 ($19,821 is a 10 percent increase over $18,053). By 1995, however, after ten additional years of compounding, the same 2 percent difference in the compounding rate will have created a 32 percent difference in the accumulated amounts. ($42,793 is a 32 percent increase over $32,330.)

Happily, you can use the same weapon of compound interest over a long period of time to offset inflation's effects. And you can bring a third powerful force into the picture: *tax deferral*. Savings grow at a snail's pace when they are accumulated with after-tax dollars, and when the interest you earn is taxed each year. But the government, recognizing the pernicious effects of inflation on our ability to accumulate sizable retirement funds, has created the Individual Retirement Account, the Keogh plan, and other tax-deferred savings vehicles to help you cope with inflation. The plans enable you to earn untaxed interest on untaxed income. When you begin to withdraw these funds after retirement, they are taxed at a lower rate because you will most likely be in a lower tax bracket than you were when you were working.

Under the Economic Recovery Tax Act of 1981, these useful grow-your-own retirement savings programs are now available to *all* wage earners, whether or not they are currently also covered by a government-, company-, or union-sponsored pension plan. Contribution limits have also been liberalized (see page 183). The benefits of these plans are incomparable. By using self-restraint to put away as much money as possible, starting as early as you can, and obtaining the added impacts of tax deferral and the highest available guaranteed rate of interest, you can harness the magic of compound interest to help you combat inflation.

Money-Expanding Tips

You have now analyzed your retirement financial needs and resources. If you are still not sure you have an adequate hedge against inflation, here are five additional tactics you can employ to increase your retirement security:

1. *Retire later.* The trend to early retirement grew steadily for several decades following World War II. This trend has slowed, as people seek to bolster themselves against inflation. When you retire before sixty-five, your Social Security and pension benefits are usually reduced, and instead of having several extra years to build your retirement nest egg, you must begin to draw on it earlier and for a greater number of years. The Age Seventy Mandatory Retirement Law has given many people the option of staying with their company longer. If you are in good health, working a few years in another field after you retire can also assure you greater peace of mind, but remember that a second career requires planning and forethought.

2. *Plan to work part time,* either in your current vocation or in another area, using a marketable skill you have or can develop. A steady source of wages will make your retirement capital last longer and, of course, wages tend to rise with inflation.

    Working part time may make you last longer, too. Chapter 13 will help you develop a plan of action for part-time work in retirement, either for an employer or in your own small business.

3. *Plan to own your home free and clear.* Housing is the largest expense in retirement, accounting for over 35 percent of the average retirement budget, according to the Bureau of Labor Statistics. If you don't have to worry about making mortgage or rent payments, you will have greater financial flexibility. Your home is an excellent inflation hedge, and if you become truly hard pressed, you could sell it and move into a less ex-

pensive one. You might also be able to obtain a second mortgage on your home, although it is doubtful that the return you could earn on this money would exceed the mortgage interest.

4. *Diversify investments*. Retirement is no time to be involved with speculative investments in the hope of hitting the jackpot. But too many people take just the opposite course. They are too conservative with their investment money, putting it all into savings accounts or bonds which do not offer the highest rate of return available. When large sums of money are involved, an interest rate differential of only 1 or 2 percent can mean several thousand dollars of income lost each year. If the extra income is important to you, by all means investigate money market funds, Treasury bills, money market certificates, and unit investment trusts (basically a mutual fund for bonds). Mutual funds geared to high current stock dividends (for income) might also be suitable for a small percentage of your portfolio.

5. *Reduce spending*. If you earn an average of 8 percent as a return on your retirement cash reserve fund after retirement, and you are in a 20 percent tax bracket, every extra 80 cents you spend must have $12.50 in capital backing it up (assuming you are spending only the interest and not the capital itself). For every additional $800 you spend, you need capital of $12,500. If your retirement income projections indicate you will not be able to put enough money (capital) away to provide for inflation, you may simply have to cut back on your spending plans. You'll be surprised at how much you can reduce your spending without truly lowering the quality of your life.

SOURCES OF RETIREMENT INCOME

Your Social Security Benefits

The New Deal spirit of the Roosevelt administration gave rise to the Social Security Act, which was approved by Congress in August 1935. This law laid the groundwork for many social programs still with us today, including unemployment benefits, aid to children and the blind, and public health programs. At the heart of the legislation, though, was a national pension plan for the aged, designed to help replace the income lost upon retirement.

Today, nine out of ten workers in the United States are enrolled in the Social Security program, and many of those who aren't are covered under similar federal pension plans. The benefits provided have expanded, too, and now assist both young and old, wage earners and dependents. Today about one out of seven people in the United States receives a monthly Social Security check.

Programs now under the auspices of the Social Security Administration include:

- Retirement benefits for workers and dependents
- Survivor's benefits
- Disability benefits for covered workers of any age and their dependents
- Medicare (partly through the Social Security fund)
- Supplemental Security Income (a federal program assuring a minimum monthly income to financially needy people sixty-five or older, blind, or disabled; administered by the Social Security Administration but financed entirely from general revenues)

Despite the significant role played by tax-free Social Security benefits with their automatic cost-of-living increases in financial planning, over three quarters of those eligible aren't sure what their benefits will be when they retire. Add to this state of confusion a continuing undercurrent of talk about the possible "collapse" of the entire Social Security system, and you may well wonder if you'll ever see any money from this source at all.

Let's take a brief look at the probable future of Social Security, and then get down to the specifics of how large a contribution to financial security your benefits will provide.

Will Social Security Survive? The most basic threat facing today's Social Security system is the ongoing increase in the number of older Americans, and therefore, the number of people collecting. Social Security benefits are funded by the payroll contributions of workers and employers, not from general tax revenues. The contributions you make now are *not* going into your own personal savings account, waiting to be paid back to you when you retire. They are being used to pay benefits to retirees today. In this ongoing system, the money which will pay *your* benefits must come out of the paychecks of the people who are working after you retire.

Therein lies the potential problem. There will be a greater number of older people collecting Social Security benefits in the future for each worker paying into the system. The deduction from each worker's paycheck would have to skyrocket to meet the needs of the larger future retirement population, so some changes are going on in the system. For example:

- The contribution rate has risen for both employers and employees and is scheduled to keep going up for the next few years. In 1982 they each paid 6.70 percent of the worker's wages into the system. Increases up to 7.65 percent in 1990 have been authorized.
- The maximum amount of earnings subject to Social Security taxes has been increased dramatically, and this trend will continue. When the system was initiated, only the first $3,000 in earnings per year were subject to Social Security deductions. The ceiling on taxable wages was $29,700 in 1981. It will continue to rise annually thereafter, to reflect the average increase in wage earnings over the prior year.
- Regulations which greatly penalized the benefits of those who work past age sixty-five have been liberalized, making a longer working career more financially rewarding.

These are the current strategies being employed to keep Social Security on its feet. And other steps could be taken to alleviate the funding crunch of the future.

The first is to finance some of the benefits with money from general tax revenues, instead of making payroll deductions bear the entire burden. Social Security is already broken up into several distinct divisions; Medicare, for example, is already financed through a combination of Social Security funds and income tax dollars.

A second possible change would be to move up the age at which benefits are paid or to establish a sliding scale of benefits. A revamped system might not allow you to claim a full benefit before age seventy but might still provide a reduced check for those who chose to retire earlier.

In the end, the future course of Social Security will be determined by the political process. The system is already something of a political football, and debate is now raging as to how the system should adapt to shifting societal conditions. As society's demands evolve, the Social Security system is subject to change by elected officials, and therein lies the primary assurance that the system will survive. Federal dollars go where the votes lead them.

Eligibility for Retirement Benefits. Social Security, in order to deal with the individual cases of over 110 million workers and their dependents, has dozens of rules and rulings to cover the diverse personal situations which affect eligibility and payment levels.

If you are not clear on your status with Social Security, contact your nearest office. There are over 1,300 offices of the Social Security Administration throughout the country, listed in the white pages of your telephone directory under *United States Government*. Your local office can provide you with full information on the many benefits provided under Social Security, including disability and Medicare.

Retirement benefits are paid to a qualified worker and the worker's dependents. In order to be qualified for Social Security retirement benefits, a worker must:

- be at least sixty-two years old (for reduced benefits) or sixty-five years old (for full benefits);

- have contributed to the Social Security fund for a specific number of years (or quarters—see the list on page 164).

Nearly all employed people in the United States are now covered, including people in the armed forces, civilian employees of the federal government, and self-employed individuals. However, if you fall into the following classifications, you should get in touch with your Social Security office to determine whether or not you are covered:

- employees of nonprofit institutions
- employees of state or local governments
- employees of international organizations
- farmers and farm workers
- household workers (babysitters, gardeners, etc.)
- employees or self-employed individuals who work outside the United States
- members of religious orders

If you are unsure of the number of years or quarters you have to your credit, you can request the information from the Social Security Administration. They will check your earnings record and tell you the *number of quarters* which have been credited to your account. At the same time, you can request an up-to-date report of the *total earnings* credited to your Social Security account.

Check to see that the total in the Social Security Administration's records matches your own records of earnings in previous years (see page 166 for the maximum contribution you could have made for each year). In addition, it is wise to send a request for your earnings record every three years, to make sure your contributions are being credited properly. This way you can straighten out any discrepancies as they arise.

In order to be eligible for retirement benefits based on your own work record, you will need credit for the number of years shown in the list on page 164.

Benefits for Spouses and Children. Dependent's benefits based on a worker's retirement benefit amount are paid to a worker's wife or husband who is sixty-two or older, or to a worker's unmarried children under eighteen (or under twenty-two if full-time students).

If you were born in:	You need credit for:
1914	6¼ years
1915	6½ years
1916	6¾ years
1917	7 years
1918	7¼ years
1919	7½ years
1920	7¾ years
1921	8 years
1922	8¼ years

If you were born in:	you need credit for:
1923	8½ years
1924	8¾ years
1925	9 years
1926	9¼ years
1927	9½ years
1928	9¾ years
1929 through the present	10 years

Widows or widowers whose spouses die after retirement age are eligible to receive checks equal to the spouse's retirement benefit if they wait until age sixty-five, or somewhat reduced checks starting at age sixty.

A Social Security provision which challenged a widow's survivor benefit if she remarried has been changed. Now she can remarry at age sixty or over and collect the full amount of her checks based on her late husband's work record. However, if a man is drawing checks on his late wife's account and remarries at any age, he forfeits the benefits. Payments will also be made to younger wives caring for disabled children, and to disabled children themselves. A divorced woman can claim benefits based on her ex-husband's earnings record when *he* begins drawing his Social Security check, as long as she is at least sixty-two years old and they were married at least ten years.

In cases where an individual is eligible to receive benefits both as a dependent and on the basis of his or her own work record, only the higher of the two benefits will be paid.

Estimating Your Retirement Benefit. You can let the Social Security Administration estimate your future retirement benefits. If you are over fifty-six, you can obtain a postcard form at your local office and send it in to receive an estimate of your future check, based on your earnings to date and the statistical tables on future earnings patterns. Of course, you can't determine *precisely* the amount of your monthly benefits, since the computations involved will include all of your earnings up until your last day of work.

To estimate your monthly retirement benefits yourself, the Social Security Administration provides the following eight-step method for those workers who reach age sixty-two in 1979–83.

What if you want to estimate your Social Security check and you will not turn sixty-two until after 1983? There are too many unanswered questions about post-1983 regulations and levels of payment to get a very accurate dollar estimate, but benefit amounts listed below can be of some help. Future adjustments for inflation will change both benefit amounts and the amount of income which is counted toward your benefit. But since inflation is integrated directly into future levels of Social Security payments, you can get a sense of what your future benefits will be by calculating what you would get if you retired *now,* and comparing that with your needs if you were to retire today. The results of this calculation will give you an idea of the *percentage* of your income which will be replaced by Social Security payments when you retire.

Calculating Your Estimated Benefit. The following instructions are designed for those born between 1917 and 1921, but if you are younger, you can use it to figure what your present benefit rate would be.

STEP 1

Your retirement check is based on your average earnings over a certain number of years. Find the year you were born, and pick the number of "earnings years" you need to include from the following list:

Year you were born	Years needed
1917	23
1918	24
1919	25
1920	26
1921	27

STEP 2

On a separate sheet of paper, list each year from 1951 to 1981 in one column. Next to each year, fill in the amount of money you earned in that year, *up to the maximum earnings covered for Social Security for that year.* These maximum amounts since 1951 have been:

$3,600 from 1951 to 1954
$4,200 from 1955 to 1958
$4.800 from 1959 to 1965
$6,600 from 1966 to 1967
$7,800 from 1968 to 1971
$9,000 in 1972
$10,800 in 1973
$13,200 in 1974

$14,100 in 1975
$15,300 in 1976
$16,500 in 1977
$17,700 in 1978
$22,900 in 1979
$25,900 in 1980
$29,700 in 1981

The maximum amount of annual earnings that count for Social Security will rise automatically after 1981 as earnings levels rise. Because of this, the base of 1982 and later will undoubtedly be higher than $29,700.

STEP 3

Cross off your list the years of your lowest earnings until the number of years left is the same as your answer to Step 1 in the Years Needed column. (You may have to leave some years of "0" earnings on your list.)

Note: If you will be sixty-two after 1983, and are doing these calculations to supply a guideline, give yourself credit for a suitable percentage of the maximum allowed earnings in some of the early years on the list if you feel that your total years of maximum contribution will be greater in the long run than your early earning years would indicate.

STEP 4

Add up the earnings for the years left on your list.

STEP 5

Divide this total by the number you determined in Step 1. The result is your average yearly earnings covered by Social Security.

STEP 6

Look at Table 9. Under the heading "For Workers," find the average yearly earnings figure *closest* to your own. Look over to the column listing your age at retirement to see about how much you can expect to get.

STEP 7

If you have an eligible spouse or child, or both, look under the heading "For Dependents" to find about how much they can get, based on the same average yearly earnings you used to figure your check.

Table 9. Monthly Retirement Benefits for Workers Who Reach Sixty-two in 1979–83

| Average Yearly Earnings | For Workers | | | | For Dependents [1] | | | | | Family [2] Benefits |
	Retire-ment at 65	at 64	at 63	at 62	Spouse at 65 or Child	at 64	at 63	at 62	
$923 or less	121.80	113.70	105.60	97.50	60.90	55.90	50.80	45.70	182.70
1,200	156.70	146.30	135.90	125.40	78.40	71.90	65.40	58.80	235.10
2,600	230.10	214.80	199.50	184.10	115.10	105.50	95.90	86.40	345.20
3,000	251.80	235.10	218.30	201.50	125.90	115.40	104.90	94.50	384.90
3,400	270.00	252.00	234.00	216.00	135.00	123.80	112.50	101.30	434.90
4,000	296.20	276.50	256.80	237.00	148.10	135.70	123.40	111.10	506.20
4,400	317.30	296.20	275.00	253.90	158.70	145.40	132.20	119.10	562.50
4,800	336.00	313.60	291.20	268.80	168.00	153.90	140.00	126.00	612.70
5,200	353.20	329.70	306.20	282.60	176.60	161.80	147.20	132.50	662.70

5,600	370.60	345.90	321.20	296.50	185.30	169.80	154.40	139.00	687.10
6,000	388.20	362.40	336.50	310.60	194.10	177.80	161.70	145.60	712.10
6,400	405.60	378.60	351.60	324.50	202.80	185.80	169.00	152.10	737.10
6,800	424.10	395.90	367.60	339.30	212.10	194.30	176.70	159.10	762.30
7,200	446.00	416.30	386.60	356.80	223.00	204.30	185.80	167.30	788.90
7,600	465.60	434.60	403.60	372.50	232.80	213.30	194.00	174.60	814.70
8,000	482.60	450.50	418.30	386.10	241.30	221.10	201.10	181.00	844.50
8,400	492.90	460.10	427.20	394.40	246.50	225.80	205.40	184.90	862.60
8,800	505.10	471.50	437.80	404.10	252.60	231.40	210.50	189.50	883.80
9,200	516.00	481.60	447.20	412.80	258.00	236.40	215.00	193.50	903.00
9,400	520.40	485.80	451.10	416.40	260.20	238.40	216.80	195.20	910.40
9,600	524.60	489.70	454.70	419.70	262.30	240.30	218.50	196.80	918.00
9,800	530.40	495.10	459.70	424.40	265.20	243.00	221.00	198.90	928.00
10,000	534.70	499.10	463.50	427.80	267.40	245.00	222.80	200.60	935.70

[1] If a person is eligible for both a worker's benefit and a spouse's benefit, the check actually payable is limited to the larger of the two.
[2] The maximum amount payable to a family is generally reached when a worker and two family members are eligible.

STEP 8

Finally, add the figures you arrived at for Steps 6 and 7 to see about how much your total family retirement benefit will be under Social Security. Remember, the total cannot exceed the amount in the "Family Benefits" column.

Timing Your Retirement. Your age at retirement determines the level of payments you will receive, and the amount you receive when you first retire will be your basic benefit for the rest of your life. Hence, if you elect to take reduced benefits at age sixty-two, that figure (adjusted for inflation) will be your level throughout your retirement years.

Does this mean that you should necessarily hang on and wait until sixty-five to receive full benefits? That depends on your personal plans. Let's say, for instance, that your average yearly earnings for Social Security purposes come to $9,200. According to present statistical tables, a man who reaches age sixty-two can expect to live about another sixteen years, so we'll assume that he will receive benefits until he is seventy-eight.

If you accept benefits starting at age sixty-two, you will receive $412.80 each month for 192 months, for a total of $79,257.60.

If you wait until age sixty-five and draw full benefits, you will receive $516 a month for 156 months, for a total of $80,496.

In other words, the three extra years of benefits you receive make up almost entirely for the lower benefit rate over the course of an average lifespan. Taking reduced benefits will not affect your dependent's benefits, since those are always calculated on the amount of your full benefit.

There are certain disadvantages to electing early retirement, including proportionately smaller increases as the benefit amount is increased for inflation; lower allowable earnings before your benefits are affected (see below); and lower widow's benefits after your death.

In addition, if you are able to continue working, you have the chance to *increase* your monthly check past the full benefit paid at age 65 by waiting to begin drawing benefits until you are older. The benefits for workers who reach sixty-five before 1982 will be increased by 1 percent for each year they delay retirement. For those who reach sixty-five after 1981 this credit will be raised to 3 percent for each year of continued work. Those additional earning years for later retirement will be averaged in when figuring your average yearly earnings, which will mean more benefit money for you if you earned more in your later working years and can replace earlier low-earning years.

It is also possible to earn money and receive Social Security payments at the same time, up to a point. The "Retirement Test" below determines the effect of your earnings once you begin to receive benefits.

The "Retirement Test" Earnings Limitation

Would you work at a job if you weren't being paid? For many retirees, the current Social Security system creates that situation, largely robbing them of the financial incentive to keep on working. At present, if you draw a salary when you are eligible for Social Security, your earnings as a worker may amount to very little more than you would have received sitting at home doing nothing.

The reason for this is that there is a limit on the amount of money which you are allowed to earn each year without reducing your Social Security benefit. For those between sixty-five and seventy-two, this earnings limitation is $5,000 for 1980, $5,500 for 1981, and $6,000 for 1982.

For those between sixty-two and sixty-five and drawing reduced benefits, the earnings limitation is $3,720 in 1980, $3,960 in 1981, and approximately $4,300 in 1982. This amount will be adjusted upward each year to reflect national economic conditions.

Currently, the earnings limitation applies only until you reach age seventy-two, after which a worker can earn as much as he or she likes and still receive a full Social Security check. Starting in 1983, the age at which you are free of an earnings limitation drops to seventy.

Just because you reach the earnings limit does *not* mean that you forfeit your entire Social Security benefit, however. One dollar of benefits is withheld for each two dollars you earn above the exempt amount.

Remember that Social Security income is not taxable, but almost every dollar that you earn on the job is. On that extra 50 cents you cleared on your hard-earned dollar, you will have to pay federal and (in most cases) state income taxes, as well as the Social Security payroll tax, which is collected even if you are currently receiving benefits. Without even taking state income taxes into account, you gain at most about one-third of each dollar you earn above the earnings limit. And even *that* figure doesn't take into consideration the costs of working itself, including transportation, meals, clothing, and so on.

One way around this dilemma is to delay taking Social Security benefits until you are really ready to retire. As already mentioned, as of 1982 your benefit will be increased by 3 percent for each year after age sixty-five in which you don't take benefits. So if you continue working until age seventy, then begin drawing checks which are 15 percent higher than your full benefit would have been at sixty-five, you can continue working after that with no reduction in Social Security payments.

The other loophole which allows you to continue to make money without diminishing your monthly checks is the distinction between earned and unearned income.

Income from a job or self-employment counts as earnings for Social Security purposes, but the money you receive from the following sources is *not* counted toward the earnings limitation:

- investment income in the form of dividends from stock you own, unless you are a dealer in securities
- interest on savings accounts
- income from Social Security benefits, pensions, other retirement pay, or Veterans Administration benefits
- income from annuities
- gain (or loss) from the sale of capital assets
- gifts or inheritances
- rental income from real estate you own, unless you are a real estate dealer or rent out a farm and participate substantially in running it

- royalties you receive from patents or copyrights which were obtained before you became 65
- if you're a retired partner, retirement payments to you from the partnership don't count under certain circumstances (details available from your local Social Security Administration office)

Certain other payments, such as trust fund payments, moving expenses, travel expenses, and sick pay are often considered unearned income. Check with the Social Security Administration if you are in doubt.

If you are self-employed, only the profit you make is counted against your retirement test limitations. You can therefore claim substantial business expenses for such items as rent or upkeep for the part of your home used for business purposes, use of your automobile, travel and entertainment expenses—in short, any business deduction which would be allowable on your income taxes.

If you own your own business, you may be able to pay your spouse a salary if you can justify his or her active involvement in the business, and thus keep your individual earnings from the business below the limit. A married couple may each earn up to that limit before their benefits are reduced. When you go over that limit, your reduction can be kept to a minimum if you share the additional income approximately evenly.

If you incorporate your business, you may be eligible for even greater business deductions. There are expenses involved in becoming a corporation, though. Discuss the possibility with your accountant to see if this option makes good financial sense in your own case.

Disability and Survivors' Benefits

The Social Security system provides certain forms of lifelong coverage to workers who make payments into the program. If a worker is severely disabled before age sixty-five, he can collect disability checks, as can his wife if she is over sixty-two (or even younger in certain cases) and unmarried children under eighteen (or twenty-two if full-time students, in some cases).

Applying for Benefits

It is a good idea to contact your Social Security office about three months before you plan to retire, so you will receive your first checks as promptly as possible. You should definitely contact them three months before you reach age sixty-five for Medicare benefits, which begin at age sixty-five whether you retire or not.

You will need to have the following items when you are applying for benefits. You can get copies from municipal offices if you don't have them now.

- *Your Social Security card* or a record of your number. (If you are applying on the basis of someone else's work record, you will of course need that person's card or number.)
- *Proof of age.* This can be in the form of a birth certificate, baptismal certificate, or other generally accepted legal documents.
- *Marriage certificate* if your marital status has a bearing on your claim.
- *Your W-2 earnings* form for the previous year, or a copy of your last federal income tax return if you are self-employed.

If when it's time to apply you are missing any of these papers, ask the people at the Social Security office about any substitutions which may be possible. Don't delay your application just because you are missing some of your documentation.

YOUR COMPANY PENSION PLAN

Somewhat less than half of American nongovernment wage earners are covered by employer-financed pension plans. If you are part of that group, you can be lulled into a false sense of security regarding your future income. We tend to think that "the company is taking care of all that" when it comes to pension plans, but that isn't necessarily true. There are important questions you must ask now to make certain that the retirement benefits you *assume* are building up in your name will actually be there when you need them.

There are important decisions to be made, too, which will affect both the amount of money you will receive and the future financial security of your spouse and children. It's conceivable that your most profitable financial planning decision would be to voluntarily withdraw from the company's pension plan and set up your own tax-deferred retirement program. The level of benefits you will eventually receive from whatever program you are now enrolled in is just not a cut-and-dried matter.

Happily, you are assured of certain safeguards on the operation of your pension plan by the Employment Retirement Income Security Act of 1974 (ERISA). This act does *not* require any company to establish a pension plan for its workers. However, it does regulate the administration of virtually all nongovernmental and nonchurch-oriented plans which are put into effect. ERISA includes important provisions to control the ways in which pension funds may be invested and accounted for.

Eligibility

The rules governing eligibility for pension benefits are now regulated to protect the employee, as are certain survivors' benefits. A worker who joins a company later in his career, for example, cannot be denied the opportunity to be covered by its pension plan. ERISA also prevents companies from firing a worker who is growing older in an attempt to avoid paying him a pension.

In the past, pension plans were often so confusing that it was virtually impossible for the employee to figure out what he stood to gain in retirement benefits. A crucial provision of ERISA is the requirement that the administrator of your plan provide you with a summary of its provisions, written in understandable language. This summary must clearly state the rules governing eligibility, how you accumulate benefits, how to file for benefits, what sort of insurance of payment you'd get if the plan is ended, and what your own obligations are under the plan.

The law further requires that you receive a statement of your present status in the plan, if you request it, indicating the amount of benefits accrued to date, and also a summary annual report, explaining the financial activities of the plan for that year.

With these documents at your disposal, you'll have the basis for making intelligent decisions about your future financial security. If you do not have them already, ask your employer for them now, and read them thoroughly.

Now answer the following questions for yourself. They are designed to help you understand both your present status in the pension plan, and the options available to you within it.

Type of Plan

Pension plans may be funded in two different ways:

Defined benefit plans determine the amount of pension benefits you will receive when you retire. Payments into the plan are varied in order to meet that goal, given current investment conditions.

Defined contribution plans, also known as individual account plans, set up separate accounts for each participant and contribute a yearly fixed percentage based on that employee's wages. In this way, the final benefit to be paid is determined by the amount of money deposited to the individual's credit at retirement. These plans, which include corporate profit-sharing arrangements, are the most common.

Pension plans also vary in the degree to which payments are tied to Social Security benefits. In an *integrated* plan, the pension amount is reduced by some percentage of the individual's monthly Social Security check. The reason for this is that employers contribute to the employee's Social Security account throughout his employment and so have already made some contribution to his retirement income. Keep in mind that Social Security income is tax-free, and so each Social Security dollar is worth more to you.

In a *nonintegrated* plan, pension benefits are unrelated to Social Security income.

- *Is your plan a defined benefit or defined contribution plan?*
- *Is it integrated with Social Security or nonintegrated? If integrated, what formula is used to determine the relationship between pension payments and Social Security checks?*

If you know that you will not be staying with your present company long enough to establish a significant amount of retirement income, it may be more worthwhile in the long run to establish your own tax-deferred IRA account instead of accepting the company plan. This retirement planning option was established by ERISA as a means for workers without company pension plans to build a retirement nest egg for themselves, by putting part of their salary into a separate interest-earning fund which will remain untouched and untaxed until they retire. For details, see page 186.

ERISA generally requires that you must be allowed to participate in a plan if you are at least twenty-five years old and have completed one year of service with the employer. If the plan provides full and immediate *vesting* (see below), you must have at least three years of service. In addition, defined benefit plans are allowed to exclude anyone who begins employment when they are within five years of the plan's normal retirement age (usually sixty-five, even though mandatory retirement has been changed to seventy).

- *Are you eligible for participation under the rules of your plan?*

Vesting

Eligibility does not necessarily mean that you will receive payments on retirement. The benefits you earn must be *vested*—that is, you must have worked a specified period of time to have those benefits made available to you. Once your benefits are vested, and you meet the vesting requirements, that money is yours even if you leave that employer.

Vesting is in effect a test of your corporate allegiance, a reward for continued service with the same firm. To curb abuses of the vesting provision by management, which could otherwise refuse to pay retirement benefits to employees with less than thirty or forty years service, ERISA sets minimum requirements. Each plan must at least meet the standards of one of these schedules:

Full and immediate vesting: Your benefits become fully vested as you earn them.

Cliff vesting: Your benefits are fully vested after ten years of service, with no vesting before then.

Graded vesting: You receive 25 percent vesting after five years of service, another 5 percent for each additional year up to the tenth year, plus an additional 10 percent for each year thereafter. (In other words, benefits will be fully vested after fifteen years.)

Rule of 45: You receive 50 percent vesting when you have at least five years of service and your age and years of service add up to 45, plus 10 percent for each additional year up to five years. (In this case, young workers gain no vested benefits at all, while older workers are more quickly vested.)

It is important to understand the vesting procedures involved in your own plan, and where you currently stand in relation to these requirements. Any job change, career change, or early retirement decision must take into consideration the number of additional years required before benefits are fully vested.

You should also know what constitutes a year of service in your plan. Generally this is any twelve-consecutive-month period in which you work at least a thousand hours, but plans vary.

- *What constitutes a year of service according to your pension plan?*
- *What are the vesting requirements of your plan?*
- *Are you now fully vested? If not, when will you be?*

There are other questions regarding your length of service:

- *What constitutes a break in service? If you do have a break in service, due to illness, a leave of absence, or some other cause, will you lose some or all of your accrued benefits?*
- *Does service in the years before you become eligible for the plan count toward vesting and benefit calculations?*
- *Will service after the "normal" retirement age increase your eventual benefit?*
- *According to company records, what is your current service and earnings status? Do their records agree with your own?*

Retirement Age

- *What is considered normal retirement age for your plan?*
- *What benefits will you receive at that point?* Your summary plan description should give you the formula used to calculate this. You can base your figuring on the vested benefit currently credited to you plus a reasonable estimate of your future earnings and their effect in the plan. If your plan is integrated with Social Security, the formula provided will include an adjustment based on the earnings ceiling for Social Security payments in effect when you retire.
- *What provisions are made for early retirement in your plan?* Most plans allow for retirement before age sixty-five, just as Social Security does, but once again you must determine whether the reduced benefits collected for a longer period of time will outweigh the larger payment available if you want to retire.

Form of Payment

- *How will your benefit be paid to you? In the form of a lump sum payment at retirement, or monthly checks for life, or some other system?* Be sure to discuss your total tax situation with your accountant to be sure you will receive the greatest possible share.

One alternative to consider with a lump sum payment is a *rollover IRA*, which will enable you to continue deferring tax payments on the bulk of your retirement fund (see page 186).

Disability and Survivors' Benefits

- *What provision does your plan make for disability payments?*
- *What are valid grounds for a disability claim?*
- *How much would the payments be?*
- *How long would they continue?*

Most pension plans that pay monthly benefits must include a provision for survivors' benefits, payable to the retiree's spouse. This will come to at least half of your monthly pension benefit and is payable for your spouse's lifetime, subject to certain conditions.

You have the option to *reject* the survivors' benefit and receive a larger monthly benefit in return. A family with two wage earners each eligible for substantial pension benefits should give this option serious consideration, although it is not generally advisable if there is only one wage earner. There are specific procedures and deadlines for filing a written rejection of survivors' benefits.

Another choice involves protection for the spouse of a worker who stays on the job past the plan's early retirement age but dies before retiring and beginning to collect benefits. This form of coverage, if available, is only provided if the employee specifically requests it. Choosing to take advantage of this extra protection will result in a reduction in your eventual retirement benefits, but the extra protection involved could be well worth the loss.

- *What are the survivors' benefits provided by your plan?*
- *If survivors' benefits are available, would you forfeit them by taking a lump sum payment of retirement benefits? If so, is it a good idea to take monthly checks instead?*
- *Would it be prudent to reject these benefits and increase your basic payments and, if so, how would you go about it?*
- *Do you have the option of providing survivors' benefits even if you don't retire after the early retirement age? If so, is it worth the price, and how would you apply for this coverage?*

Plan Termination

If your company goes out of business, what happens to your pension? Suppose your employer simply decides to end the pension plan—he has the right, and many employers are doing so because of the more stringent ERISA requirements on funding and benefits.

ERISA provided a certain amount of protection for retirement benefits in this case by setting up the Pension Benefit Guaranty Corporation (PBGC). There are very definite limits on the extent to which you are protected, though: Only vested benefits in certain defined benefit plans are insured, and there is a limit on the amount of benefits covered by PBGC insurance. This turns out to be slightly over a thousand dollars per month if you're at least sixty-five when you retire, somewhat less for early retirees. Your summary plan description will state whether your plan is insured by the PBGC.

Insurance protection is just one factor in assessing the stability of your future pension payments. If you have any doubt about the future ability of your pension plan to pay monthly benefits, this should be a key factor in your decision whether or not to take a lump sum payment on retirement, if that option is open to you.

- *Is your plan insured by the PBGC?*

Benefit Adjustments

One of the hottest topics of conversation among pension planners and regulators at the moment is the question of increasing pensions to adjust for inflation. The retiree who had the level of his monthly pension check fixed ten years ago may be in trouble today—each pension dollar buys less than half of what it did when he received his first check. In the interest of fairness, unions and many legislators argue, pension benefits should be indexed, as Social Security payments are—tied directly to increases in the cost of living.

Corporations are fighting any mandatory linking of pensions and prices, and with good reason. Double-digit inflation would mean double-digit increases in pension benefits, which would increase costs to the companies by as much as 30 percent, and possibly much, much more.

In recent years, many major corporations have voluntarily provided cost-of-living increases to their pensioners. These adjustments are certainly helpful, but they are rarely substantial enough to keep up with the present soaring inflationary spiral. And they are given only at the discretion of the employer—there are no guarantees. The number of companies who have agreed to *mandatory* increases tied to the Consumer Price Index is minuscule—most estimates say only about 3 percent of private pension plans have such a provision.

Where does this leave you? You should certainly check on your company's recent history in granting voluntary pension increases. You might consider taking as much money as you can from your pension plan as soon as you can get it in order to invest it so that it can work for you. You can retire later, if those years count toward your pension benefits, since your wages should go up as inflation does, and your pension check would then be figured on the basis of more years of higher, inflated dollars.

Above all, you must plan your other sources of income to provide more support as your monthly benefit decreases in buying power.

- *Is your pension benefit indexed to the cost of living, and to what degree?*

Applying for Benefits

Some employers automatically submit your application as you near retirement age, but there are often forms to fill out and decisions to make in advance, so you should check on the procedure now. Delaying that process could postpone the arrival of your benefits check.

- *How do you go about filing for pension benefits?*
- *If your application for benefits is denied for any reason, what is the procedure for appealing this decision?*

IRA AND KEOGH ACCOUNTS—SETTING UP YOUR OWN PENSION PLAN

Among the biggest winners under the tax law of 1981 are those people who wish to set up a tax-deferred personal pension plan. Whether you are self-employed or work for a company with or without a pension plan, you can now set up *your own* pension plan, which will give you substantial tax advantages right now, in addition to the ultimate payoff of a secure retirement fund in the future. Previously, only those not covered by an employer pension plan were eligible for an IRA.

The basic appeal of both IRA and Keogh plans is that they enable you to take a portion of today's income to save for retirement without first paying income taxes on it. The money is put away in a special retirement account, and you pay income taxes on this money only as you take it out after you retire. You come out a winner in three ways:

1. By reducing your current taxable income by the amount of your retirement plan contribution, you may lower the tax rate on the remainder of your present income.

2. The interest earned on the money you invest in your plan is not taxable until you use it, as opposed to interest received on a regular savings account, which is taxable annually. Therefore, you can use those untaxed interest earnings as additional capital to earn further interest or investment income.

3. When you finally do begin to withdraw money from your retirement account, you will probably be paying taxes at a much lower rate, since taxable post-retirement income is generally lower than income during the working years (remember, Social Security benefits are not taxable), and you gain additional tax deductions and allowances once you reach sixty-five.

In short, these plans let you put Uncle Sam's money to work to make more money for you. The government is, in effect, helping to finance your retirement investment program.

Who Is Eligible?

IRA: Effective January 1, 1982, anyone who has earned income is entitled to his or her own Individual Retirement Account (IRA).

Keogh: Generally, any self-employed person is eligible for a Keogh plan, in addition to an IRA. However, if you have employees, you must include them in your Keogh plan as well, and contribute for them at the same percentage of their salary as you do of your own. Since this money is a tax-deductible business expense, you may still come out ahead, since a Keogh allows you to shelter far more of your own income than an IRA does.

Who Runs the Plans?

Financial institutions of all kinds are lining up to sponsor these plans. Banks are only one alternative. As with any investment decision, you must assess the degree of risk you are willing to accept in exchange for the possibility of higher returns. Your choice of sponsors includes:

- banks
- savings and loan institutions
- brokerage houses
- mutual funds
- insurance companies

Check out each of these sources and choose the one that best fits your personal set of priorities. If your concern is security—a fixed rate of interest—start your account at a bank, but, especially since banking regulations are currently being liberalized, be sure that you are getting the maximum rate of interest allowed by law.

You may be able to increase your rate of return by investing in a more flexible mutual fund. And if you are interested in managing your own funds, you can set up an IRA or Keogh with a brokerage house. They will allow you to make the decisions as to where your money is invested, from a wide range of stocks and bonds, mutual funds, government securities, and other investment opportunities. This option would let you use your tax-deferred funds to build a nest egg, and let Uncle Sam share the investment risk.

Once you choose a plan sponsor, you *are* allowed to move your funds to a different account, or to contribute to several different accounts simultaneously, as long as your total contribution does not exceed the legal maximum. You may not change plan sponsors more than once per year, however. When making your choice of sponsor, be sure to find out how much of a fee or commission you will be charged.

How Much Can You Contribute?

Under the 1981 tax law, the maximum contribution to an IRA in each taxable year is 100 percent of earned income, up to $2,000. If a husband and wife both qualify for an account, they can each contribute up to this limit in individual accounts and take a combined $4,000 deduction on their taxes.

If you have a nonworking spouse, you can set up a marital IRA and increase the maximum contribution level to $2,250.

One of the latest wrinkles in the pension scene is the Simplified Employee Pension (SEP). Since ERISA led to the folding of many company pension plans due to increased time and money demands, Congress approved the SEP plan, under which a company sets up an IRA on behalf of each of its employees and makes contributions to it. Employers can overstep the personal IRA contribution limits, though, and contribute up to $15,000 or 15 percent of an employee's wages to a SEP account per year.

Another special form of tax-deferral is the rollover IRA. If you receive a lump sum pension payment when you leave your job, you can put all or part of it into a rollover IRA account and continue to defer taxes on that sum except as you withdraw the money. This account is entirely separate from any previous IRAs you might have started, but there is a time imperative. You have just sixty days to start a rollover IRA after receiving your pension check.

The basic limit for Keogh plan contributions is $15,000 or 15 percent of earned income, whichever is less, per taxable year. Keogh plan holders are now also eligible to contribute $2,000 to an IRA.

If you are interested in contributing more than the basic maximum, you may be interested in a Defined Benefit Keogh Plan, sometimes called Keogh Plus. Instead of paying in a fixed, limited proportion of your earnings, you set the final goal for your retirement fund and then make annual contributions at a rate commensurate with this goal.

Another possibility for the self-employed, if they are really bringing in a substantial income, is to incorporate and set up a defined benefit pension plan. You can get a much larger tax deferral this way than with either a Keogh or a Keogh Plus plan, but of course you will incur the fees and hassles of incorporating. If you feel that you might earn enough money to compensate for the expenses of incorporating through an improved tax position, consult your lawyer or accountant.

Establishing a standard IRA or Keogh plan doesn't mean that you have to put *anything* into it, after the initial contribution; you can just put money aside when you can. If you begin an IRA or Keogh plan and subsequently take a job which provides a company pension plan, you will be unable to continue contributing to your own plan, but you will not be penalized for the money you have already put in. It will continue to earn compound interest, and be available when you need it in retirement.

When Can You Start Receiving Retirement Benefits?

You can begin withdrawing funds from an IRA or Keogh plan at age 59½ without penalty. You can take out funds before then if you need to, but you will pay an additional 10 percent income tax penalty on those withdrawals. The rules also state that you *must* begin withdrawing your funds by age 70½.

When you make withdrawals from your account, that amount will be taxable as regular income. If you decide to take the proceeds of your plan as a lump sum, you may be eligible to save some money by using income averaging when figuring your taxes. Ask your accountant or the IRS for further details on income averaging.

TAX ASPECTS OF RETIREMENT

Throughout life we wage a quiet, ongoing war with the government. They gain control of as much of our income as they can, and we fight like hell to keep the maximum amount of that hard-earned paycheck in our own pockets. Most of us find ourselves either grappling with complex tax regulations to squeeze out a few more spendable dollars, or hiring a professional to do it for us.

As you grow older, some important changes take place. The tax regulations actually start tipping the scales in your favor *if* you have structured your financial planning properly. The various tax breaks available for older Americans can make the difference between just squeaking by and a very comfortable retirement income.

Your sources of income will change substantially after retirement, from weekly wages to some combination of Social Security payments, pension benefits, annuities, proceeds from buying and selling property, bonds, stocks, and other returns on your investments. Do you know how much of the income you have established for retirement will disappear in taxes? You should.

Your most accessible, inexpensive source of advice is the Internal Revenue Service itself. They publish hundreds of free booklets detailing the various issues confronting taxpayers, and will answer particular questions by phone or in person at their local offices. An essential part of anyone's preretirement reading is the IRS booklet "Tax Benefits for Older Americans." This publication addresses the issues which are of special interest to retirees and presents sample forms which you are required to file for certain tax benefits.

You will also want to consider the effect of changing residences on your tax situation, if you are thinking of moving. On pages 353–65, you'll find a chart listing the tax requirements in all fifty states, including income taxes, sales taxes, and any special advantages for retirees in each state. The difference in tax liability between two localities could be a deciding factor in choosing a retirement community. If you are planning to operate a business in your new community, it is particularly important to consult a tax expert in that area, to advise you on your tax responsibilities as a local businessman and also on any tax breaks given to new businesses.

Where you will live also has a bearing on your investment decisions. The proceeds from certain investments gain or lose their tax-exempt status depending on your legal residence. Interest you receive on bonds issued by your home state will not be taxable, for instance, but if you move out of that jurisdiction, you may be liable for a state tax on your earnings. Be sure that you understand your tax liability on any investment return. Your personal level of income, place of residence, and overall tax situation after age sixty-five will all be determining factors.

The Basic Tax Breaks for Senior Citizens

Extra Personal Exemption. Anyone sixty-five or older is entitled to claim an extra personal exemption when paying federal income taxes. This means that a single person can claim two exemptions, and a married couple can take four exemptions on a joint return.

More Tax-Free Income. Social Security benefits are not taxable, so if you substitute nontaxable Social Security dollars for earned income, you also lower the tax rate on any additional income you may receive.

You may well have other tax-free income. Benefits you receive from an employer-funded pension plan are taxable as personal income, but any contribution *you* made into the plan are generally tax-exempt. Veteran's benefits, gifts, inheritances, and health and accident insurance policy benefits received are also nontaxable.

Tax-Free Sale of Residence. Older taxpayers who sell their principal residence get a substantial tax break.

If you are fifty-five or older and sell your home, the first $125,000 of your gain over the initial purchase price will not be taxed. There are other provisions which allow homeowners of any age to sell their residence and not pay taxes on the transaction if they reinvest the proceeds in another home within two years. Therefore, the one-time exclusion of gain for those over fifty-five should generally be used only if you are not planning to buy a new home in the near future—for instance, if you plan to live in rental housing from now on.

The residency requirements and eligibility restrictions for taking advantage of these tax breaks are outlined in detail in ''Tax Benefits for Older Americans'' and another IRS publication, ''Tax Information on Selling or Purchasing Your Home.''

The basis for much of your preretirement planning is postponing your tax liability until your later years when you enter a lower tax bracket. If you gain a clear understanding of your retirement tax situation now, when you are making your investment, savings, pension, housing, and estate-planning decisions, you can provide well for your financial future.

8

INVESTING FOR FUTURE SECURITY

It's a great country, but you can't live in it for nothing.
WILL ROGERS

YOUR RETIREMENT INVESTMENT STRATEGY

IN the last chapter, we asked you to total up the value of assets you intend to convert to cash upon retirement—your *retirement cash reserves*. We assumed you could earn an average annual return of 8 percent on these cash reserves over the long run through conservative investments such as high-quality bonds or long-term savings accounts. You projected how many years your reserves would last on the basis of this 8 percent return.

In an era of high inflation, though, the traditional "conservative" investments often do not *conserve* at all. With a fixed return on principal, the real purchasing power of both the return and the underlying principal can be seriously diminished over time. For example, suppose you put $10,000 in the bank tomorrow at 8 percent, and inflation is running at 10 percent. Every year, before taxes, you receive (and spend) $800 in interest. Five years from now, your $800 annual interest will buy only $472 worth of goods and services by today's standards, and your $10,000 will have shrunk to an amount equal to $5,905 in today's dollars.

There is no surefire solution to this investment problem, but it is possible to maximize the total return on your reserves without incurring so much risk that you can't sleep at night, by developing a diversified portfolio of investments. Your goal is to achieve a balance of investments that preserves the real purchasing power of your capital without robbing you of your peace of mind.

Before embarking on an investment program of your own, you should have a pretty good idea of what the various types of investments are, how different economic forces tend to influence investment markets, and what choices are available to you in selecting, buying, managing, and selling these investments. Unless you have the time, interest, and temperament to investigate these subjects, you may be better off putting your money in a nice safe long-term savings account.

Investing is something of a cross between a game of chess and a game of chance. Your chances in chess certainly improve with practice and expert advice. Also while anyone can win on one throw of the dice, the experienced player who understands the odds will nearly always come out ahead in the long run. And investments are a long-run game.

Good investment advice is difficult to obtain for the small investor, so you have to seek it out for yourself. Start by delving into a couple of the excellent resource guides mentioned at the end of this chapter. If you find yourself intrigued, read more, talk to some friends who dabble in the market, and rough out a preliminary strategy of your own for retirement investments. On the other hand, if you find the subject boring, or unpleasant, at least try to familiarize yourself with the basic concepts and jargon, and then take the route that's easiest for you.

*   *   *

Savings

The experts advise that your first $10,000 of surplus cash should always be kept in a high-interest savings account. These funds are your emergency cash reserve, and must be readily available at all times. At this writing, both six-month bank savings certificates (usual minimum deposit, $10,000) and brokerage firm money market funds are paying over 12 percent annual interest—significantly higher than a conventional passbook savings account with about the same degree of safety. Money market funds are not insured by the federal government, however.

A money market fund is similar to a mutual fund, except that its capital is invested in a variety of high-quality, short-term government and corporate obligations whose interest rates rise rapidly in times of high inflation. Some money market funds allow you to invest as little as $1,000. There is no minimum time requirement or sales commission for participation, although there is a management fee of about three fourths of one percent, which comes off the top of the interest they pay. You will receive a monthly statement indicating your balance, and the rate of interest paid during that month. When and if this interest rate drops to savings bank levels, you can transfer your money to a savings account. To learn more about money market funds, ask your broker or write for and compare the prospectuses of these organizations:

Scudder Managed Reserves
175 Federal Street
Boston, MA 02110

Dreyfus Liquid Assets
600 Lincoln Blvd.
Middlesex, NJ 08846

The Reserve Fund
810 Seventh Avenue
New York, NY 10017

Merrill Lynch Ready Assets
One Liberty Plaza
New York, NY 10006

Oppenheimer Monetary Bridge
One New York Plaza
New York, NY 10004

The Prime Reserve Fund
T. Rowe Price Associates
100 East Pratt Street
Baltimore, MD 20202

Stocks and Bonds

When you hold shares in a corporation, you literally own a portion of its assets and earnings. You participate in the growth of both the corporation and the economy, because as corporate earnings grow, so does the market value of the stock. During the 1970s, unfortunately, many stocks performed poorly and small investors abandoned the stock market in droves, seeking greater safety for their capital. Historically, however, stocks held over the long term have performed significantly better than either savings accounts or bonds. According to one study, for every fifteen-year holding period between 1930 and 1976, the New York Stock Exchange listings as a group provided an annual return (assuming dividends were reinvested) of between 8 and 22 percent, with the majority of these periods in the 11-to-16 percent range. There was only one fifteen-year period out of some thirty that did not reach 8 percent. In the same study, ten-year holding periods were found to be somewhat more erratic, but only two periods out of thirty-five registered lower than 8 percent average annual growth.

By contrast, bonds have performed quite poorly overall since World War II, because steady increases in interest rates have caused the market value of bonds to drop to allow their yield to match that of currently available investments. For example, if you buy a newly issued $1,000 thirty-year bond with a *coupon rate* (stated interest rate) of 5 percent, the bond will pay you $50 a year in interest. If next year, market rates are 10 percent, the market value of your bond will decrease to $500, so that its *annual yield* of $50 will now equal 10 percent for the investor who buys the bond at that time. When your bond matures, it will be redeemed at its original $1,000 face value.

There are tactics you can employ to minimize this problem with bonds, however. One way is to buy a variety of bonds selling at a discount (as in the example above) which have *staggered maturities,* so that you can later redeem a certain number of bonds each year and at least receive the face value of each of them. Another approach could be to buy into several bond mutual funds or unit investment trusts, which would give you a certain amount of diversification and still preserve your principal.

Financial pros tend to agree that investing in stocks with a strong record of dividend growth may be the best strategy for retirement income. The following list of twenty high-quality stocks, compiled in 1979 by David L. Babson and Company, a Boston investment counseling firm, includes companies which raised their dividends by an average of 10 percent annually in the ten-year period 1968 to 1978, and 15 percent a year in the five-year period 1973 to 1978. These companies are to some degree protected against rising cost pressures which would dampen profits, and for this reason the Babson investment professionals believe they will continue to outperform the market in dividend yield and growth rate.

The New York Stock Exchange has created an "Investor's Information Kit," available for $2.50 by writing the New York Stock Exchange, Publication Section, 11 Wall Street, New York, NY 10005. The Exchange also publishes a bibliography of investment information sources, and a list of member stock brokerage firms throughout the United States which serve the smaller investor, both of which you can request at no charge. Other New York Stock Exchange booklets on investment are distributed chiefly through brokerage firms, and you can probably obtain them at no cost by calling one or two local brokerage offices.

*   *   *

Table 10. Companies With Strong Dividend Growth

| | May 8, 1979 | | Annual Dividend Growth | | |
	Price	Yield	1968–78	1973–78	1979–84 (Est.)
American Express	30	5.9%	17%	25%	23%
American Home Products	25	6.0	12	15	11
American Telephone	59	8.5	7	9	7
Atlantic Richfield	62	4.5	9	18	12
Avon Products	48	5.9	11	13	12
Beatrice Foods	21	5.7	8	11	11
Citicorp	24	5.5	8	9	12
Coca-Cola	39	5.1	11	14	10
Colgate-Palmolive	18	6.2	11	15	9
Combined Insurance	17	6.9	14	18	11
Continental Corp.	27	7.4	8	8	13
CPC International	49	6.2	5	9	9
Dow Chemical	25	5.6	12	21	12
Exxon	51	7.0	6	8	9
General Electric	49	5.3	6	10	10
IBM	78*	4.4	17	21	12
Marsh & McLennan	62	5.2	13	18	12
Prentice-Hall	25	5.5	8	8	10
Stauffer Chemical	41	5.4	8	16	12
Tecumseh Products	63	7.6	17	29	10
Average 20 Cos.	—	6.0%	10%	15%	11%
Standard & Poor's 500 Average	—	5.5%	5%	9%	8%
Consumer Price Index	—	—	7%	8%	?

* Adjusted for 4-for-1 split effective 5/10/79

Mutual Funds

Here is renowned economist Paul A. Samuelson's "main recipe for no-fuss canny investing: make great use of no-load mutual funds, preferably those with low expense ratios." This strategy makes particular sense for retirees or preretirees who want to make more than savings account interest on their money but want to avoid the risk of investing heavily in a few speculative issues.

A mutual fund is a way for many people to pool their money, buy a variety of different investments, and share the proceeds. The initial investment required is almost always quite modest, and money invested in mutual funds is readily available to you when you need it: You simply sell your shares in the fund.

The mutual funds on the market follow different overall investment strategies, and you should take some care in choosing the fund which best suits your purposes. Some spread their capital over a wide range of properties, in order to assure general stability and modest return. Other funds specialize in riskier areas, hoping for faster, more substantial gains. You will find mutual funds that concentrate on particular industries or geographical regions as well as funds that deal exclusively with stocks, or bonds, or Treasury bills, or some combination. The money market fund is one variety, specializing in the short-term loan market. If you are thinking about investing in mutual funds, you should consider the following:

Goals. The mutual fund prospectus will give you a clear statement of its goals. Your choice of fund will depend on whether you prefer a steady source of income, long-term capital gains, rapid growth, or something in between. The tax liability you incur on the proceeds of your mutual fund will vary, depending on the investment vehicles the fund employs. You can buy into a fund specializing in tax-free municipal bonds, for example, and gain the same federal tax exemption you would have if you had purchased the bonds themselves.

Past performance. A mutual fund is only as good as the investment decisions of the fund managers. By checking into the fund's record in past years, in both good and bad market conditions, you will have some indication of the potential for success in the future.

The annual *Forbes* magazine ratings on the relative performance of mutual funds are published in early January of each year.

Closed-end or open-end. Most of the mutual funds available are open-end funds, meaning that shares are generally available to the public. There are also closed-end funds, which issue only a certain fixed number of shares. These can only be purchased when one of the initial investors is ready to sell and are only available through brokerage houses.

Load or no-load. You have to pay a sales commission (the load) to buy certain mutual funds (including the closed-end funds mentioned above). No-load funds can be purchased directly, without a sales charge. If you use a broker for any of these transactions, you will be paying him a fee as well. You can receive a free listing of no-load funds by writing to the No-Load Mutual Fund Association, Valley Forge Colony Building, Valley Forge, PA 19481.

Services. One of the primary reasons that the average investor uses a mutual fund is that the fund management takes care of the bookkeeping and paperwork involved in investment transactions. Most funds charge an annual fee for their services—about one half of one percent. If the fees outlined in a prospectus are substantially higher than this, it may be wise to look elsewhere.

In addition to basic investment services, mutual funds often provide additional conveniences. These may include IRA and Keogh programs, automatic dividend reinvestment in the fund, a systematic monthly payment plan, the ability to make purchase and withdrawal transactions over the phone, and so on. Compare the features of the funds you are considering to find the service package which best fits your needs.

Annuities

An annuity is a contract, generally with an insurance company, by which you give the company a large sum of money and the company promises to send you a check for a set amount every month for as long as you live. In the best of all possible worlds, this would mean that you would never have to worry about outliving your income. Whether you lived to 70 or 170, those checks would keep arriving monthly. The snag, though, is the amount of those checks.

The most visible problem with buying an annuity is that each check you receive represents a very small percentage of the original purchase price you paid. And those checks are not just interest payments on principal. Once you buy an annuity, that money is spent, and those monthly checks are all the money you will ever see.

The size of the payments you receive is determined by your sex and your age at the time your checks begin to arrive, based on standard life expectancy tables. If a man pays $10,000 for the simplest form of lifetime annuity at age sixty-five, he will receive $80–85 a month for life; if a woman pays the same amount, she will receive about $70–75 (less because her life expectancy is greater). If the man waited until age seventy-five to buy, his check would be $105–115; a woman's about $100–105. In other words, buying at age sixty-five provides you with less than a 10 percent annual return on the money you put in, and you lose the original purchase price.

With their fixed, relatively low rate of return, annuities are certainly not the place for all of your savings dollars. However, there are certain conditions which make them a more attractive investment. If you wait to buy until you are older, for instance, you will receive a higher payment level, albeit with the probability of a shorter payout. Security is the primary selling point of an annuity. You know for certain that you will receive a monthly sum despite possibly adverse investment conditions, and without any effort at managing your money on your part. Annuities are also sold by many charitable organizations, combining the promise of lifetime income with the satisfaction of making a sizable donation. The payments from these annuities are usually smaller than those from life insurance companies, though.

If you are interested in exploring the possibility of buying an annuity, here are some of the options open to you:

Guaranteed minimum payments. "What happens to all my money if I buy an annuity which pays me $100 a month and I die three months later?" is a common question. If you object to the idea of the insurance company getting something for nothing, you can buy a *refund* or *years certain* contract. A refund annuity guarantees that if the contract holder dies before receiving payments at least equal to the original cost of the annuity, the difference will be refunded to his estate. A years certain contract addresses the same question by guaranteeing that payments will be made to his survivor for a given number of years, even if the annuitant dies before that time. Each of these options, of course, will yield substantially smaller payments each month in exchange for the added protection provided.

Joint lifetime annuities. If you are concerned with providing continuing income for both yourself and your spouse, a joint lifetime annuity will carry on throughout both of your lifetimes. These contracts vary widely in the amount they pay after the death of one of the annuitants, sometimes continuing with the same monthly rate, sometimes providing some fraction thereof.

Savings Bonds

Investment counselors generally frown on United States savings bonds today, since they pay only 6.5 percent interest compounded semiannually when held for five years. That is hardly the key to combating double-digit inflation. However, there are practical considerations which might make government savings bonds a worthwhile part of your overall financial package. Savings bonds are sold at banks everywhere, or through an automatic payroll deduction savings plan where you work. There is no charge for either buying or redeeming the bonds. By making bond purchases a systematic part of your savings program, you can set aside just a few dollars a week and have it amount to a substantial sum in the long run.

In addition to being free of state and local taxes, savings bonds are also a means of deferring your liability for federal income tax. The interest you earn on your savings account is taxed as income in the year you earn it, but the interest on savings bonds does not become taxable until you cash them in. This way, you can buy bonds while you are working and cash them in after retirement, paying income taxes on the interest in your new, lower tax bracket.

There are two types of bonds currently available:

- *EE bonds.* The interest on Series EE bonds, which are sold with face values of $50 to $10,000, is paid at the time you cash in the bond. They sell at half their face value, and earn 6.5 percent per year for nine years, at which time they mature. If held to maturity, the average annual return becomes 8 percent. The proceeds are not taxable by state or local governments.
- *HH bonds.* The bearer of a Series HH bond gets an interest check every six months. Instead of buying a bond at less than face value and waiting for it to reach maturity, as with EE bonds, holders Series of HH bonds buy at face value, which ranges from $500 to $10,000. The bonds pay increasing rates of interest during the first ten years, to average 7.5 percent over that period. They reach maturity at ten years but continue to pay 7.5 percent if held longer.

Real Estate

Most people agree that the best investment they ever made was their home. They made a down payment, took a hefty portion of their mortgage payments as a tax deduction, and can now sell their house for many times what they paid for it. This initial real estate venture may be the only investment they've ever made which has kept up with inflation. Why not, then, expand their real estate activities and sink their investment dollars into more speculative purchases of land, or rental property, or maybe part ownership in a shopping mall?

Real estate investment just isn't a casual matter. After all, you devoted years to managing your home. You selected it carefully, arranged for financing, and made sure that everything was in order before moving in. You then served as an on-premises manager, spotting maintenance problems, improving the property, and keeping up the grounds, as well as getting involved in the community.

Are you willing to give the same kind of dedication to buying property which will serve only as an investment? When you consider putting your money into real estate, you must make a commitment similar to that of any small businessman opening a store for the first time. The more time and energy you devote to learning the ins and outs of the business, the greater your chances of success.

In order to make money in real estate, you must play several roles at once. First, you have to be an investigator. The key to being successful in real estate is finding both a location and an individual property which will increase in value and, possibly, generate spendable cash flow in the meantime. This sounds a great deal easier than it actually is. You must first learn enough about property to be able to spot its assets and flaws, and accurately assess what effects improvements will have on its value. You must judge the condition of not only a building but the community as a whole, spotting social and economic trends that will affect property values in the years to come. There is always the possibility of the unforeseen factory closing, the change in zoning laws, or the natural disaster which pulls the rug out from under your property's profit potential. You can minimize the risks involved, if you are willing to do quite a bit of research and footwork on your own. Real estate brokers and other professionals are helpful, but you must be a skilled investor to take advantage of their services.

Next, you must be a financier. One of the advantages of purchasing real estate is that, through mortgages, you can control a property with a large value by making a relatively small initial payment. This is known as *leverage*. You have to understand the ways in which you can find adequate financing, and recognize a good deal when it is presented.

How much risk can you afford? Even with the availability of financing, you will have to put a substantial sum up front, and pay off the mortgage each month. The enormous rise in real estate prices in recent years may look like a good sign, but it also means that you will have to *buy* a property at current inflated prices and hope that the market will bear still higher prices in the future. At this point, if a property is inexpensive, there is probably a very good reason why it has not gone up in price already. A cheap property may be an opportunity, but be extremely wary.

Remember that the money you put into real estate will not be readily available to you if you need it and that the monthly rent paid to you will be only a small fraction of the initial purchase price. On the other hand, there are the tax breaks. Discuss your entire financial situation with your accountant to get a good idea of the amount of money you have to play with, and the tax benefits which might result in your bracket. Then evaluate your own nervous system, and honestly assess your ability to take on large financial burdens in a risky enterprise.

Finally, you have to be a manager. With rare exceptions your property will not run itself. You will have to put in time making sure that it is kept up properly, arrange for repairs and other services, keep up with the situation in the neighborhood and, if you have tenants, collect rents and answer complaints. One way to keep a tight rein on your property and derive some personal benefit at the same time is to buy a property you can live in yourself. You could buy a home which needs work, live in it until the work is completed (possibly doing some of the repairs yourself), then sell the improved property at a profit and move on to another house in a similar situation. Another alternative is to own a house with rental units, ranging from a two-family dwelling to an apartment building, live in one of the units, and rent out the others.

Real Estate Investment Trusts. One way to invest in real estate without taking on the burdens of management is to buy into a Real Estate Investment Trust (REIT). An REIT is essentially a mutual fund which deals exclusively in real estate, in the form of both property ownership and mortgages. After the bankruptcy of one of the largest REITs in 1974, these trusts acquired a reputation as a particularly risky investment, but they have shown far better performance in recent years. REITs are sold through brokerage houses, and your broker will be able to give you an appraisal of their suitability for you.

RETHINKING YOUR INSURANCE NEEDS

You probably have some form of life insurance coverage today, but there is a good chance that you are wasting money in the way you carry your insurance. The older you get, the more likely it is that you are paying for "protection" you don't really need, and quite possibly letting a valuable financial asset go to waste.

It's very easy to make mistakes when it comes to buying insurance. The basic problem is that there is no simple standardized system, no unit pricing or estimated miles per gallon figure to fall back on when comparing the relative merits of different insurance policies. Each has its own distinctive set of features, options, guarantees, and promises.

Too often, a fast-talking salesman plays a large part in insurance purchases. He comes into your home and explains how buying the policy he recommends will guarantee not only college for your kids but a secure widowhood for your wife and, if you should live, financial security for your old age. Very attractive package. What few people realize is that very often their best choices, the policies which most successfully combine economy with lifelong security, are precisely the ones which offer the insurance agent the *smallest* commission on the sale. Comparison shopping for insurance is essential to a sound purchase, and too many of us don't know enough about the insurance business to shop effectively.

It isn't really that difficult to wade through the morass of straight life, term, renewable, refundable, cash values, and paid-up policies. You can learn to deal with the insurance industry on your own terms by taking an hour or two to read an informative, consumer-oriented survey of insurance policies. Jane Bryant Quinn's *Everyone's Money Book* has an excellent section on life insurance. It could save you hundreds or thousands of dollars in wasted premiums and lost investment opportunities.

Being well informed about insurance becomes even more crucial as you approach retirement. You probably first bought insurance when your children were small and your primary interest was assuring their financial safety in case of emergency. However, whole life insurance is sold with two goals in mind—to insure against the death of the family breadwinner, and also to serve as a form of investment. Your needs in both these areas change drastically as you enter your forties or fifties, when you want to leave the greatest possible amount of money in your pocket. You must ask yourself two major questions before you mail in the next premium check—how much insurance do you really need now, and how effectively does a given policy fill those needs?

The answer to the first question is undoubtedly not the same as it was when you first bought life insurance. Do your children still rely on you for support? Is there still a large mortgage on your home? If the answer to these questions is no, you can justify a substantial reduction in the amount of insurance you carry.

If you are a man, the primary purpose of your insurance may well have been providing for your wife in the event of your death. But what other sources of income will she have at her disposal? A combination of Social Security widow's, survivor's, or disability benefits, continuing survivor's benefits from a pension plan, any retirement benefits she has earned herself at her own job, and the savings and investments you have amassed over the years may well provide all the security she really needs.

When no one is depending on you for support, there are only two reasons to carry life insurance—as a means of leaving money to your beneficiaries directly (individuals or charitable organizations) outside of your will, or as a form of investment to provide continuing income.

As a money making investment, insurance has come under heavy fire in recent years. It is a form of enforced savings, but is more useful as protection for your survivors than as a tool for building a retirement nest egg. Experts today generally advise selecting the cheapest life insurance policy you can find that will provide your survivors with sufficient protection in the event of your death, and using more lucrative forms of investment to earn money for you over the years.

Evaluating Your Coverage

The comparatively expensive policies which offer a financial return on your premiums as well as death benefits are called *whole life* or *straight life* insurance. As you pay your premiums, you build up a *cash value,* a sum which is yours if you choose to discontinue the policy, or which will be paid back to you in some form after you reach a certain age. A whole life policy represents a commitment on the part of the insurance company to continue insuring you throughout your lifetime, as long as you continue paying the premiums, which remain at their original fixed level.

When you buy *term* insurance, on the other hand, you are covered for a shorter period. The term of the policy may be as little as one year or as long as twenty. You build up little or no cash value—the insurance company pays off only in case of death. In return, you pay far less than for whole life. It often works out that by choosing term insurance, you can buy coverage providing the same death benefit amount as whole life at a fraction of the price. You can then invest the money you save and allow it to grow to be significantly larger than the cash value you would have built up by paying for whole life over the years.

The decision, unfortunately, is not that simple. The major complicating factor is your insurability. Remember, once you buy a whole life policy you are guaranteed continued coverage throughout your lifetime at a fixed premium rate. Each time your term insurance expires, you have to sign up for new coverage, paying progressively higher premiums as you grow older and running the risk of being denied coverage altogether if your health is not up to par at renewal time.

If you have already held life insurance policies for several years, you should take a little time to consider the following issues.

IF YOU NOW HAVE A WHOLE LIFE POLICY

- Determine how much cash value you have already built up and the ways in which you can use this reserve within the terms of your policy. You could simply cancel the policy and take the cash in a lump sum, or you could use that cash value to convert your policy to a paid-up policy with a lower face value. This would make it possible for you to stop paying premiums and retain coverage. Another alternative is converting to term insurance through your present company and using the cash value to pay the premium for the next few years. You might borrow against the cash value at low interest rates, or arrange for an annuity payment based on your cash value. When assessing the merits of any of these possibilities, be sure to check on the tax liability you incur when you receive the money.
- Consider the possibility of integrating your policy in your estate planning, possibly by changing the beneficiaries now named. This way you can pass a portion of your wealth to an heir via life insurance, free of estate taxes.
- Generally, try to change your policy and retain the same company. You should be able to alter your policy at no cost, but a new insurer means paying new sales commissions.
- In evaluating any policy, be sure that the disability provisions adequately protect you in the event that you cannot continue to pay premiums because of serious illness.

IF YOU NOW HAVE TERM INSURANCE

- Check on the renewability of your policy. Generally term policies are renewable only until age sixty or sixty-five at the discretion of the insurer, but there are somewhat more expensive policies which may be guaranteed renewable up to age one hundred, although at substantially higher premiums. You must weigh the increased cost of renewable coverage against the probability that you will or won't need it.

- Explore the conversion feature of your policy, which allows you to change over to whole life coverage within certain limitations. Once again you will pay for the privilege of lifelong coverage, and the premiums charged for the converted policy may be quite high.

IF YOU HAVE GROUP LIFE INSURANCE THROUGH YOUR JOB

- In some cases, employers pay for continued participation in the company's life insurance policy after retirement, but early retirement or a short service history could affect this. Some group policies include the right to convert to individual payment, without having to pass a medical exam to prove eligibility. This can be a great boon considering the stringent preinsurance health requirements as you grow older.

The face value of the group policy usually drops considerably when you pass a certain age. But even if the value drops and you have to pay for continuing the policy yourself, the group rates may still make this your most economically attractive insurance choice.

Personal Property Insurance

While you're thinking about life insurance, you might as well make sure that the rest of your coverage is adequate. Since inflation has had an enormous effect on the value of your house and other possessions, you undoubtedly need increased insurance protection. Higher coverage will, of course, mean higher premiums, but that is the only way to be sure you will be able to replace expensive personal property in the event of catastrophe. One way to keep the price of your policy low and still increase your coverage is by raising the deductible amount on your policies.

You will need a reasonable appraisal of the value of the property you wish to reinsure, and your insurance agent can help you in determining the current replacement costs of any possessions in question. There are also private appraisal services which will assess the value of your home or property for a fee.

HEALTH INSURANCE

Medicare

Medicare is a wonderful system to *help* people deal with the high cost of health care, but it pays *only* about 40 percent of the total medical expenses of the over-sixty-five segment of the population. This is not to say that Medicare is not good insurance—you could never beat the price with a private insurance company, since the coverage is heavily supplemented by federal funds. The entire Medicare package for retirees eligible for Social Security costs less than twelve dollars a month.

However, too many people rely on their Medicare coverage as their only form of health insurance, and are rudely, sometimes tragically, awakened when enormous medical bills face them at the end of some necessary treatment. For virtually everyone, some form of private health insurance is needed to pick up costs which Medicare fails to cover.

When dealing with insurance companies, the younger you are, the more options are open to you, so the better time to get your coverage together is right now. Many plans will not accept applicants over a certain age, or will require a stringent medical examination to determine your insurability. The health insurance policies you now hold may seem perfectly satisfactory, but they can change drastically when you retire, or when you turn sixty-five.

This section will point out some of the potential pitfalls in your health coverage future and provide a framework for choosing the insurance package which best fills your needs.

Medicare Coverage. Medicare is a two-part federal health insurance program directed by the Health Care Financing Administration. It was inaugurated in 1966. Virtually everyone sixty-five or older is eligible for Medicare coverage, and more than 97 percent of those eligible participate in the program.

The first part of Medicare is hospital insurance, designed for inpatient care. This coverage, called Part A, is free to all those sixty-five or older who are entitled to Social Security benefits, either on the basis of their own work record or as a dependent. Those who don't have enough work to their credit can enroll in the hospital insurance program by paying a monthly premium of $89 (as of July 1981).

The medical insurance part of Medicare, Part B, helps pay for doctors' bills, outpatient bills, outpatient hospital services, and other medical costs. It is available to everyone who pays the monthly premium, which in July 1981 was just $11.00. This is one of the greatest bargains around, and you should certainly take advantage of it. This premium is deducted from your Social Security checks each month, or is billed quarterly for those not yet receiving Social Security.

There are several points to keep in mind regarding eligibility for Medicare:

- You are not covered until you apply for Medicare, and you should do so about three months before your sixty-fifth birthday, even if you don't plan to file for Social Security benefits at that time.
- When you check on your eligibility for Social Security benefits, you can determine whether you have enough work credit for Medicare. In certain cases it may be worthwhile to take a part-time job just to earn the few more quarters needed to make you eligible for Medicare.

- The spouse of a qualified worker becomes eligible for Medicare as a dependent on reaching age sixty-five, even if the worker is not yet sixty-five. Once again, however, you must file for coverage.

In the chart on page 212, in the column labeled ''Medicare Coverage,'' you will find a brief rundown of the medical services which are and are not included as Medicare benefits. For a fuller description of the program, ask for a copy of ''Your Medicare Handbook,'' available free from your local Social Security office. The guide covers every provision of every service, from home health care and physical therapy to chiropractors and Christian Science practitioners.

Part A: hospital care. The basic expenses which you may incur beyond covered charges are the deductible amounts and certain services. For any hospital stay, you must pay the first $260 charge, and Medicare pays the rest for sixty days. If you are hospitalized for thirty additional days, you must pay $65 per day for that period; Medicare will pay the balance. After a ninety-day stay, you have an additional sixty-day reserve period of coverage to draw on, but you pay $130 a day for each reserve day, and once you've used them all, you never get any more. From that point, and in any subsequent illness which surpasses a ninety-day hospital stay, you are responsible for all hospital charges from day ninety-one on.

On a dollars-and-cents basis this means that a ninety-day hospitalization would leave you to pay a bill of $2,210 out of your own pocket, above and beyond Medicare's contribution, and a longer illness would result in a far larger bill, both in basic hospital charges, and the full price of private nursing, should you need it. There are certain other areas which are also excluded from Medicare coverage.

Part B: medical coverage. The deductible amount is not the major problem here—it is only $75 per year. However, Medicare pays only 80 percent of ''reasonable'' fees after that point. And what is considered ''reasonable'' by Medicare standards? There is a set schedule of charges considered ''reasonable'' by insurance companies, and they pay their share of that predetermined charge. However, your doctor is free to charge whatever he chooses, and the ''reasonable'' fee is often only a small fraction of the actual bill. You must pay not only

Comparison of Services Covered

Services Covered	Medicare Coverage	Private Insurance Policy*	Blue Cross Blue Shield	Health Maintenance Organization (HMO)
Outpatient services Routine physical exams	not covered			
Immunizations	"			
Eye examinations (for glasses)	"			
Eyeglasses	"			
Hearing examinations	"			
Hearing aids	"			
Prescription drugs (out of hospital)	"			
Mental health therapy	$250/year			
Physical therapy	limited			

Speech therapy	"			
Physicians' services (including surgery) In hospital	80% of reasonable fees after $75/year			
In progressive care facility	"			
In doctor's office	"			
In nursing home	"			
In your home	limited			
Inpatient services (hospital) Room, board, special rooms drugs, lab + others	full cost after deductibles for 60 days +			
Special-duty nursing	not covered			
Mental health hospitalization	limited			

Comparison of Services Covered (Continued)

Services Covered	Medicare Coverage	Private Insurance Policy*	Blue Cross Blue Shield	Health Maintenance Organization (HMO)
Posthospital skilled nursing	20 days + 80 days @$20			
Home health care				
Part A	100 calls			
Part B	"			
Entrance requirements	Medicare eligibility		exclusion riders	health screening
Effective times	age 65 open enrollment periods		6 months for certain conditions	
Exceptions			limits on drugs & alcoholism	

Cost				
Part A		0 or $89		
Part B		$11.00/ month		
Deductibles				
Remarks				

*Examine specific policy provisions, as plans offered by different companies vary widely.

Note: Entries on this chart are not intended to be all-inclusive. Specific coverages may be added as desired for comparison.

your 20 percent, but any additional charges over the Medicare-determined "reasonable" amount. For instance, if your surgeon charges you $800 for an operation and Medicare says the "reasonable" fee is $350, you must pay $520 out of your own pocket.

There are also medical charges which are completely excluded from coverage. The most substantial noncovered items in Part B are prescription drugs taken at home, which are entirely your responsibility.

You can make your comparison shopping for additional health insurance easier by making a chart similar to the one presented here and using it to keep track of the provisions of the different policies you look at.

Shopping for Health Insurance

Here are some points to consider when evaluating the policies available to you:

- You may find that, instead of buying a single plan, you are better off with a combination of two or more policies which include different features. Many of the insurance policies now being offered to supplement Medicare are designed to deal with very specific types of problems. This does not mean you should buy policies aimed at specific *diseases*, though. Insuring against specific ailments (cancer, for example) is an overly expensive, highly impractical form of protection, and should be avoided. Your goal is reliable overall coverage.

- For most people it is impractical to insure against every possible contingency. By paying "deductibles," you put your insurance dollar to work where it is most needed—to provide for the larger expenses incurred when serious illness strikes. Trying to find an insurance company to pay the first $160 of hospital costs, which Medicare excludes, is far less important than making sure that your hospital bills after ninety days are covered, and that private nursing will be paid for.

- Inquire into the availability of major medical coverage. This type of policy supplements most standard health insurance to provide for the unmanageable costs of extended hospitalization, often providing benefits up to $250,000 or more.
- Remember that you are buying insurance for the long run. Don't look at your present, hopefully sound, state of health and assume the best for the future. When it comes to buying insurance, a little pessimism is useful to ensure that future emergencies will not be complicated by financial pressures.
- Keep in mind the rapidly escalating price of medical care, and the effect that it will have on the policy. You are probably better off with a policy which pays a percentage of the fee charged, or all expenses over a certain amount, than a policy which pays a fixed sum for a particular service, even though it may cost you more in the form of escalating premiums. The fixed sum may seem like a reasonable estimate of the charge right now, but within a few years it could represent only a small fraction of the cost.

What About Your Present Policies

The first step in shopping for health insurance is to check out the provisions of your current policies.

If you have group insurance through your job, find out how it will be affected by your retirement. Will your coverage continue after you leave the company as part of your employee benefits? If not, can you arrange to pay for it yourself? If you are married, be sure that your spouse is fully protected as well.

There are undoubtedly special rules in your policy to account for the availability of Medicare. When you take these changes into account, how much protection does your formerly adequate health insurance provide? Try to find supplementary insurance to fill the gaps which will occur.

You should almost certainly try to maintain your current policies. The rates for continued coverage will probably be lower than a new policy, and you can waive the medical exam. When you switch from one company to another, you run the risk of going through a period when you have no coverage at all, or of the new company refusing to pay any expenses incurred in the treatment of a "pre-existing condition." Some policies guarantee to insure you in the future, despite changes in your health. If you have experienced medical setbacks, this may be the only way you will be eligible for private medical insurance.

Shop around and explore all of the alternatives. Just be sure to think twice before letting any of your present policies lapse.

Other Private Plans

The insurance industry has a mind-boggling array of policies designed to fill the "medigap"—the broad area where Medicare leaves off. Start off your search for coverage with a call to your present insurance agent, who may be able to offer valuable advice. Next, contact your local chapter of Blue Cross and Blue Shield. The policies written by this organization to supplement Medicare have achieved an excellent reputation for both fair price and reliable protection.

Another source to consider are the various groups you belong to which may sponsor medical plans. Fraternal organizations, professional associations, trade unions, and many others offer their members coverage at group rates which are substantially below the costs of individually written policies, and also provide greater benefits.

Health Maintenance Organizations

One recent attempt to make the costs of medical care more reasonable has been the establishment of health maintenance organizations

(HMOs). Under an HMO system, you pay a single fee which covers all of your medical expenses for the year, with very few exceptions. Not only medical emergencies, but routine checkups, visits to investigate minor complaints, health services, and supplies are included in the coverage. This type of protection is not cheap, but it does encourage you to see a doctor when something bothers you. In an HMO, you have already paid in advance. Studies show that this availability of preventive medicine leads patients to catch relatively minor problems before they escalate into serious ones. It keeps them healthier and keeps overall medical costs down at the same time.

You may find that it is difficult to meet HMO acceptance standards, since their evaluation of your present state of health can be rather stringent. In addition, there are only a limited number of HMOs currently operating, and you must use the facilities of the community HMO for your medical care.

Still, it is certainly a possibility worth investigating. To get the name and address of an HMO operating near you, write to the Group Health Association of America, Suite 701, 1717 Massachusetts Avenue NW, Washington, DC 20036. They will also provide you with informative booklets about HMOs in general at your request.

Once you have provided for your financial security during your retirement and have your investments and insurance in order, you are going to feel infinitely more comfortable and better able to enjoy the life you're secure enough to lead.

FOR FURTHER READING

General Money Guides

Porter, Sylvia, *Sylvia Porter's New Money Book;* Doubleday, 1979.

Quinn, Jane Bryant, *Everyone's Money Book;* Delacorte, 1979.
These two substantial volumes are to handling your money what
Dr. Spock's book was to raising your children. Comprehensive, com-
prehensible, and encyclopedic, they provide answers to all the common financial problems you are likely to encounter, from budgeting
and bank services to home sales, insurance, investments, divorce, fu-
nerals, estate planning, and more. One or the other should form the
backbone of your personal financial library.

Investment Guides

ESPECIALLY RECOMMENDED

Tobias, Andrew, *The Only Investment Guide You'll Ever Need;*
Harcourt Brace Jovanovich hardcover, 1978; Bantam paperback,
1979.
Staff of United Business Service, *Successful Investing;* Simon and
Schuster hardcover, 1979; Simon and Schuster paperback, 1980.

ADDITIONAL SOURCES

Jessup, Paul E., *Competing for Stock Market Profits;* John Wiley
paperback, 1974.
Malkiel, Burton, *A Random Walk Down Wall Street;* W. W. Nor-
ton and Co., Inc. hardcover and paperback, 1973.
Meltzer, Yale L., *Putting Money to Work: An Investment Primer;*
Prentice-Hall paperback, 1976.
Rukeyser, Louis, *How to Make Money on Wall Street;* Doubleday
hardcover, 1974; Doubleday paperback, 1976.

Real Estate Investment Guides

Case, Fred E., *Investing in Real Estate;* Prentice-Hall paperback, 1978.

de Benedictis, Daniel J., *The Complete Real Estate Adviser;* Pocket Books paperback, 1977.

Harney, Kenneth R., *Beating Inflation with Real Estate;* Random House, 1979.

Hatfield, Weston P., *The Weekend Real Estate Investor;* McGraw-Hill, 1978.

Lowry, Albert J., *How You Can Become Financially Independent by Investing in Real Estate;* Simon and Schuster, 1977.

Lowry, Albert J., *How to Manage Real Estate Successfully in Your Spare Time;* Simon and Schuster, 1979.

Seldin, Maury, and Swesnik, Richard H., *Real Estate Investment Strategy;* Wiley, 1979.

Stern, Walter H., *The New Investor's Guide to Making Money in Real Estate;* Grosset and Dunlap, 1976.

Watkins, A. M., *Buying Land;* Quadrangle, 1975.

One good source of up-to-date advice is the *Real Estate Investing Letter,* a monthly newsletter published by United Media International, a division of Harcourt Brace Jovanovich. While a subscription is fairly expensive (about $40 a year), the newsletter provides detailed information on current trends in the real estate market along with solid general advice on such essential matters as taxes, mortgages, tenant relations, and property evaluation. You can get a free sample issue along with current subscription rates by writing to Real Estate Investing Letter, 757 Third Avenue, New York, NY 10017.

Health Insurance

The AARP/NRTA publishes an excellent booklet entitled "Medicare and Health Insurance for Older People." This publication provides not only information on the ins and outs of Medicare, but worthwhile information about what to look for in a health insurance policy, and a glossary of the terms you'll be running into during your research. To obtain a copy free of charge, write:

AARP Fulfillment
Dept. M-H
P.O. Box 2400
Long Beach, CA 90801

The Health Care Financing Administration has also prepared a valuable free booklet explaining Medicare benefits and providing tips on the types of supplemental insurance coverage available and how to choose the right policy for you. Its title is "Guide to Health Insurance for People with Medicare," and it is available from your local Social Security Administration Office.

9

WILLS AND ESTATE PLANNING: PROVIDING FOR CONTINUITY

PART OF WAYNE'S ESTATE IS SOLD TO PAY TAX BILL

Phoenix, Dec. 16 (UPI)—Tax problems have forced the sale of the Red River Land Company, co-owned by the late actor, John Wayne, for more than $30 million. It is one of the largest farm and ranch sales in Arizona history.

Michael Wayne, who announced the sale yesterday, said that his father never planned for his estate, "so the taxes have created a burden for the estate." He said that "a lot of taxes" were owed on the ranch.

YOU may not have a multi-million dollar estate, but that doesn't mean you can avoid the problems which can result from inadequate estate planning. This chapter explains what estate planning is all about and why it is important to think about it now.

ESTATE PLANNING

In the course of your lifetime you have accumulated investments, property, and personal possessions worth a great deal more than you may realize. This wealth is your *estate,* and it has both monetary and sentimental value. Inflation has greatly increased the value of your estate over the years. You may have substantial company insurance, profit sharing, pension, and other benefits whose total value you've never calculated. When these assets are taken into account, the average middle-class American approaching retirement age can easily find his estate to be worth in excess of $100,000. What will happen to it all after you die? The problem of estate planning is no longer limited to the very rich.

Estate planning is the process of arranging financial and legal affairs for the present and the future. You want to afford the maximum comfort to you and your spouse during your lifetimes, while enabling as much wealth as possible to pass directly to your heirs at your death. A carefully drawn will is the cornerstone of good estate planning. Other elements include arranging the ownership and distribution of assets so that as little as possible is lost to state and federal taxes, and providing for the preservation and management of funds on behalf of your heirs. We cannot possibly discuss the subject of estate planning in enough detail here to substitute for in-depth professional advice, since each state has different laws regarding wills and estates, and every individual's circumstances and requirements deserve specialized attention. This chapter will make you familiar with some of the concepts, issues, and complexities of estate planning. This background will better enable you to formulate a plan to fit all of your personal needs, with the help of the appropriate professionals.

Note: The Economic Recovery Act of 1981 (Reagan Tax Bill) made substantial changes to the laws governing estate and gift taxes. If your will was drawn prior to 1981 and designed to minimize tax liability under prior law, it could be seriously outdated under the new law. You would be well advised to consult a competent estate planning attorney as soon as possible.

When to Start

Many people are willing to sacrifice some of their own comfort in retirement to preserve capital so they can leave it to their heirs. They draw less income from their assets than they could, so that their children and grandchildren might be well provided for. Yet these same generous folks often fail to undertake aggressive estate planning to safeguard these funds. The government becomes their only real beneficiary, which makes no sense at all. With the proper use of trusts and other estate-planning devices, most people could not only leave more to their loved ones but even pay for a few more years of comfortable retirement living on tax savings alone!

A good time to begin active estate planning is ten to fifteen years before you expect to retire. By that time the end of your conventional working career is in sight and you have begun thinking seriously about your retirement needs. You have some idea of what your estate will ultimately be worth and you may also have a clearer sense of the special needs of your children and other heirs. Bringing all these factors together, you can begin to arrange your affairs to achieve the greatest possible benefits for all concerned.

Managing Your Legal Affairs

When we consider consulting a lawyer in connection with growing older, we may think first about his importance in drawing up a will. There are, however, several other aspects of retirement which require a lawyer's special skills as well.

It is a good practice to develop an ongoing relationship with your lawyer and consult with him about all decisions that require you to take on any new legal obligations. If possible, your family lawyer should be familiar with your general situation, your family's needs, and your personal goals. In much the same way that your family doctor knows you and not just your individual ailments, your lawyer will be able to make more reasonable, personally appropriate suggestions for your legal needs if he knows your personality and your history. This relationship of familiarity and trust becomes especially important when you consider that a lawyer, like a doctor, is often called upon to help in emergency situations, where quick judgments are required.

If you do not already have a family lawyer whom you feel comfortable consulting, now is a good time to find one who can serve you in the years ahead. Perhaps in conjunction with reviewing your will, you can have a thorough legal checkup. After all, you have signed a great many documents over the years, entered into a number of binding agreements, and set up several financial and personal contracts which carry legal liability. There may be ways in which you could improve these arrangements which you would never think of, and that is where your lawyer's special abilities come into play. A good family lawyer is a valuable adviser, who has experience and training with the same sorts of problems you may have. By taking advantage of his knowledge, you can avoid many mistakes.

The following are just a few of the areas in which your lawyer should be included in the important decisions you will make in your preretirement and retirement years.

Living Arrangements. If you are planning to buy or sell your home, consult with your lawyer before you even approach a real estate agent. Your lawyer will go over the pros and cons of your decision, taking into account all aspects of property ownership.

Even if your mind is made up, a visit with your lawyer should still be your first step. People are often amazed, and sometimes unpleasantly surprised, by the force of an "informal" agreement. You can make substantial commitments without ever signing your name to a contract, and your lawyer will be able to caution you about the pitfalls of verbal agreements. He will also advise you of your rights and responsibilities at every stage of the buying or selling process, and review any contracts for you before you sign.

Family Arrangements. When it comes to marriage and divorce, a lawyer can be a valuable stabilizing force in the midst of high emotions. Marriage can mean many problems of property and prior legal commitment when undertaken later in life. With grown children and ex-husbands or wives in the picture, a new relationship can become a source of turmoil in the family. This can be avoided to some extent by spelling out the legal side of the marriage with your lawyer, possibly in the form of a prenuptial agreement, a written contract which sets down the rights of the marriage partners before the ceremony ever takes place. If divorce is unavoidable, he will naturally advise you on your rights and obligations, but one of the partners will have to select a second lawyer for the proceedings.

Your lawyer can also be helpful in determining the best ways of dealing with older, dependent parents or other relatives. He can be empowered to make decisions for an infirm individual, and will be a human as well as a professional link to provide continuity in the life of that relative.

Setting Up a Business. The success or failure of a new business, even a relatively modest venture, can be tied to the legal form of organization you choose. Your attorney will be familiar with the various forms of partnership, incorporation, and so on, and will help you keep both your tax liability and personal liability for a lawsuit at a minimum. Many businesses also require you to enter into agreements with suppliers, franchisers, customers, or landlords, and your lawyer should be consulted on any and all of these contracts.

Financial Arrangements. Your lawyer is an important consultant on investment decisions, along with your accountant. He can also defend your rights to any benefits which you believe you should receive from government or private pension plans, inheritances, business deals or sales of property or services. Getting what you deserve from pension or insurance plans can be difficult, and your lawyer will be familiar with the procedures to follow in order to assure you of your rightful share.

Estate Plan. A good lawyer can play a key role in the success of your estate plan. You need to be very candid with him to get the best results. It is important to know whether or not your attorney specializes in estate planning; if he does not, find out what percentage of his practice involves estate and tax planning. Many lawyers who can write a legal, clearly drafted will do not have the special up-to-date expertise in estate planning you may require.

Your lawyer should help you outline the important issues and objectives in your estate plan, and as in all other legal matters, should respect your personal concerns and family circumstances. After all, he is going to administer your affairs and advise your family after you are no longer around.

Your attorney should be familiar with your will, your family situation, and the contents of your estate. If you do not have such a relationship, your executor will have to choose an attorney after you go. The lawyer's fee for settling an estate is usually figured according to the estate's value, less insurance proceeds. Like the executor's fee, it is tax-deductible. If your lawyer is going to serve as executor, in general he should get only one fee—either the lawyer's fee or the executor's fee, but not both.

WILLS

It is estimated that more than 50 percent of Americans die *intestate*—without a properly drawn and executed will, one that is legal and binding. Many of them probably feel that their estates aren't large enough to require a will or that the "most logical" people will end up with their property; or some who know that it is necessary to make a will feel they can postpone it until they are on their death bed. They apparently have little idea of the agony, conflict, confusion, and waste that results from this oversight.

Nobody really dies without a will. If you haven't prepared one, the state in effect writes it for you after you're gone, according to its own peculiar statutes. And each state's *intestacy* laws are different.

*   *   *

If You Die Without a Will

In most states, the formula awards a wife only one third to one half of her husband's estate, and the balance goes to the children. The result is often financial hardship for the widow, who must depend on her children for future support.

In some states, your estate would be divided equally among your wife and your children. In others, if there are two children or more, your wife might receive only one third of your estate. If the children want to return a portion of the funds to their mother, they may have to pay a gift tax on these amounts. If there are no children, your state's laws may require that portions of your estate go to your parents, brothers, and sisters, regardless of their financial circumstances.

Without a will specifying an *executor* (a trusted person or institution such as a bank) to oversee the administration of your estate according to your wishes, the state will appoint such a person, who may be a complete stranger to your family. Executor's fees will be deducted from your estate, and the person appointed to be executor may also be required to post a bond (to ensure against his or her absconding with the money). These costs reduce the estate's value.

In certain "community property" states, your wife would automatically receive the majority of your estate, leaving less to the children than you may have desired.

If you die without a will, nothing—not personal possessions, collections, or cash—goes to grandchildren, stepchildren, friends, aunts, uncles, cousins, charities, or others who may have been important to you in life.

While your estate is being settled by the state-appointed administrator, your bank accounts, safe deposit box, and other assets may be frozen for a lengthy period, up to a year or more, and this could deprive your survivors of necessary living funds.

Real estate, such as your house, may be divided up among your heirs in such a way that it creates bitter squabbling. If two married daughters both want to live in the house, should one have to pay the other rent? Or should they sell the house, depriving both of them of its use and its sentimental value? If your spouse is no longer living, the law of most states grants each child an equal say in the administration of your affairs. This situation can cause an ongoing struggle among siblings with differing beliefs about your desires—and their own.

Finally, there are a number of tax consequences in the passing of property to your heirs. Through careful estate planning, and an understanding of the legal methods available for minimizing estate taxes, your heirs can avoid some very harsh and unpleasant tax consequences.

I don't think I have to say any more. *Everyone* needs a will.

Clearing Up Misconceptions About Wills

- A will does not restrict you from doing anything you wish to do with your property while you are alive. You may buy, sell, alter, or give away your property in any manner, just as before.
- You can change your will anytime you wish, so long as it is done in proper legal form; you always have control over your bequests.
- Your will can be completely confidential, if you wish. It is not publicly recorded anywhere while you live.
- You do not have to do a complete "spring cleaning" of all your possessions before making a valid will. You do not have to itemize at all. Some people simply refer to general categories and percentages in their wills. It is a good idea, however, to have a pretty clear knowledge of the property you own and its value.
- Making a will is not bad luck. A will shows that you care about the comfort of those you love and want them to be provided for as well as possible.

Kinds of Wills

Some people are under the impression that any document they have signed which specifies how their property should be distributed can serve as a will. Not so. Every state has specific requirements which must be met for a will to be considered binding. If you move to another state, your will should be reviewed by a lawyer to ensure its continued validity.

Contested will cases cause much unhappiness, expense, and delay in the orderly distribution of an estate to its intended beneficiaries. Often these cases result from homemade attempts to draw a legal will. If your will is successfully contested, it may be declared totally invalid by the state and either a previous will or the state's *intestacy* statutes will take effect.

There is simply no such thing as a foolproof do-it-yourself will. Handwritten, or *holographic,* wills are not regarded as valid in most states, and even where they are, imprecise language makes them highly vulnerable to contest. Oral wills are even less likely to be valid. A few states recognize oral wills when made on the deathbed with a certain number of witnesses present. But this is not a real alternative.

Alternatives to a Will

A form of property ownership known as *joint tenancy with right of survivorship* (called *tenancy by the entirety* in some states) causes jointly owned property (a home, an automobile, bank accounts, and investments) to pass automatically to the surviving spouse upon the death of one of them, so long as both names are indicated as joint owners on the title document or deed. Such property cannot be passed by will. This arrangement has been used by so many people that it is known as "the poor man's will," because it overcomes the need for a will in terms of the property affected. It also obviates court

validation of the will (*probate*), executor's fees, and certain administrative costs in settling the estate. This works fine in some relatively
simple estates, where there is only a house and a jointly owned bank
account, some life insurance, and some personal effects.

There are several pitfalls in this "will substitute," however; for
example, if both you and your spouse die in the same accident or disaster, and there is no evidence that one lived longer than the other,
your property and personal effects will be distributed under the state's
intestacy laws. The state will also determine who should be the
guardian of any minor children.

Joint Tenancy. In joint tenancy with right of survivorship, each
spouse has full, 100 percent ownership of the property. Neither
owner can sell his or her interest without the other's consent. Both
names must appear on the ownership document. Upon the death of
one spouse, sole ownership of the property passes immediately and
automatically to the survivor, without requiring mention in a will. In
fact, jointly owned property with right of survivorship cannot be
passed by will. For example, if you will your children your interest in
property you own jointly with someone else, the will has no bearing
on this property.

The tax law of 1981 allows for unlimited transfers of property between spouses after 1981, and levies no estate or gift taxes on such
transfers. This is a substantial change from prior law, as it creates an
unlimited marital deduction and makes joint ownership more attractive for those with potentially taxable estates. You should seek the
advice of an attorney for your best course of action under the new
law.

In second marriages, joint tenancy with right of survivorship is not
advisable. Too often, say experienced estate attorneys, when the surviving spouse makes a will after the death of the former joint owner,
he or she gives the former joint property to his or her own children.
The children of the now-deceased joint owner become completely
disinherited.

Because each joint tenant owns all joint assets, any joint tenant
can, for example, withdraw all the funds from a bank account at any
time, to use as he or she wishes. In the event of a marital dispute,

such an action could create a serious hardship for the other spouse.

Jointly owned assets can be used to pay the debts of one of the joint owners if his or her personal assets are not adequate. For example, parents often put the names of their children as joint owners of bank accounts and other kinds of property in order to avoid probate (see page 249). The child may not even know of this joint ownership. Suppose the child is involved in an automobile accident, and a judgment is made against him or her. The lawyer for the plaintiff (who will probably get a percentage of the damages award) runs a computer check in your community to determine whether there are any bank accounts jointly held with the child. This practice is reportedly growing; it could result in major losses of your savings and property.

Property Passing Outside the Will. Certain kinds of property are transferred by means other than a will. The tax treatment of such property is a more complicated issue and should be discussed with your lawyer.

In addition to property held jointly, pension benefits and IRA and Keogh accounts and United States Savings Bonds, which require you to name a beneficiary, pass directly to the named beneficiary. Bank accounts in trust for another person, and other trusts set up while you are alive, pass to their beneficiaries in accordance with the trust documents.

Proceeds from life and accidental death insurance can be passed outside your will, and if the beneficiary is other than your spouse, these proceeds are not taxed as part of your estate so long as ownership of the insurance policy is held by others. You must not retain any policy rights, such as the power to change beneficiaries to borrow against the policy. Under the tax law of 1981, which allows unlimited transfers of property between spouses without taxation, if your *spouse* is the beneficiary, proceeds from such insurance can pass to him or her free of taxes regardless of who owns the policy. Transfers of *community property* do not qualify for the unlimited marital deduction, though. If you live in a community property state, it may be wise to transfer ownership of a life insurance policy to your spouse, and be sure to waive *community property rights* on the transferred document or in an attached letter, or else half the life insurance proceeds will jump right back into your estate when you die.

Tenancy in Common. This is a form of joint ownership in which there is no right of survivorship, and each *tenant* owns a partial share of the property. This share can (and should) be willed at death. It is commonly used for property jointly held by friends or relatives. Each owner is free to dispose of his or her share at any time, and the new owner becomes a tenant in common with the other owner or owners.

Community Property. This category of ownership exists in eight states, and is imposed by state law. In these states—Arizona, California, Idaho, Louisiana, Nevada, New Mexico, Texas, and Washington—all assets acquired during a marriage are considered to be jointly owned, regardless of who paid for them or whose name appears on the deed or certificate of title. Certain property can be kept outside "community property," such as property owned before marriage, and gifts and inheritances received during marriage. Your half of community property can be willed to whomever you wish (except that each state requires a minimum bequest to the spouse). If you die without a will, this property will be distributed according to your state's intestacy laws. These drawbacks can often be overcome with the help of a competent attorney, but if you are going to work with an attorney at all, you might as well have him or her advise you on a will.

Preparation of a Will

The first step is to compile a list of the assets and liabilities in your estate, using the worksheet on page 244. This list will prove vital in planning strategies for minimizing taxes, and the process of writing up the list will help you remember any *specific legacies,* such as an especially prized heirloom or collection, which will need a special mention.

When you have completed the description of your estate, you are ready to consult with your lawyer. He or she will charge somewhere from $50 to $200 for a legal and binding will. This fee could save your estate (and your heirs) thousands of dollars, months of delay, and untold emotional hardship.

In your initial meeting with the attorney, you will review the contents of your estate and whether each item is owned individually or jointly. You should also bring a list of your intended beneficiaries, with their names, addresses, ages, and relationship to you.

Most wills follow a pretty standard format, similar to the following example. This is provided here for general background only. It should *not* be used as a guideline for writing your own will.

1. There is a general declaration which states that you are the author of the will, and that this will replaces any previous wills or *codicils* (additions or amendments) to such wills.
2. Generally you instruct your executor to make prompt payment of burial expenses, debts, taxes, and administrative expenses. These are the first claims on your estate and must be taken care of before any other distributions are made, unless you provide otherwise for their payment.
3. The core section of the will lists *specific legacies* (the old grandfather clock, perhaps, and the family silver service), and *general legacies* (to my faithful friend Harry, $1,000). A specific legacy indicates the source of the bequest; a general legacy is paid from nonspecified assets. Many experts recommend stating large bequests in percentage terms rather than in specific amounts. Unforeseen circumstances can cause an estate to shrink in total size, causing a large bequest stated in dollar terms to virtually empty the estate and deprive other heirs of a share.
4. The remaining assets, if any, are known as the *residual estate,* or residuary, and are bequeathed to your principal heir. It is important not to make so many general legacies that the residual heir is left with little or nothing—unless that is your intention.
5. There will be an executor named to handle the administration of the estate. A substitute should also be named (see below, *Choosing an Executor*).

6. If you wish to create *trusts* to manage and invest funds for specific heirs, or to shelter the estate from taxes, these should be described and *trustees* named to oversee them.

7. Your wishes concerning burial arrangements are often included, to spare the family unnecessary confusion in determining the best approach, but these instructions should be included with your personal documents that are available *prior* to the reading of the will.

8. Specific instructions to your executors and trustees are often included, enabling them to manage the affairs of your estate according to your explicit desires, rather than the decrees of the state.

9. You sign (*execute*) the will in front of witnesses and they sign in your presence and in the presence of each other.

Choosing an Executor. The person you name to carry out the provisions of your will is called the *executor* of your estate. He or she is responsible for seeing the will through *probate*, paying your debts and taxes, arranging for the appraisal of property, distributing the estate according to your will, and making a final accounting to the state.

If your estate is simple, a responsible member of your family, with the aid of your attorney, can probably handle the job. But if your estate is complicated—involving trusts, shares in a business, or multiple real estate holdings—you will be better off with a competent professional, either an experienced attorney or the trust department of a local bank. Executors in most states are now personally liable for their mistakes.

You may want to appoint a family member as coexecutor, so that there will be some personal involvement to the management of your affairs. If you do, the attorney coexecutor will handle the administrative burdens, but all legal documents must be approved and signed by the family member.

You should be sure that the person you select is willing to serve as executor, and you should discuss beforehand whether a fee will be expected. Maximum executors' fees are set by statute in each state and are usually figured as a percent of the estate's value. If you have two executors, your estate will pay two fees unless the relative agrees to serve with no fee. This should be indicated in the will. Some executors are paid an hourly rate. In many states, executors are required to post a bond, which is paid for by the estate, but you can waive this requirement in your will. If the family member is in a distant state, a local attorney coexecutor can do all the required work and communicate with your relative by mail.

Witnesses. Most states require either two or three witnesses who sign and certify that they saw you sign your will. It is always a good idea to have one more witness than is needed in your state in case one dies or cannot be located later. Witnesses must sign in your presence and in the presence of each other.

Anyone who is a beneficiary named in your will should *not* serve as a witness. If the will is challenged and this person is called to testify as a witness, he or she may be totally or partially disqualified as an heir by the court.

Wills for Both Spouses. Wives with little or no property in their own names often feel they do not need a will, but there are excellent reasons why a wife *should* have one:

1. Even if you do not have substantial financial assets, you may possess jewelry, antiques, family heirlooms, furs, works of art, and other valuables. By consulting with children and other loved ones, and setting the information down in a will, you can be certain that each receives what is important to him or her.
2. If your husband dies before you, you will most likely receive the bulk of his estate. If you were to die shortly afterward and did not have a will, the property you both owned would be administered under the state's intestacy laws just as if your husband had died without a will.
3. The process of estate planning—conserving and preserving assets, minimizing taxes, bequeathing special gifts to loved ones—does not end with the death of the principal breadwinner. If you die without a will, the estate you inherited from your husband might be dissipated regardless of precautions taken in his will. There is no marital deduction (page 244) to

shelter the surviving wife's estate from taxes, and for this reason estate planners are placing more and more emphasis on preserving this "second estate."

The best way to plan for the future is the way you planned the other elements of retirement—by doing it together, writing both wills in consultation with each other. This way, the two wills agree with each other from a legal standpoint, and both of you will understand all the provisions of your two wills. Your spouse is the one who will have to live under the terms of your will, and therefore deserves a voice in how it is written.

Statistically, wives tend to outlive their husbands by an average of seven to eight years, and often longer. Odds are that the woman will have to carry on your numerous financial aspects by herself, so it's only fair that she share in financial planning. Both spouses should have a complete understanding of the family finances, no matter who has previously borne the money responsibilities.

Updating the Will. If any of the five circumstances below apply to you, or if your will was drawn prior to 1982, when major revisions in federal estate tax laws went into effect, you should consult a lawyer and possibly have your will legally changed.

1. *You move to a new state.* Even if your old will is legal in your new state (and it may not be), it might not do the best job possible to preserve your estate and provide for the efficient distribution of your property.

2. *You change your mind about the amounts you want to leave, or to whom.* Deaths, marriages, divorces, births, your remarriage, changes in the health or financial condition of loved ones—all these events can affect your feelings concerning planned bequests and may make you decide to revise your will.

3. *Changes in federal or state tax laws.* Major revisions, such as the Economic Recovery Act of 1981, can totally alter the picture. To enable the maximum to be passed to your heirs, new strategies must be employed to minimize estate, gift, and other taxes. Changes in state laws affecting forms of property ownership, wills, inheritance taxes, and probate should be incorpo-

rated in an up-to-date will. The best way to ensure that your will is not outdated is to make an annual phone call to your lawyer.

4. *Changes in cash availability or the value of major assets.* Your estate plan takes into account the debts, taxes, funeral expenses, and other cash needs that arise immediately when you die. Will there be enough cash available to meet these obligations without necessitating the sale of assets you intended to bequeath to heirs? Has there been a significant change in the value of your taxable estate, giving you greater tax obligations? Or perhaps your estate is not as large today as it was, because of investment or casualty losses, or a prolonged illness. In that case, certain specific cash legacies should be reduced.

5. *Change in executor.* Has your executor died or moved away? Has your relationship with your executor changed? Has the increasing complexity of your financial affairs made it sensible to appoint an attorney or bank trust department as executor?

Should your will require a simple addition or revision, your lawyer can generally write a *codicil,* or amendment, to update it. If a major revision of your will is necessary, have it redrawn. Keep in mind that a legal, well-drafted, up-to-date will is the best insurance against undue taxation, expense, and family conflict.

Will and Other Vital Papers. Do not keep your will in your safe deposit box. Many states require that a safe deposit box be sealed immediately upon the death of its owner, and your executor would then have to get a court order to open it. Most experts advise you to keep the executed (signed and witnessed) copy of your will *in your lawyer's safe,* or in the vault of a bank's trust department, if they are to serve as your executor. If a relative or friend will serve as executor, have that person retain your original will in a safe place.

Keep a photocopy of your will handy in case you need to refer to it, and be sure several of your key beneficiaries know where the executed will is kept. Never mark or make notes on the executed will: in many states, this would automatically invalidate it.

In addition to your will, it is advisable to prepare a letter which details key personal information as well as the whereabouts of vital papers pertaining to your estate. Your attorney or your executor can hold this for you. This comprehensive "personal affairs checklist," from *Sylvia Porter's New Money Book for the 80's,* is a good guideline to follow:

- List the names, addresses, dates, and places of birth of yourself, your wife or husband, your children, your father and mother, your brothers and sisters.

Write on separate lines and in clear detail:

- Your Social Security number and where your card is located.

- The location of your birth certificate and, if you have one, veteran's discharge certificate.

- If you have more than one residence, the address of each, where you vote, and where you pay income taxes.

- The date and place of your marriage and where your marriage certificate can be found.

- If you have been married previously, your deceased or former wife's or husband's name.

- If you are divorced, the place of the divorce, whether it was contested, who brought the action, where your divorce papers are. This will help your lawyer determine whether your former spouse has any inheritance rights remaining. If separated by agreement or court action, all the details and the place where your separation agreement can be found.

- Where a copy of any prenuptial agreement into which you entered can be found.

- Whether any of your immediate relatives are handicapped or incompetent.

- Other family information, such as the state of health of its members, whether you have any adopted children, marital problems, family feuds; "difficult" family members, if any.

- The names and addresses of others you intend to make your beneficiaries.

- If you are the beneficiary under a trust or have created a trust, where your lawyer can obtain a copy of the document.

● If you have the right to exercise a power of appointment under someone's will or under a trust, also where this document can be found.

● A statement of your approximate income and general standard of living for the past several years.

● The name and address of your accountant if you have one.

● The place where copies of your income and gift tax returns may be found and the name and address of the person who prepared them.

● Name and address of your employer.

● Details of any employment contract or stock purchase plan in which you are enrolled.

● Whether you are entitled to a pension, profit-sharing benefit, stock options, or any other employment benefits. Give the name of the person who handles your company's fringe benefits plus information on how the benefits are payable on your death.

● Any union or unions to which you belong and appropriate details.

● Life insurance policies owned by you on your life; policies owned by others on your life (stating who pays the premiums on them); and policies owned by you on the lives of others. Also list annuity policies owned by you. Include the name and address of each issuing company, name and address of your insurance agent, policy numbers, principal amount of each policy, the beneficiaries, and whether there are any outstanding loans against any of the policies.

● An itemization of all your real estate. Give the location of each property, its approximate value, the price you paid for it, any mortgages on the property, and whether you own the property by yourself or jointly with others. Give the location of deeds to any property you own.

● The location and total of stocks, bonds, and other securities you may own, the name and address of your broker or brokers.

● A complete rundown of all your other assets, the approximate value of each, its cost basis, and location of each. This would include bank accounts, any business ownership, as well as your more valuable personal effects, such as jewelry, furs, art objects, and the like. (Don't overlook details of debts due to you).

- The location of your safe deposit box and the box key.
- A complete outline of your debts, including mortgages on your house or business, leases, and other obligations. Give the names and addresses of persons to whom you are indebted and the terms under which you are supposed to repay.
- The names and addresses of whomever you wish to name as your executors, trustees, and guardians.
- The name of your lawyer, his address, telephone number, and a list of your papers in his safekeeping.
- The name and address of any person to whom you have given power of attorney.
- The names of organizations—such as fraternal or trade societies—to which you belong. Make a special note here about any benefits which may be coming to your family from these organizations.
- If you have been in active military service, the branch and period of service and the date of your discharge.
- Funeral arrangements you prefer and any preparations you have made.

In preparing your checklist, consider once more:

- Have you married since you made your will? If so, call your lawyer, tell him so, and ask him what you should do about your will.
- If you have acquired a business interest, have you provided for its disposition at your death? No matter what the size of your interest, make a sound plan for its disposition. If your interest must be sold in a hurry to pay death taxes, it may be sacrificed—and your family may be badly hurt.

These questions are primarily designed to intrigue your interest. Your lawyer surely will bring up others.

*   *   *

Calculating the Value of Your Estate

The worksheet on page 244 will help you itemize your assets and liabilities so that you can judge the true size of your estate. If you are married, use this exercise first to calculate the taxable estate of the *husband*.

There are three good reasons to go through this exercise. First, it will help you be more specific about how you would like to divide your wealth and possessions among your heirs. Second, you will be able to determine roughly the extent of your estate tax obligations, and thus begin to think about ways of reducing these taxes, if necessary. Third, the worksheet will help save time when you meet with an attorney to discuss estate planning.

WORKSHEET TIPS

Equity in Home—Figure this amount conservatively, since national and local economic conditions might require selling at a price lower than the top of the market. Deduct the balance remaining on your mortgage, and an estimate of closing costs and the broker's commission.

IRA and Keogh Plans—These are not subject to estate taxes as part of your estate. They are taxed as ordinary income to their designated beneficiaries.

Collections—If you have spent years collecting rare books, stamps, art, coins, guns, or other items, you should have your collection appraised by a reputable dealer. In recent years some items have appreciated substantially, and knowing the value of your collection might affect your plans for its disposition.

Pension, Profit Sharing—Determine the lump sum value of these benefits by consulting employee benefits literature or the personnel department where you work.

Liabilities—Exclude loans in your name only which are covered by credit life insurance.

Total Value of Your Estate—Effective 1982, amounts considered to be part of your estate and subject to federal estate taxes include all property which is in your name, and one half of property owned jointly with your spouse, irrespective of who paid for it.

For estate tax calculations, *the adjusted gross estate* is the relevant figure. Table 11 can help you establish the *tentative tax*. Then there are certain deductions and credits which can greatly reduce your estate tax obligation.

First, the Tax Act of 1981 repealed previous limitations on the tax-free transfer of most property between spouses. The *marital deduction* (which was formerly limited to the greater of $250,000, or 50 percent of the total adjusted gross estate) *is now unlimited*.

Estate Planning Worksheet

Assets	Estimated Value	How Owned? Husband	Wife	Joint
Equity in home	$_____	_____	_____	_____
Checking accounts	_____	_____	_____	_____
Savings accounts	_____	_____	_____	_____
IRA and Keogh plans	_____	_____	_____	_____
Other real estate	_____	_____	_____	_____
Inheritances and trusts	_____	_____	_____	_____
Money owed you	_____	_____	_____	_____
Autos, boats, other vehicles	_____	_____	_____	_____
Household, personal effects	_____	_____	_____	_____
Collections	_____	_____	_____	_____
Stocks	_____	_____	_____	_____
Bonds	_____	_____	_____	_____
Annuities	_____	_____	_____	_____
U.S. Savings Bonds	_____	_____	_____	_____
Government securities	_____	_____	_____	_____
Mutual funds	_____	_____	_____	_____
Other investments	_____	_____	_____	_____
Equity in own business	_____	_____	_____	_____
Individual life insurance	_____	_____	_____	_____
Group life insurance	_____	_____	_____	_____
Pension, profit sharing benefits at death	_____	_____	_____	_____
TOTAL	$_____	$_____	$_____	$_____

Liabilities

Current bills $_____
Auto loans   _____
Installment loans   _____
Loans against life
  insurance   _____

TOTAL $ _____

TOTAL VALUE OF YOUR
  ESTATE $_____
(Subtract liabilities from
  assets)

Deductions from Your Taxable Estate

    Less:
Burial expenses $_____
Lawyer's fee   _____
Executor's fee   _____
Cost of liquidating assets   _____

    Total Deductions $_____

TOTAL ADJUSTED
GROSS ESTATE
(Total value of your
    estate, minus total
    deductions) $_____

    Less:
(Total value of $_____
    property willed
    to surviving spouse)
Charitable bequests $_____

NET TAXABLE
ESTATE $_____

Table 11. Federal Estate Taxes

Amount of Net Taxable Estate	Tentative Tax (before application of $62,800 estate tax credit)
Under $10,000	18 percent
$10–20,000	$ 1,800 plus 20 percent of the amount over $ 10,000
$20–40,000	3,800 plus 22 percent of the amount over 20,000
$40–60,000	8,200 plus 24 percent of the amount over 40,000
$60–80,000	13,000 plus 26 percent of the amount over 60,000
$80–100,000	18,200 plus 28 percent of the amount over 80,000
$100–150,000	23,800 plus 30 percent of the amount over 100,000
$150–250,000	38,800 plus 32 percent of the amount over 150,000
$250–500,000	70,800 plus 34 percent of the amount over 250,000
$500–750,000	155,800 plus 37 percent of the amount over 500,000
$750–1,000,000	248,300 plus 39 percent of the amount over 750,000
$1,000–1,250,000	345,800 plus 41 percent of the amount over 1,000,000
$1,250–1,500,000	448,300 plus 43 percent of the amount over 1,250,000
$1,500–2,000,000	555,800 plus 45 percent of the amount over 1,500,000

Second, there is an *estate tax credit* of $62,800 (as of 1982, increasing each year through 1986), which you deduct directly from your calculated tentative estate tax. In effect, this credit allows the next $225,000 (after deducting property transferred to your spouse tax free) to pass to your other heirs free of estate taxes. This credit will increase annually until 1987, at which time it will provide an exemption equivalent to $600,000 for property passing to other heirs.

So the tax picture is really very nice. If you are married, you can leave an unlimited amount to your spouse, and you should be able to leave at least $225,000 (in 1982) to your other heirs without paying a dime in federal estate taxes. The simplified examples below will show you how the tax is calculated. Example A, which applies to married couples, includes the unlimited marital deduction. Example B, which would apply to most single, divorced, and widowed people, does not. Note the vast difference in estate taxes due when this deduction is not available.

	A	B
Adjusted Gross Estate	$650,000	$650,000
Less: Amount to Spouse (Example)	400,000	—
Net Taxable Estate (Other Heirs)	$250,000	$650,000
Tentative Estate Tax (from Table 11)	$ 70,800	$211,300
Less: Allowable Tax Credit	62,800	62,800
Federal Estate Tax Due	$ 8,000	$148,500

If you plan to will the bulk of your estate to your surviving spouse, and the amount to be willed to other heirs is $225,000 or less, *why worry about estate planning?* Here are some very important reasons:

- Generally speaking, if you are ten years from retirement with an estate valued at $375,000, an annual inflation rate of only 8 percent could lift the value of your estate to more than $800,000 by the time you retire. These inflated estate dollars may go no further in 1990 than today's dollars do, but your estate tax obligations would increase substantially under current laws. If you don't provide for inflation your heirs will end up with a great deal *less real wealth*. Careful tax planning can prevent this outcome.

- If your estate grows in real terms as a result of new assets, capital gains, increased annual income, or an inheritance, your estate tax problem could grow proportionately.

- After your death, the combined effects of inflation and loss of the marital deduction could greatly diminish your spouse's estate, and less real wealth would be passed to your children and grandchildren. However, the 1981 tax law liberalizes the gift tax, and now allows your spouse to transfer up to $10,000 per year to each child or grandchild, tax free. If you have three children and two grandchildren (by that time), over ten years the surviving spouse could transfer $500,000 out of his or her estate to theirs, tax free. These gifts will not impair your spouse's financial security if you plan carefully now.

- Suppose you are in a second marriage and want to make sure that children from your first marriage will inherit from you. You might want to set up a trust for your second spouse to be activated at the time of your death. Upon your spouse's death, the principal would pass to your children.

- Suppose you have an elderly parent who is dependent on you and you want to insure that your parent will have adequate financial support should you die first. You might set up a trust to be administered by a trustee or guardian after your death, for your parent. The principal could be transferred to your spouse or children upon the parent's death.

- Suppose you plan to leave equal amounts to each of two children. Upon your death, one receives a savings account worth $30,000, and the other receives stock worth $30,000. The Internal Revenue Service discovers that the stock was purchased for $12,000. This "equal gift" of stock creates a capital gains tax liability for its recipient.

Probate

In recent years there has been a lot of talk about "beating probate." Books and articles promise that a great deal of time and money can be saved by avoiding it. But experts in the fields of estate and tax planning caution against simplistic approaches to probate. Most of them can cite cases in which an estate was stripped of thousands of dollars and tied up for years in bitter court battles—all because of homemade estate plans designed to avoid probate.

Probate is the orderly passing of your property through the court to your heirs according to the terms of your will. It is the function of the executor, usually with the aid of an attorney, to oversee each step in this process. The court first determines whether or not the will is valid. If there is no will, or the will is declared invalid, this probate court (sometimes called *surrogate's* or *orphan's court*) distributes the estate according to the state's intestacy laws.

Why avoid probate? In some cases, especially in first marriages when the rapid transfer of all assets to the wife is the prime consideration, avoiding probate can save time and expense in administering the estate. Probate is, in effect, delayed until the death of the wife; in some cases, estate taxes are postponed as well.

A key consideration here is the state you live in, since each state has its own machinery for passing an estate through probate. Some have expensive and complex requirements involving multiple fees, court-appointed administrators, and practices which tie up a case for months with red tape. Other states have simplified their probate laws, so that an uncomplicated estate can be fully distributed quickly and at minimal cost. You could read volume after volume and still not be familiar enough with your state's practices to decide intelligently whether or not to avoid probate.

The property arrangements we mentioned earlier as ways of avoiding probate (pages 231–34) can be risky and inconvenient for you while you live. The only way you can make a sound choice between the possible hazards and rewards of avoiding probate is to plan your estate carefully with the guidance of a trusted attorney.

PLACING ASSETS IN A TRUST

A trust is a legal arrangement by which some or all of your assets are held by a *fiduciary*—usually a bank trust department or other trustee—who has legal responsibility to manage these assets for your benefit or for the benefit of others you have specified. A *living* or *inter vivos* trust is set up while you are alive and passes to your beneficiaries outside your will. A *testamentary* trust is established after your death, when you have included such provisions in your will.

Trusts can be highly effective in accomplishing a variety of desirable estate-planning goals. They can:

- assure expert management of varied assets and investments while you are alive, thus relieving you of this day-to-day responsibility;
- reduce state inheritance taxes and federal estate taxes;
- prevent the dissipation of your investments in the event of a long-term illness;
- provide for competent financial management of funds left to a widow, elderly parent, or someone else inexperienced in business affairs;
- place restrictions on the use of particular assets or property after your death;
- require that your assets be used in a particular way after you are gone.

When you create a living trust, you are turning over all or a portion of your assets to the trustee, who will manage it for your benefit. The trustee can hold, sell, manage, invest, and carry out other activities involving your assets, and you receive the income or dividends from the assets. A detailed legal document, prepared by *your* estate-planning attorney (not the bank's legal department) specifies the purposes of the trust and the powers and responsibilities of the trustee. Initially, you should make the trust *revocable*, meaning that you can cancel it, change the terms, or change beneficiaries. A revocable trust is considered part of your estate for tax purposes. After you feel you've had enough experience with your trustee, you should make the trust irrevocable. If he is managing your funds effectively and regularly reporting the results to you, he is doing his job well and can probably take care of the trust.

You might want to establish a trust while you are alive to "try out" the services of a particular bank which would be managing these assets for your dependents after your death. Before you choose a bank, it's worthwhile to check into their track record with trusts— how well they have done with investments over time. Or you may simply want to free yourself of everyday involvement with the management of your investments after retirement. In some trusts, called *directed living trusts,* you can have a say in how your investments are managed, although you are probably better off relying on the expertise of a good trust department to help preserve your capital.

Bank trust departments operate for profit, and there are numerous costs. There is usually a minimum fee, an annual fee, figured as a percentage of the trust's assets and the income they generate, a fee for withdrawal of principal, and a termination fee at death. Larger banks will usually not accept individual trusts of less than $100,000 but will sometimes accept smaller trusts which are managed in a pool with other trusts, much like a mutual fund. The amount you must contribute to such a pool varies from bank to bank and depends on your existing relationship with that bank.

A *testamentary* trust works very much like a living trust, but it is created through your will and does not take effect until after your death. This form of trust is especially useful in providing a well-managed base of assets for the education of children, for support of elderly parents, or to provide income to a widow without adding taxable assets to her estate. Upon her death, the trust passes to the children. Since the "second estate" is not eligible for the marital deduction and is usually taxed heavily, it is most useful for preserving your children's legacy. In this type of trust, where the primary objective is to reduce taxes, you should always empower the trustee to draw upon principal if your spouse requires it.

Whatever type of trust you find beneficial for your estate plans, be sure to discuss its purposes and restrictions openly with your spouse.

It is tragic but true that many widows and their families have been bound up in trust arrangements dictated by a husband who unwittingly created inflexible or undesirable restrictions without consulting the people who were later going to live under them.

Although this chapter has merely scratched the surface on most of these important financial points, it has given you the groundwork to start planning the management of your assets in retirement. Once settled and secure, you can concentrate on the really enjoyable part—building a new lifestyle for the future.

3

BUILDING YOUR LIFESTYLE FOR THE FUTURE

10

PLANNING TO ENJOY YOUR LEISURE TIME

Dost thou love life? Then do not squander time, for that is the stuff life is made of.

BENJAMIN FRANKLIN

As we advance in life, we acquire a keener sense of the value of time. Nothing else, indeed, seems of any consequence: and we become misers in this respect.

WILLIAM HAZLITT

THERE is a windfall in store for you when you reach retirement, and now is the time to start dreaming about ways to spend it. I'm not talking about money, but about time: thousands of hours of precious, irreplaceable time, which will be yours to invest in the most exciting, rewarding activities you can find.

Nearly three-quarters of your weekday waking hours are now controlled by your job, counting travel time. Your "free time" on evenings and weekends is often spent recuperating from the strains of a full week's work. Then suddenly you reach retirement age, and the rules change dramatically. Social Security, pensions, and returns on investments provide a flow of income; your financial responsibilities are considerably smaller with children on their own and the mortgage paid off. For the first time in forty years or so, the focus of your daily activities can shift from what you *have* to do to what you *want* to do.

This brings up a very difficult question, however—what *do* you want to do?

WHAT DOES IT MEAN TO RETIRE?

A life of uninterrupted relaxation in retirement has, over the years, become an accepted aspect of the Great American Dream. The ultimate aspiration was to just sit back and do nothing. That sounded awfully good to many harried young workers, who saw the prospect of restful retirement as a welcome reward for their years of hard labor. The seemingly attractive picture of perpetual idleness was used to sell everything from retirement homes and fishing rods to insurance policies and political programs.

On closer examination, the joys of doing nothing were found to be vastly overrated. The retiree who expected to take it easy for the rest of his life found that he was powerless to combat the effects of inflation, or any other major drain on his financial resources. What was worse, he was overwhelmed by a sense of uselessness. The society which encouraged him to leave his job as soon as possible failed to help him with his problems once he had taken that step. In fact, he found himself shut out of the mainstream of American life.

I can remember imagining days sitting on the south patio, taking in the beautiful Arizona scenery and climate, watching the sun go down over the colored rocks, and asking my wife, "What would you like to do this evening?"

It never happened: We *always* knew what we were doing, each evening for two or three weeks ahead (and sometimes a lot further than that). And I'm not sure we wouldn't have been bored silly if it *had* been the way I had pictured it. We weren't the kind of people to simply drift along and not know what our plans would be. So the vision sometimes isn't congruent with what is best for your own happiness. Ours turned out to be a happy experience, but different from our original idea of what it would be like.

Living without trying to accomplish something—for us or for anyone—is boring. When you work for most of the week, you use your leisure for relaxation. In retirement, you will have to get more out of your leisure activities—a greater sense of challenge, accomplishment, success—or your retirement freedom can become a burdensome lack of direction.

Roles for Retirees

From the time we were children, we were taught that our main purpose in life was either to earn a living or to keep house and raise children as a partner of someone who worked for a living. In retirement, new roles must be developed.

We have made some significant progress in expanding the possibilities for a satisfying later life. The mandatory retirement age has been raised to seventy and may be eliminated altogether in the near future, as it already has been for federal employees. There is more opportunity for part-time work than ever before, especially for skilled older workers. Retirement communities and adult community centers have grown rapidly, and there are large numbers of charitable organizations actively courting older Americans for meaningful volunteer work. There is a great deal to do, but you must go after it and not expect it to come to you.

You are given a certain amount of freedom throughout life and are expected to make the most of it. Now that you have the new freedom of more time and fewer obligations, your boundaries are greater than they have ever been. The fact that there is no clearly defined path for you to follow could leave you feeling that you have nowhere to go.

By accepting the challenge of retirement planning, however, you can choose the leisure activities that fit your preferences and build an engaging, invigorating, fulfilling life for yourself.

A CREATIVE APPROACH TO LEISURE PLANNING

Retirement planning is a creative process. It takes imagination, preparation, and determination to shape the time you have at hand into a way of life that will give you balance, pleasure, and value. How to go about it? I'd suggest paring the task down to its essentials.

Step 1: Setting Goals. The first step in planning is to decide what the end result of your creative efforts should be. Like any builder, take a good look at your raw materials and ask yourself:

- What do I have to work with?
- How does that limit what I can do?
- What possible projects are suggested by the nature and shape of my raw materials?
- What elements do I want to include in the finished work?
- How can I combine and structure these elements so they'll fit together well?
- How will I go about turning my raw materials into the finished form I have chosen?

Expand your horizons. This could be your chance to turn that dormant talent or interest into the retirement activity you can thrive on.

Step 2: Gathering Your Tools. Now you can start assembling the tools you need to turn your vision into reality: information, skills, money, and other people. The abilities, equipment, and acquaintances you have gained through years of work and recreation will form a major resource in planning for the future.

Don't let your past dictate your future plans too strictly, though. There are new skills to acquire, new people to meet, and new fields to conquer at any age. If you want to feel young, you must continue to learn, to explore, to discover. Justice Oliver Wendell Holmes, Jr., of the United States Supreme Court, had the right idea. At age ninety-two, still actively serving on the Court, he was discovered sitting in his library reading Plato, "to improve my mind," as he put it.

If you begin today expanding interests that you can continue to pursue in retirement, you will be several steps ahead of the game. The skills you build up over the years will be your best asset, since they will provide immediate enjoyment as well as future pleasure.

Step 3: Executing Your Plan. Planning doesn't mean you have to map out each waking hour in advance. Your desires, circumstances, and abilities may change in ways you can't possibly foresee now, and besides, too much structure is as tedious as none at all. A little spontaneity adds spice and joy.

But planning a rich, full lifestyle for the future is a critical part of avoiding upheaval. If you know where you're headed before you get there, you can make the transition from job to retirement far more smoothly. You won't be facing a threatening void; instead, you'll be gaining the opportunity to devote more time to familiar activities, along with the new interests that come your way. If you are able to do many different things, you'll have the necessary resources to adapt to changes when they occur.

What Activities Are Available?

I call myself the world's champion dilettante, and I do dabble in almost everything. I'm almost like Alexander Woollcott, who once said, "I am interested in everything except incest and folk dancing." I've taken up many things—dabbled in them a little, dropped them, and maybe never returned to them. Experimentation is the way to find the things that will come back to haunt and grab you; that's how you'll sift out the things that are really right for you.

There is virtually no field in which reasonably healthy adults can't participate in some way, regardless of age. All over the world, men and women in their sixties, seventies, eighties, and beyond are busily enjoying sports, art, music, politics, theater, travel, volunteer service, religious work, crafts, hobbies, education, and work, among other activities.

Why do I mention work? Well, why not? If you can get rid of those factors which bothered you on the job, you can make working a valuable part of a balanced retirement lifestyle. As one sixty-two-year-old woman we spoke to put it, "You have an altogether different outlook on work if you don't *have* to work. You're doing something you like."

As you compile a set of activities for your retirement, you should keep in mind the areas of work satisfaction for which these other interests may substitute. For example, let's examine the following elements of your life and see which ones are primarily centered in your work:

- *Sense of Identity*—Are you Joe Smith, attorney, or Joe Smith, Executive Vice-President? How would it feel to wake up one morning and be just Joe Smith?

- *Enjoyment of Work*—Do you take pleasure in simply doing your job well? Is this your sole or dominant source of pleasure?

- *Social Contacts*—Are most of your friends people connected with your job? Or can you enjoy the company of people totally outside your field of work?

- *Feeling of Self-Worth*—Do you judge yourself on the basis of how successful you are on the job, especially on how much money you make? Or do you also consider your opinions, affections, advice, and other human qualities to have value?

- *Sense of Progress*—Have you advanced regularly in your position? Is this the element of your life that gives you the greatest pride? Or do you have other areas of personal progress, such as an enhanced ability to achieve a sense of well-being, new insights, ways to give and to enjoy comfort, etc.?

The prospect of leaving work can be threatening unless your feeling of self-identity goes beyond your job. There are myriad other possibilities for self-satisfaction. I am not suggesting that an abrupt switch to a life of leisure activities can curtail a determination to continue important work—nor should it. But adjusting the job itself to fit your desires and your retirement schedule can be the key to undreamed of new satisfactions, if the planning and approach are sound. The next section will show you how to narrow down potential areas of interest, and shape the best ones into a carefully crafted new lifestyle.

Personal Preference Profile

This brief questionnaire may help stimulate insights and ideas buried in the recesses of your mind. Write down the responses which occur to you in each of the following categories:

Current Leisure Activities. What do you enjoy doing now? Make a list of recreational and occupational activities which give you pleasure. Now look at each individual item and ask yourself:

- How many years have I been doing this? Am I improving at it, or have I learned just about all there is to know?
- When was the last time I did this? If it's been a while, is it because I don't have the time, or money, or energy? How could I make it easier to engage in this activity? Or have I neglected it because I really don't get much enjoyment from it?
- How will retirement affect my participation in this activity? Will growing older have any effect?
- What is there about doing this that I enjoy?

Over the years, you've learned by trial and error. You may have tried half a dozen sports before deciding that you enjoyed swimming, or read books on dozens of topics before you discovered a passion for astronomy or ancient history. You can now benefit from past experience to help set your course for the future.

Examine each item on your list and try to come up with a few related activities that you might consider. An avid freshwater fisherman might like to try his hand at surf casting, for instance, or an expert pastry chef might enjoy experimenting with sausage-making. Write down each of your ideas for expanding your horizons next to the current interest to which it relates.

Then try stretching your imagination and reaching for more distantly related ideas. The fisherman may have developed an interest in the fish themselves and might decide to study them, to take a course or set up an aquarium at home. He might feel that the time has come for him to learn how to cook the fish himself, or to learn about the white wines that go with the fish he eats.

Even if your list of current activities is quite small and you find most of your satisfaction on the job, you can come up with an impressive array of recreational ideas which appeal to you by building on the basis of what pleases you now.

Add to your list any ideas which come to you now, but don't stop there. Keep the question of leisure activities in mind as you go about your daily chores and be receptive to new ideas. Add them to your list for future reference.

Current Plans. Now think about what you actually expect to do when retirement comes along. Make a list of the activities you plan to indulge in when you reach age sixty-five or seventy. See if you have some new things to add to those you are already engaged in. Ask yourself:

- *Will my current interests be enough?* Many people latch on to one leisure pursuit and look no further. Telling yourself, "When I retire I'll have more time for my fishing," or "At last I'll be able to travel," may be a way to avoid the main issue. How much more time do you really *want* for your fishing? How much time do you want to spend traveling? How much travel can you afford?

  If you move up and out and diversify your interests, you will open up more possibilities for the future. This approach is terrifically energizing. It allows you to look forward to something else each day and makes growing older feel like growing better.

- *Am I underestimating my future abilities?* Don't sell yourself short. Never mind the stereotypical negative images. Plan to be active, alive, interested, and interesting. If you gain nothing else from reading this book, you should get a sense of the richness of experience available to you as you grow older.

Of course, you may overestimate what you will be able to accomplish. So what? Just rev up and keep moving. You can always hit the brakes if you have to.

Skills and Interests. What do you know how to do? What did you learn to do in school? What knowledge and abilities have you used on the job? What skills have you mastered in your free time?

Most people don't realize how much they really know, and assume their abilities are very ordinary. But abilities are relative. Retirement is a new situation; the relative value of what you know can change drastically. A highly trained air traffic controller will find little opportunity to use his professional skills once he's retired, but may be grateful for the tennis lessons he took, which can provide a major source of exercise, social activity, and self-esteem.

For me, the activities that I would call hobbies are the ones that really haunt me, the ones I'm driven back to time and again: sailing, flying, and horseback riding. Those three are really the prime ones. But I've tried everything from car racing to scuba diving in icy winter waters. Of the sedentary ones, I'm a virtuoso on the phonograph. I'm sure I play more classical music than anyone I know, probably twelve hours a week. I actually plan concerts, such as a program of Bach, or Beethoven, or Brahms. I play chess, but months could go by without it and I wouldn't feel any void. I couldn't stand not listening to music.

One of the reasons I pursue the active hobbies now is that when I'm ninety-five, if I can't spend three days in the wilderness on horseback, I sure as hell hope I can listen to music, read, write, and pursue other sedentary interests. I might even become more serious about chess. I keep these things active and "in the bank" in case I get so I can't do some of the others.

With a little imagination you can turn your present abilities into interests which will make up an important part of your retirement lifestyle. That's what Henry McNeill did. A retired machinist of sixty-seven from Pittsburgh, Mr. McNeill is now known as Santa's Helper. He spends most of his time fixing broken toys in preparation for Christmas, when they are distributed to needy children. He has repaired everything from bicycles to Raggedy Andys. He loves his new work—both the doing of it and the pleasure it gives others.

Milton Williams was a mining engineer and estimator of industrial steel products until he retired in 1973. He had enjoyed geology when he was in college, and as he approached retirement he learned the art of making jewelry. He spends several hours a week at his lapidary work in the retirement community in Arizona where he lives and sells some of his silver pieces to pay for supplies for future projects.

What do you have to work with? Make a list of all of the special skills you have acquired in the course of a lifetime. Include your technical skills, of course, but don't forget the sports you have mastered, your creative and artistic flair, and your personal skills, such as leadership and organizational abilities. Next to each of these abilities jot down a few possible activities that might call for these talents. When you go back over your list, you may find ways to adapt seemingly impossible undertakings to fit your personal circumstances. Perhaps all it takes is a little determination and some additional training.

Successful Leisure. You have now made a shopping list of attractive possibilities for the years ahead. You may be surprised to find that you have a broadly based assortment of ideas to choose from and to incorporate into your present and future plans.

Your choices will naturally be influenced by circumstances, economics, and health, but you still have a large spectrum to work with, regardless of your situation. There are many ways and many different levels on which to satisfy your needs.

Keep the following ten goals in mind when making your choices. After reading through them, go back to your Personal Preference Profile and see how the activities you are considering can provide these keys to a happy retirement.

Ten Keys to Choosing Retirement Activities

1. Continuity

Work has always been the basic force scheduling our days. If you take that away, you need some other regular, reliable activities to form the backbone of your life. Waking up on an occasional Sunday and wondering what to do with the day is a welcome relief from the ordinary grind, but you wouldn't be very comfortable if it happened every day. You need some sort of routine.

By planning now you can ensure that your schedule will mostly consist of enjoyable pursuits, not just regularly delegated household chores. There's no real trick to filling up hours. Using them to your best advantage, though, calls for some forethought and a number of interests which you can follow on a regular basis.

2. Peaks

Routine can lead to monotony if you are not building up to certain peak moments. Whether it is a trip, a performance, a goal reached, or a project completed, there has to be a place on the horizon when you will be able to stop and say, "Thank goodness, I've finally done it!"

3. Growth

Plan to have interests that will challenge you to improve, to become continually better at what you do. You may grow in skill through practice, or in knowledge through studying, or some combination of the two.

4. Exploration

The process of discovery and seeking can continue on many levels throughout life. There is always a new sight, a new thought, a new experience, and a new acquaintance waiting for us. Travel, intellectual and philosophical pursuits, curiosity about other people, questions on how and why things work as they do are all valid means of exploration. Plan to look for answers in some organized way once you retire, whether through books, group discussions, formal education, or firsthand observation.

5. Balance Social and Private Activities

Try to be open to activities which you can pursue on your own as well as those which require other people's participation. It is sometimes too easy to become retiring in retirement. People often cut themselves off from the outside world and closet themselves in their own isolated lifestyle. Remember that people will rarely come knocking at your door to ask you to join in, especially if you have previously shown no signs of interest. The answer is simply to keep some group activity—a team or a club, not to mention your family—as a vital element in your retirement planning.

One excellent way to bridge the generation gap is to enjoy an activity with your whole family—children and grandchildren and even great-grandchildren. By exploring different interests together, you can change your relationship from a static, passive appreciation to an exciting, cooperative partnership which will be stimulating to young and old alike.

I get a lot of satisfaction from horseback riding with my ten-year-old grandson. He's been at it since he was four, and now, even though he's not fully grown, he can take care of the horse himself. He can do everything except lift the saddle onto the horse's back. And he loves nature as I do.

I first took him into the wilderness in Arizona when he was five or six. It was the first time he had stayed out all night, and he was very impressed. We went about seven miles up toward what's called Mormon Girl Mine, and made camp on a moonless night. When the sun went down it got *dark* dark—you saw stars, but when you're out away from all lights (and you forget this when you spend a lot of time in the city) it is *dark*. You could stumble right into a cactus.

We had a campfire, and we had eaten, and we started to hear animal sounds. There are a lot of animals in that part of the country: there are mountain lions, wild boars, deer, coyote, and at higher elevations, bear, but none of these got near us. The sound was range cattle, and they made noises in the dark because they sensed the feed we'd stashed for the horses in the morning.

My grandson was obviously afraid and he sat near the fire after we'd finished eating. After a moment, he turned to me and said solemnly, "How do you know we'll be alive tomorrow?" Coming out of a little kid like that it cracked me up. He wanted some assurance we were going to make it through that inky night. And I said, "Well, I intend to be, and I hope that you'll join me." At the time I'm not sure he was too convinced.

6. *Balance Indoor and Outdoor Activities*

For your health and your general self-image, you need to get out and move around in the world, whether your preference is gardening or motorcycling. To combat a tendency for staying indoors too much of the time, establish yourself as an active participant in some form of outdoor recreation.

7. *Structured and Flexible Activities*

Some activities require a steady natural progression. For instance, if you are building a bookcase, you must assemble wood and nails in a precise order if you want the structure to stand and hold weight. Other activities are more flexible. The photography buff, for instance, can take out his camera and go off in search of interesting pictures any time he feels like it.

In your assortment of retirement activities, try to include some structured pursuits, which will give you a source of regular, progressive involvement, and some activities which you can pursue whenever the spirit moves you.

8. *Worthwhile Activities*

There is certainly nothing wrong with engaging in activities strictly for pleasure. However, everyone needs to feel that part of his or her time is spent doing something worthwhile. For some, the goal is self-improvement; for others, the feeling that they have helped someone else. Whatever your personal thoughts on the matter, you will undoubtedly want to take on some projects which seem important and constructive to you.

9. *Balance Active and Passive Pursuits*

You can plan to make both forms of leisure more rewarding. For instance, watching television, that most time-consuming of all American leisure activities, is essentially a passive undertaking, yet it can be done in a way that involves you a little more deeply.

By being selective about the programs you choose, you can make watching educational, inspirational, informative, challenging, and emotionally stimulating. The same can be said for other leisure activities in which you are basically a spectator. Reading or going to a play or listening to music are relaxing pastimes which can enrich your life experience as well as entertain.

The active pursuits you choose are all creative in some sense, whether they offer new self-assertiveness through physical exertion or self-expression through artistic endeavor.

10. Economically Rewarding Activities

Which of the activities on your list would reap financial bonuses? If you are planning to turn one of your leisure interests into a moneymaking proposition, you should right now be gathering together the know-how you'll need in order to make the transition from hobbyist to business person (see pages 315–23).

It is always a good idea to be able to turn a profit at something you like to do, even if you don't need the extra money. That way, you always have the security of knowing that the possibility exists in case you do decide to sell your goods or services.

11

POSSIBILITIES
IN YOUR
OWN BACKYARD

Most people say that as you get old, you have to give up things. I think you get old because you give up things.
SENATOR THEODORE F. GREEN, before he retired from a distinguished career in the United States Senate at age ninety-three.

ONCE you have a pretty good idea of what is possible in your range of experience and interests, you should decide where you want to spend most of your time. It is often a great revelation to many people to discover that their own home can be the base of all their activities—entertainment, artistic creation, recreation, and moneymaking ventures. It's all there in your own backyard.

I have met numerous retirees who converted basements into workshops or ham radio centers, who built greenhouses in their extra wing to expand gardening activities, who refurbished kitchens for evergreater gourmet cooking pursuits. Others spent some extra savings to put in the swimming pool or tennis court, where they had decided to improve their own physical skills or to give lessons. And these are only a handful of ideas for enriching your life at home.

CRAFTS

Building an object with your own two hands produces a feeling of accomplishment. It has become fashionable lately to disparage crafts activities for retired people, but it cannot be denied that a craft can produce immense rewards for the person who develops skill in it.

There are hundreds of "established" crafts, some very expensive, such as cabinetmaking and silversmithing, and some which cost virtually nothing at all.

In looking for craft ideas, ask yourself what materials and what skills you have at hand. One of the most exciting approaches to this work is developing an original idea. Experiment with two or three until you settle on one you really want to pursue.

Making money from your crafts is largely going to depend on how well you master the technique, how much originality you bring to your projects, and how successful a salesperson you are. If this is a major consideration to you, look around in local shops to see what handmade goods are now being sold. Think of what *you* would consider buying, especially as a gift. You might also pick up a clue from ads in organization newsletters and bulletins placed by craftspeople with items to sell.

While crafts work is basically an individual undertaking, there *are* opportunities here to meet and work with other people. Classes in crafts bring together people with a common interest and often involve sharing facilities, like a kiln for ceramics or power tools for woodworking. There are clubs organized around a particular craft, in which the members hold regular meetings to discuss techniques, show each other their work, and sometimes organize group projects.

Crafts fairs, which have recently become popular, offer opportunities
to display items for sale and meet other craftspeople.

Here is a list of crafts you might want to consider. The suggestions
are meant to serve as inspirations only. A trip to your local library will
reveal many more specific craft ideas.

Acrylic and lucite crafting	Found-object sculpture	Papier-mâché
Basket weaving	Glassblowing	Quilting
Batik	Jewelry making	Scrimshaw
Cabinetmaking	Leather tooling	Stained-glass crafting
Candle making	Macrame making	String and yarn crafts
Ceramics	Model building	Weaving
Embossing metal	Needlecrafts	Whittling
	Net making	

Action Plan for Crafts Involvement

- *Research*. Start at your public library. You will find many
  books on individual crafts, as well as anthologies which bring
  together information on several different ones.

  Even if you are considering a craft which you think is
  uniquely yours, you may find project ideas in these books
  which will work well with your chosen material, as well as
  techniques and tools which you can adapt to your own needs.

  Magazines are an excellent source of craft ideas. *Woman's
  Day, McCall's,* and *Family Circle* often feature articles on
  crafts projects, particularly on gift ideas. There are also
  dozens of specialty magazines which cater to the home crafts-
  person. Some, such as *Handweaver and Craftsman* and
  Modern Carpentry, deal with particular skills, and others,
  such as *Family Crafts Ideas,* survey a broad spectrum of possibilities.

- *Experimentation*. The only way to find out if you will really
  enjoy a craft is to try it. For your first effort, pick a project

that goes quickly and is inexpensive and easy to do. Be sure that you will need only a minimum number of tools.

One way to approach a new craft is by purchasing a kit. Everything from needlepoint and lacemaking to stained-glass crafting and kite building has been put together in kit form, and your local hobby or department store should have a good selection. If not, there are several catalogue companies which sell crafts kits by mail, including Dick Blick, P.O. Box 1267, Galesburg, IL 61401; C.C.M. Arts and Crafts, Inc., 9520 Baltimore Avenue, College Park, MD 20740; Economy Handicrafts, 47-11 Francis Lewis Blvd., Flushing, NY 11361; and Sax Arts and Crafts, 207 N. Milwaukee Street, Milwaukee, WI 53202.

- *Getting Instruction.* If the craft you are considering requires expensive equipment, like power tools or an electric kiln, your best bet would be to find a club or an adult education course which offers these facilities. Some basic instruction will provide the direction you need to get started, and the group environment may prevent you from becoming discouraged with the results of your own first efforts. Everyone improves with time.

SPORTS AND GAMES

It was Satchel Paige who posed the intriguing question, "How old would you be if you didn't know how old you was?" The question was particularly relevant when considering Paige's accomplishments. He liked to keep his chronological age a mystery, but he was certainly no kid when he became the first black major league baseball pitcher in 1948, after over twenty years pitching in the Negro leagues.

Sports

Gordie Howe was no youngster either as he skated into his fifties side by side with his own kids in the violent, demanding world of professional ice hockey.

And when the 1912 Olympic gold medals for the Running Deer team shooting event were handed out to the victorious Swedish squad, Oscar G. Swahn was there to receive his award, aged 65 years 258 days. He must have enjoyed Olympic competition, because he won another medal, a silver this time, at the 1920 Games and qualified for a berth on the 1924 team as well. This at seventy-seven!

You don't have to compete at the championship level to get the full measure of fun from your leisure athletics. If you are in reasonably good health now, don't limit your choice of sports and games too strictly. Fishing can be very pleasant, but if you feel that you'd prefer shooting the rapids or racing powerboats, at least do yourself the favor of investigating the possibility. This is not to say that everyone over sixty-five should be encouraged to take up parachute jumping— but Ardeth Evitt of Paris, Illinois, made her first jump at seventy-four years of age, and she told reporters she enjoyed it immensely. Publisher Bernarr Macfadden made his first jump at age eighty-two.

Speaking of parachute jumping, that's one thing I haven't yet done, but I plan to. I wear a parachute a lot when I fly, and even though I have all kinds of weird ratings for different types of aircraft, I've never jumped out of one. My wife jokingly says I'm so Scottish I would probably try to save a disabled ship and ride it down to earth too late to jump out anyway. But I'd like to go through a training course and do at least one free jump so I know what I'm doing. It's not likely to become one of my passionate hobbies—it's just something else I'd like to try.

Preparation now is of primary importance for active sports participation in the future. The younger you begin to train your body for a particular sport, the easier learning will be. Once you have mastered the basics, your steadily increasing skill will keep you fit for competition as you grow older, even if you can't run quite as fast or hit quite as hard as you once could. And you *will* keep your strength and agility well into retirement if you are physically fit through your middle years.

If you are already a weekend athlete, you have a distinct edge over your neighbors who spend their Saturdays sitting around. If you have already made sports part of your life, build your participation in retirement from a few hours stolen between work and family commitments to a greater portion of the week.

Here are four key steps to help make sports a vital part of your future plans.

Step 1: Check Your Health. Ask your doctor if there are any limitations on your ability to participate in sports, and make it clear to him that you *want* to be athletically involved. He may prescribe an exercise program to build you up for sports involvement, or steer you toward more suitable sports than the ones you have chosen, but it is unlikely he will absolutely forbid you to take part in some sort of sport. He will probably just remind you of the cardinal rule for beginners of all ages—take it easy when you're starting out, and work up gradually.

Step 2: Explore the Possibilities. To find a sport which suits both your own preferences and the facilities available to you, ask yourself the following questions:

- What sports do I enjoy now? What sports did I like to play when I was younger? What is appealing about them, and what other sports share these elements?
- What sports do I enjoy watching?
- What sports do my friends play?
- What special opportunities are available to me because of my geographical location? Can I get to the ocean, or a lake, or mountains? Are there indoor sports facilities I can use at a school, a YMCA, or a health club?

Step 3: Learn. For a sport like sailing or swimming, good instruction is essential for safety. But even seemingly harmless activities can be done incorrectly, or with improper equipment, and lead to unnecessarily pulled muscles and twisted ankles. At the very least, stop at your public library and check out a book on the sport you are going to try. If you can find the time and facilities to take some lessons, that's even better. Your local YMCA or adult education program probably has the course you're looking for.

Step 4: Participate. If you can find time on a fairly regular basis to get out and play, your sports ability and enjoyment will grow proportionately.

- Make a regular appointment with a partner to play. Whether it's for a few holes of golf or a few miles on a bicycle, having someone else's plans hinging on your activity will give you an added incentive.
- Join a team or a league. For many sports, like softball or basketball, this is the only way you are going to get enough people together to play. If you can't find a team, you might try posting a notice at a community center, school, or at work and see how many others are interested.
- Get your family involved. If you share a sports interest with your spouse, children, or grandchildren, you will be able to plan a leisure schedule—even vacations—around your common interests. By teaching each other the fine points and sharing the laughter, frustration, and success of sports, you can reach across age barriers and achieve a precious sense of solidarity.
- Check into the possibility of competitive events for your age group. In recent years, special events have been initiated for athletes of all ages.

Since 1970, Senior Sports International, a nonprofit organization, has sponsored the annual Senior Olympics, a competition in a wide variety of sporting events, including archery, fencing, gymnastics, skating, track and field, weightlifting, and at least twenty others. For information about the annual Olympics and membership benefits in the organization, write to Senior Sports International, 5670 Wilshire Boulevard, Los Angeles, CA 90036.

Another group, the National Senior Sports Association, has been founded to meet the specific needs of men and women fifty or older who wish to engage in sports for recreation or competition. They distribute educational information on sports for older people, sponsor competitive events, and offer discounts on sports equipment to members. For further information write to National Senior Sports Association, 1900 M Street, N.W., Washington, DC 20036.

Games

There are many games you can play without donning sneakers or breaking into a sweat, even when the competition becomes fierce.

Chess, checkers, and backgammon have been played and pondered with passion for centuries by serious gamespeople. I once read of a Los Angeles resident whose passion for chess was threatened when his doctor ordered him to give it up in favor of a more physically active pastime. The man rescued his imperiled hobby and satisfied the doctor as well by building an enormous outdoor chess board: alternating squares on grass and concrete three feet on edge with sloping terraces on each side of the field. Using three-to-five-foot-high chess pieces made of plywood with weighted bases and handles, he and his opponent would survey the field from the terrace, run down, pick up a piece and move it to another square, then run back up until it was time for the next move. Plenty of exercise.

Card games are also suitable for regular continued play, as any dedicated bridge devotee will attest. Major tournaments are now held across the country to find the top players in Monopoly, Scrabble, and a more recent innovation, Othello. Crossword puzzle enthusiasts also carry their fervor to regional and national tournaments.

With the recent growth of computer games, it is now possible to play traditionally two-person games like chess and backgammon by yourself against an electronic rival who is always available and rarely bad-tempered.

One of the prime advantages of developing a real skill at a particular game, though, is the enjoyment of head-to-head competition with others. You also open the door to interesting reading, a common family interest, a collection of game pieces or associated materials, and travel to competitive sites outside your immediate area.

One interesting source of information on formal competitions, new games, tips on strategy, and articles on background and history is *Games* magazine, which is published bimonthly. For subscription information write *Games*, 515 Madison Avenue, New York, NY 10022.

COLLECTING

If you can find it, buy it, or make it, chances are that someone somewhere collects it.

Whatever objects you find worth collecting, you can always spend additional time learning more about them through reading, taking courses, or talking with other collectors. If your collection consists of expensive objects, such as fine coins, stamps, antiques, or paintings, then the amount of time you spend acquiring your prized possessions will be limited by your budget. If your primary joy in building a collection is searching for new items and recognizing their hidden value, then you will want to pursue a collection which requires more effort than money. Some examples of items to consider in this regard are:

autographs	magazines
baseball cards	matchbooks
bells	newspaper clippings
bottles	postcards
butterflies	rocks
buttons	seashells
comic books	thimbles

This list is far too brief; with a little perseverance and imagination you can build an interesting collection of very nearly anything that strikes your fancy. It is still possible to amass a perfectly respectable collection of any of these items without taking out a second mortgage on your home.

Some collectors, however, are mainly interested in the rarity and monetary value of their acquisitions. In the face of skyrocketing inflation, there has been a growing trend to invest in collectibles, rare items whose value has steadily increased over the years, such as antiques, coins, gemstones, stamps, rare books, and works of art. If you are considering building a collection as a form of investment, beware of two important pitfalls.

First, it takes money to make money in this area. The items that rise in value rapidly are the rarest ones, most prized by collectors, and right now these will be very expensive. This is not the time to buy an inexpensive trinket and watch its value go through the ceiling. Today you will have to buy expensive and hope that the item becomes substantially more so in the future. You are buying at top dollar as a retail customer and will eventually have to sell to a dealer or through an auction house, accepting a price substantially below list value and paying hefty commissions in the process. There are still good investments in collectibles, but few produce short-term profits.

Also, it is extremely difficult to pick out the items which will appreciate markedly in value over the next few years. At best, you can devote many hours to studying the market, the availability of certain pieces and probable future supply, and buy according to your research. Even with a fair degree of expertise, it is hard to spot trends.

Make sure you fully understand the field in which you are planning to start a collection of expensive objects, and do not invest in it heavily enough to jeopardize your economic security if your guesses don't work out.

GARDENING AND COOKING

Even city dwellers can enjoy the pleasures of tilling the soil. You may enjoy gardening for the beauty of the plants themselves or for the incomparable taste of fresh homegrown fruits and vegetables, not to mention the exercise value you can get depending on the size of your planting area and the intensity of your efforts. You may also be able to earn some money if the crops you raise help to feed your family or can be sold to neighbors at a roadside stand. Or you may choose to channel your energies into investigating new ways to prepare those fruits and vegetables.

The joys of cooking have spread around the country lately. Millions of men and women have started to explore exciting new ways to prepare food, delving into foreign and domestic cuisines which offer different, distinctive dining experiences. A greater interest in what you eat can also be a key point in maintaining your good health, and many retirees take advantage of their time at home to learn more about nutrition and create a better diet through the excellent recipes available for low-fat, healthful cooking.

COMMUNICATING

If you love to talk to people, a CB (Citizens Band) or ham radio set may open up a richly rewarding world. CB radios, the short-range receiver-transmitters which were once basically the realm of long-haul truckers, have now found their way into the homes and cars of civilians across the country. Although the frequencies have become a bit crowded, they are still there for your use. For those who prefer conversing with people in faraway places, a ham radio set is the answer. It will allow you to send and receive signals across town or halfway around the world. Neither type of setup is prohibitively expensive, and each provides a ready source of interesting discussion at the flip of a switch.

People who feel uncomfortable with a microphone in hand might prefer the time-honored pastime of letter writing. Becoming a pen pal to someone you have never met can be an engaging hobby, opening doors to different cultures and unusual experiences. For help in getting in touch with another correspondent who has expressed interest in finding a pen pal, write to: International Friendship League, 22 Batterymarch Street, Boston, MA 02109 or Letters Abroad, 209 East 56th Street, New York, NY 10022.

FIXING, REFINISHING, REFURBISHING, AND INVENTING

Tinkerers of the world, retirement may well be the perfect time of life for you. If you took your first clock apart at the age of seven and have been dismantling, adjusting, repairing, renewing, and reclaiming broken or out-of-shape objects ever since, you have built up an invaluable skill.

Karl Hoff is now seventy-four, living in a major retirement community and still busy using his repairing skills, looking after the neighbors and relatives. He doesn't mind not being paid for his labor, but he certainly could have made money with his talents if he had chosen to. He simply decided he would feel more relaxed and have more fun by solving other people's problems in their homes.

Another possibility for someone with these skills is to find broken items or run-down furniture, work at them until they are in good shape, and sell them. Some tinkerers are inventors as well, and enjoy coming up with imaginative solutions to problems. If you invent a patentable device, you may be able to sell it to an existing company or even market the gizmo yourself.

Whether you plan to use your workshop just for fun or to make a profit, you should investigate the possibility of honing your skills further by reading manuals and repair guides or taking courses through adult education, a vocational or trade school, or a university extension service.

Again, I've just scratched the surface. There are other possibilities in your own particular background that will come to you with a little thought.

But perhaps you'd prefer to get out and develop a new lifestyle through academia, or travel, or the arts. The next chapter will explore some activities that will expand your horizons in these areas.

12

LEARNING
AND GROWING
DON'T STOP WITH
RETIREMENT

Let us think of education as the means of developing our greatest abilities, because in each of us there is a private hope and dream which, fulfilled, can be translated into benefit for everyone.

JOHN F. KENNEDY

To relax the mind is to lose it.

MUSONIUS

EDUCATION

WHAT a terrible waste it is to concentrate all our formal education in the first quarter of our lives! We can absorb only so much information in those few brief years, and the overflow is just memorized for an examination and forgotten immediately afterward. Besides, there is so much to learn which cannot be fully appreciated by a child, no matter how bright he or she might be.

Right now I'm finishing *The Great Books* for the second time, and I may even read them a third time. It's a seven-year process, fifteen pages a day. The first time I read them, it was 131 works, and it took me thirteen years. And I'll tell you: It's a different set of books at this age. I started the second time around exactly thirty years to the day from when I started the first time. If I'm alive, I may start *again* thirty years from the day I started the second time. And it would be a whole different set of books, I'm sure.

Your life experience brings a lot to the literature that you read. I read *Huckleberry Finn* three times; actually my mother read it to me the first time, when I was eight. I read it later when I was in my late twenties, and again when I was forty-five, and it was different every time. That's what makes great literature—it has its appeal on a variety of levels.

At last, adults, and especially older adults, are returning to the classroom to expand their knowledge in everything from television repair to classical Greek literature, and it's about time. As leisure time has increased over the years, going back to school has become more and more acceptable for grown-ups. The growth of adult education programs has brought a wide range of subjects within reach of a large segment of the population. More recently, the decrease in the number of students applying for college has brought financial pressure to bear on institutions of higher learning, and they have responded by reaching out to the public and inviting adults to become students once again. The junior colleges, undergraduate schools, and universities have set up special counseling programs to help adults get back on campus. They have expanded their course offerings to include more practical, adult-oriented subjects, and made funds available for scholarships and subsidies for senior citizens who want to further their educations. At this point, the educational community will not just accept you—they will welcome you with open arms.

*   *   *

Why Continue Your Education?

One of the educational advantages you now have is the ability to choose your own subjects. Now you know what your interests and abilities are. You have gotten a taste of virtually every possible subject through your exposure to the mass media, your discussions and dealings with other people, and your efforts to survive in the real world. Your educational planning, therefore, is made easier by the curiosities you've built up over the years. Your choice for home study or formal education will depend on your personal circumstances and abilities, and on your own goals.

First decide on what you want to learn and why. Sir Francis Bacon said, "Knowledge is power." Which of your mental muscles would you like to develop? The following are just a few of the reasons for devoting some of your time and energy to further education:

- *Career advancement.* If there are courses you could take which would give you the credentials to get ahead in your present firm, or move into a better job elsewhere, now is the time to do it. Improvement in your job status gives you more financial security now and in the future, and you will also be able to demonstrate—to others and to yourself—that you are really getting better at what you do as time goes on.

- *Preparing for your own business.* You may be thinking about being your own boss when you retire. If so, then the more you know about the business you are going to start, and about business practices in general, the greater your chances for success. You will be more competent and feel more confident if you take advantage of as much preparatory training as possible long before you plan to start on your own.

  The success rate for small businesses is notably low, and one of the key reasons for this poor performance is inadequate understanding of cash flow and profits and losses. For this reason, even if your career has been in business, it is important to brush-up on the basics of small business book-keeping and money management.

- *Intellectual curiosity.* Learning for its own sake, challenging your mind to deal with problems and projects in a field which interests you, can be the most self-fulfilling part of life at any age. If you have always wanted to learn about some topic which fascinates you, do yourself a favor and study it now. Aristotle was reportedly asked how much educated men were superior to the uneducated, and he replied, "As much as the living are to the dead." By continually expanding your knowledge and mental abilities, you will maintain the vitality and progressive attitude essential to happiness in later life.
- *Social contacts.* The classroom is a wonderful place to make friends. When faced with a common goal, like learning the subject matter at hand, or a common problem, like an up-coming test, the class members develop a real sense of unity. If you would like to meet people your own age who share a common interest, and especially if you would like to keep in touch with the concerns of the younger generation, there is no better means at your disposal than enrolling in a course.
- *Self-help.* Many of the skills which you can learn will make your life richer and more exciting. For instance, you could learn a sport, or dancing, a craft or hobby, and add an enjoyable leisure activity to your lifestyle. By studying a foreign language you open up lines of communication with other people particularly if you plan to travel abroad. There are many courses available which provide expert assistance in ironing out any personal difficulty you have, whether it is a philosophical question that disturbs you or your persistent inability to balance a checkbook. Think about what you would like to be able to do now and can't, or what you would like to do better than you do now, and explore the educational opportunities available.

*   *   *

No One Is Too Old to Learn

I have already mentioned examples of famous men and women who have continued to learn, create, and innovate at really advanced ages. You are no different—with health you can do the same. If you have the curiosity and determination, age itself is no barrier.

What have you learned today? This week? This year? Have you followed the news on television? Then you've studied history and current affairs, with some economics, politics, and sociology mixed in. Have you seen a movie lately? Then you've learned a lesson in film studies, mass media, drama, and critical techniques. Did you hear some gossip about a couple you know who are getting a divorce? There's a healthy dose of sociology, some psychology, and a bit of practice in the art of human communication.

The point is that your education never stops, even when you are not following a formal course of study. Most of what you learn in life is not confined to the classroom. Material presented in a course is just more clearly *directed* at teaching a specific body of related facts, and it is more *intense* in its concentration of information.

Accepting direction in your learning shouldn't be any problem— after all, you will be studying a subject which you have a real desire to master. As for the intensity of your commitment, you can choose the educational method that suits you, from simply reading books to taking correspondence courses to enrolling at a college or university. Whatever method of study you choose, you can proceed at your own pace. And there's no pressure—if you do receive a report card, you're the only one who will see it. With the negative aspects of education gone, you can enjoy the greatest rewards of learning—the excitement of discovery, the challenge of problem solving, and the pride of achievement.

*   *   *

Earning a Degree

- *High School.* If you never graduated from high school, you are not alone—almost half of the United States citizens over age twenty-five today are not high school graduates. Whatever your age, you can still benefit from receiving a high school equivalency diploma, whether it enables you to improve your job status, continue your education, or simply enjoy a sense of personal satisfaction. Call or visit the guidance department of your local high school, or contact your local board of education or the department of education in your state capital.

  In nearly every state and most United States territories you can earn your high school equivalency diploma by passing the General Education Development (GED) examination and satisfying certain residency requirements. Many communities offer evening adult education courses to prepare you for the GED. If you are confident of your skills in the five areas tested—writing skills, social studies, science, reading skills, and mathematics—you may be able to pass the exam with the aid of one of the fairly comprehensive review books on the market, such as *Barron's How to Prepare for the New High School Equivalency Examination (GED).* These books provide sample questions and answers, with detailed explanations.

- *College or Graduate School.* The admissions offices of local colleges and universities will be happy to tell you about your options for returning to school for an advanced degree. Admissions policies in recent years have become more favorable to older students, the number of night and weekend courses has grown, and increased attention has been focused on making the curriculum more attractive to nonresident, part-time students.

  As an adult student today you are very attractive to an institution of higher learning, and must not sell yourself short. Ask questions about any program which is suggested to you. Are the courses standard college courses, or a special program for older students? Will the classes be made up of students of mixed ages, or restricted to senior citizens?

Are the instructors regular faculty members, professors and assistant professors, or part-time instructors? If they are part-time instructors, what standards of qualification do they meet?

What is the goal of the program? What degree will you receive? How many credits must you earn? Can you take as much time as you may need to fulfill the degree requirement, or is there a time limit?

Can you receive financial assistance? More money than ever before has been targeted toward helping older students in recent years, and you may be eligible for a share, depending on your level of financial need. Ask the admissions department how to apply.

Another place to turn for financial aid is the company you work for. Many companies refund all or part of your tuition and expenses for any work-related courses you take as part of their employee benefits package. Ask the personnel department about assistance available from your firm.

- *CLEP.* You may be eligible for college credit for knowledge you have gained through your own informal studies, or in the course of earning a living. The College Level Examination Program (CLEP) gives older students the opportunity to earn credit toward a degree. Their standardized tests are accepted by many colleges and universities across the country. Any credits you can earn in this way will not only cut down on the time you will have to spend taking courses before earning your degree, but will save you money as well. Write for information to the College Level Examination Program, P.O. Box 582, Princeton, NJ 08540.

- *Community and Junior Colleges.* Many of the most interesting educational opportunities are found in the community and junior colleges. These schools offer two-year programs that entitle you to an associate's degree on completion. There are many technical and professional degrees available, preparing you for a job as a dental hygienist, an equipment technician or repair specialist, a paraprofessional in a school or hospital, or any number of other positions requiring special training.

Community colleges are notable for their reasonable tuition fees; in many of them local residents are entitled to enroll with no charge at all. On the basis of your completed two-year associate's degree, you can apply for admission to a four-year college and fulfill the requirements for a bachelor's degree in only two more years of full-time study.

● *Correspondence Courses.* If you don't live near a campus, or don't want to deal with transportation, you may want to inquire about correspondence courses, which are available for high school or college credit or for noncredit subjects. The National University Extension Association will send you a guide to the institutions offering independent study programs by mail. Write to them at Suite 360, 1 Dupont Circle, Washington, DC 20036.

You can request a copy of the "Directory of Accredited Home Study Schools" to find out about the accreditation of such schools from National Home Study Council, 1601 18th Street NW, Washington, DC 20009.

Other Educational Opportunities

Trade Schools. If you are interested in learning a trade, be it animal grooming, television repair, or computer programming, there is a private school ready to teach you. These schools advertise in magazines and newspapers, or you can check the telephone directory. Before signing up for a course of study, though, speak to someone who is already employed in the trade you are considering, and make a call to the local Better Business Bureau to get some background on the school you are considering.

Adult Education. Inexpensive adult ed programs are thriving across the country. Some are affiliated with local public school systems, others with colleges and universities, and all offer wonderful opportunities to find out about practical skills and enjoyable pastimes. If you have an itch to learn auto mechanics, typing, plant care, or sewing, you can find a qualified instructor who will charge a minimal fee at your local adult education center.

Public Libraries and Museums. In addition to the obvious availability of cultural materials at these institutions, many libraries and museums offer special educational programs. You may find films, lectures, discussion groups, and other valuable opportunities available at little or no cost.

Elderhostel. If you are over sixty, the Elderhostel program could be a fantastic summertime learning experience for you. The program began as an experiment in 1975, when 230 participants paid nominal fees to attend classes at five New Hampshire college campuses. They lived in the college dormitories and attended liberal arts courses during the one-week sessions. The program has become an enormous success since then, and coordinators estimate that by 1983 the program will accommodate nearly 60,000 participants in all of the fifty states.

Courses cover a broad spectrum, from literature and history to botany and astronomy, and the curriculum is supplemented by field trips and social events. In 1979 the cost for a week was $115 per person, which included room and board and all other basic expenses.

For current information on Elderhostel opportunities in your area, write to the national office: Elderhostel, 55 Chapel Street, Newton, MA 02160.

Special Programs for Older Americans. The number of educational programs specifically designed for people over sixty has mushroomed in the last few years. Some of these provide practical information about how to live well after retirement, but the majority involve qualified instruction in more general areas. You can learn about these programs from your state office of the aging, community adult centers, local chapters of the American Association of Retired Persons (AARP), or other retirement organizations, the local papers, or by contacting local educational institutions directly.

*   *   *

THE ARTS

The arts are demanding, and successful artists are generally seen as the bearers of some mysterious talent. But we can be involved in the arts just by being enthusiastic, informed members of an audience or by performing just for the fun of it. There is nothing wrong with being an amateur. Writers, artists, and performers who pursue their artistic endeavors just because it gives them pleasure accomplish valuable works even if they don't approach the standards of the professionals they emulate.

By increasing your own involvement in the arts both as a watcher and as a doer, you can develop an interest which can be enormously rewarding and absorbing when you retire.

Action Plan for Increasing Your Arts Involvement

AS A PARTICIPANT

Step 1: Find out about available learning experiences. You may be able to start a new artistic endeavor, or build your skill in an area which already interests you, by reading instructive books and periodicals or taking a course. Learning the basics right at the start will help you to turn in a respectable effort early on.

Whether you are interested in learning to paint, to dance, or to play an instrument, you will have to set aside a block of time not only for learning but for practice as well. Make a firmly scheduled commitment and don't deviate from it.

Step 2: Join an organized group. Instruction and practice often are available through clubs and groups. Painting and sculpture groups generally meet with an instructor, as do guitar clubs or writing clinics. In the performing arts, anything beyond reciting a soliloquy or playing an instrumental solo requires a group effort and generally an audience too.

Try your local community center, YMCA, and church groups and check the listings in your local newspaper for casting calls and announcements of new performing groups. Ask at your local high school or other community facility that rents its auditorium to such groups for the name of the president or manager. The same is true of other school and community facilities which are used by adults after hours, including art departments and meeting rooms for writing workshops and dance groups.

Step 3: Share your creations. There are many aspects of putting on a play which draw on talents other than acting. You may not want to get up on a stage, but you might be able to use your artistic ability or carpentry skill for set design or construction, or use your sewing and tailoring knowledge to help make costumes. Lighting, ticket sales, and publicity all require dedicated, able volunteeers.

If you have developed your musical talents to a respectable level, you will have little trouble finding a community orchestra, band, glee club, chorus, or choir which will provide an opportunity to display your abilities.

Clubs and classes in painting and sculpture frequently organize exhibits of the group's achievements, and there are often annual art shows in the community which welcome local work. You might approach a gallery owner directly about taking on some of your pieces for possible sale. Though you may get a few rejections when you first start out, you may yet discover that your talent can provide welcome extra retirement income.

When it comes to getting your writing published, it may be somewhat more difficult to find an audience, but there is always hope. The purpose of writing is communication, and the only way you'll know if you are getting your point across is to see how it affects your readers. Start with friends and family. It may take some probing to get past their initial politeness, but if you ask for an honest response, you'll probably get one.

Next, take a good, hard look at your writing and try to come up with the most appropriate form of publication for you. There is no reason not to submit your work to the major book publishers and magazines, but be prepared for the rejection slips when they arrive, and don't be downhearted.

Your chances may be better with local publishers, and with regional newspapers and magazines, small literary magazines, and specialty publications and journals. You might also decide to try your hand at journalism and write for a community newsletter.

You will be most likely to have your work accepted if it is:

- *Targeted to a specific audience.* For example, an article on the history of Spanish gold doubloons could be just the thing for *The Numismatist,* the magazine of the American Numismatic Association. Read through a few copies of any magazine to which you plan to submit your work, and get a feel for their style and content.
- *Informational and concise.* If you have special knowledge of an interesting subject, try to use your expertise in your work. Make your points in a few well-chosen words.

A book that will be of invaluable help to budding writers is *Literary Market Place,* an annual directory published by R. R. Bowker Company. LMP, found in most libraries, lists addresses and telephone numbers of book, magazine, and newspaper publishers, agents and agencies, courses, conferences, and contests, complete with brief descriptions of who is looking for what.

A word of caution about vanity presses, also known as subsidy publishers. These are the companies that actively solicit authors who have not been able to sell their work to traditional publishers, and charge them a substantial fee for the honor of publication. This will indeed get your name in print, but it will almost never make you any money, and may be a very expensive way to soothe a bruised ego. It isn't easy to get published by legitimate houses, but it can happen, and unknown authors are having articles and book manuscripts accepted every day. Just put your best effort down on paper, and try to enjoy the writing process for its own sake.

As an Enthusiast

Step 1: Specialize. A general appreciation of music or art offers enjoyment, certainly, but if you want to develop a more substantial involvement in your cultural interests, you should zero in on a particular segment of the arts which fascinates you. This might mean acquiring detailed knowledge of the life and times of a particular author or composer, or possibly exploring one era or school of thought.

When you have invested time and energy in building up your expertise, your passive appreciation of the arts becomes an active enthusiasm which adds substantially to your enjoyment of life.

Step 2: Join a group. The arts stimulate our thoughts and emotions, and sharing our reactions with other interested observers offers new perspective. We have all enjoyed debating the merits of a new movie or play with a group of friends. You can make that kind of lively discussion a regular part of your schedule by joining a group organized around a selected interest.

Many community centers sponsor art or literature appreciation clubs, and public libraries often have regularly scheduled book discussion groups.

You can take a class in your area of interest. There is no reason to think your instructor will be infallible, but he will at least have a broad background in the subject and be able to use his knowledge to add clarity to your thinking and present controversial viewpoints for consideration. Professional artists and writers may come as guest speakers or to meet with your class or group to discuss their work. There may also be group trips to galleries or museums, screenings of new movies, or trips to theatrical performances at discount prices.

Step 3: Be a paid or volunteer worker. There are many positions in every cultural area that will make you an active member of an artistic community. Here are some ideas to get you started in exploring your own opportunities for paid or volunteer employment in the arts.

- *Visual Arts*

  Paid worker: Jobs at art galleries, museums, art supply stores, art schools, bookstores specializing in art books, government councils on the arts. Writing a column on the arts for local newspaper.

  Volunteer: Positions in museums or on museum planning boards, on community councils on the arts, on organizing committees for art shows and fairs.

- *Music*

  Paid worker: Jobs at concert halls, music schools, record stores, musical instrument shops.

  Volunteer: Organizing committees for public concerts, volunteer organizations supporting concert facilities.

- *Literature*

  Paid worker: Jobs at bookstores, publishing houses, magazines, newspapers, libraries.

  Volunteer: Volunteer organizations supporting library facilities, community newsletters, literacy advocacy programs such as RIF (Reading Is Fundamental), local tutoring programs.

Whatever your talents, whether in fund raising, organizing, or publicity, you can help support the activities of creative artists and at the same time satisfy your own aesthetic needs.

TRAVEL

Travel is a way to satisfy your curiosity. We all wonder how people live in other countries, what the world looks like outside our neighborhood; how it really feels to be in the famous places we've read about in magazines or seen on television. I was over twenty-one

296 THE BEST YEARS BOOK

before I was even west of the Mississippi, and it was a great thrill when I first traveled outside the United States. There were signs I couldn't read, and people talking in languages I couldn't understand. I've been sent to many parts of the world now, but there are still countries and latitudes I'd like to explore.

Different kinds of travel appeal to different people. Some prefer trips which offer rest and relaxation, while others like to go on stimulating, action-packed whirlwind tours. You may look forward to meeting new people along the way, or simply enjoy building closer bonds with your traveling companions by sharing new experiences.

Retirement brings welcome advantages for the inveterate traveler. With freedom from a job schedule and family responsibilities, you'll be able to enjoy a trip free of the pressure you might have felt on earlier vacations. There are hefty savings available to retirees—off-season rates and senior citizen discounts, to name just two. But best of all, travel in retirement is often a dream-come-true opportunity. You have built up a rich supply of healthy curiosity about the people and places around you over the course of time, and now you can find out just what you've been missing.

The Power of Positive Travel Planning

People love to hear horror stories about traveling. Maybe it's jealousy, or a shared fear of the unknown, but everyone's ears seem to perk up when a tale of traveling woe is told. There's a never-ending supply of stories about lost luggage, canceled flights, ferocious wild animals, small-town speed traps, and Montezuma's revenge. Somehow these afflictions don't seem to deter many travelers—perhaps that hint of danger appeals to a suppressed adventurousness.

In any case, none of those afflictions is unavoidable. By becoming a well-informed traveler you can plan your way around the potential pitfalls which stand between you and an enjoyable trip. There are a host of practical matters to consider in your planning, from finances to getting your plants watered, but that's jumping ahead of ourselves. The most crucial step of all is deciding on a trip you really want to take. Let's explore the personal preferences you've built up about traveling over the years, and see what they suggest.

PERSONAL PREFERENCE PROFILE

Take out a sheet of paper and number it from 1 to 19. Then respond to each of the following questions about general likes and dislikes by writing in the appropriate letter-symbol next to each number:

D if you *disagree* with the statement
D+ if you *strongly disagree* with the statement
N if you have no particular preference on the matter
A if you *agree* with the statement
A+ if you *agree strongly* with the statement

PART I

1. To feel that I've gotten the full benefit of my vacation, I have to be away from home for a fairly long stretch.
2. I start to feel uncomfortable when I've been away from home for too long.
3. I like to have all the luxuries when I travel.
4. I like to feel that I've gotten a bargain.
5. I like the social atmosphere of the group of people vacationing together.
6. I prefer to be on my own, without feeling I have to accommodate myself to the wishes of others.
7. I like to participate in sports and explore nature when I'm on vacation.
8. I find sightseeing especially enjoyable.
9. I enjoy nightclub-style entertainment.
10. I like to rest and relax on vacation.
11. I enjoy having planned activities to fill up the day.

12. I especially enjoy cultural experiences, such as visiting museums and attending the theater.

13. I like to reach my destination and then stay put.

14. I like to hit a lot of interesting spots on a trip.

15. I like to set my own itinerary as I go.

16. I have to get rid of as much responsibility as possible to enjoy traveling.

17. Fine food is a major part of enjoying a vacation.

18. I take a lot of baggage with me when I travel.

19. I generally travel light.

Evaluating Your Responses. In the listing below are several popular styles of travel arrangements. To see whether these choices are well suited to your preferences, see whether your responses to Part I of the Personal Preference Profile indicate agreement (A or A+) with the statements indicated.

Accommodations

LUXURY HOTEL: Agree with 2, 3, 5, 7, 9, 11, 12, 13, 16, 17.

MOTEL, GUEST HOUSE: Agree with 4, 6, 8, 14, 15, 19.

CRUISE SHIP: Agree with 1, 3, 5, 9, 10, 11, 13, 16, 17, 19.

APARTMENT OR PRIVATE HOME (rental or temporary exchange): Agree with 1, 4, 6, 8, 10, 13, 18.

CAMPSITE: Agree with 1, 4, 7, 10, 13, 15, 19.

Transportation

BUS, TRAIN: Agree with 1, 4, 8, 10, 14, 15, 16, 19.

AIRPLANE: Agree with 2, 3, 10, 13, 16, 19.

CAR: Agree with 1, 6, 7, 8, 14, 15, 18.

CRUISE SHIP: See above.

Destination

CITY: Agree with 3, 8, 9, 12, 14, 15, 17.

COUNTRY AREA, PARK, WILDERNESS: Agree with 1, 4, 6, 7, 8, 10, 15, 19.

BEACH: Agree with 4, 6, 7, 10, 13, 16, 19.

FOREIGN COUNTRY: Agree with 8, 9, 12, 14, 17.

Arrangements
GROUP TOUR: Agree with 4, 5, 8, 9, 11, 12, 14, 16.
INFORMAL TOURING: Agree with 6, 8, 12, 14, 15.
PERSONALLY DESIGNED TRIP (prepared with travel agent):
Agree with 3, 11, 14.

Your responses so far have been designed to indicate the general availability of the type of traveling pleasure you seek within each of the areas discussed. Go back over the agreement responses for each category and see which of these you particularly *disagreed* with. You may find that you have strong leanings toward a particular form of travel, but dislike one aspect. For instance, the relatively reasonable expense and busy schedule of a group tour might appeal to you, but you may not be able to stand the idea of traveling with a crowd. The important lesson to be learned here is to spot the conflicts early, decide beforehand on any compromises necessary, and accept them as well as you can before you set out on your trip.

PART II

Now let's explore some particularly appealing destinations.
Make a second list and number it from 1 to 6. Answer each of the following questions with as many responses as you can come up with.

1. What countries do you have a particular interest in visiting?
2. What attractions in the United States have you been wanting to see?
3. Do you have relatives whom you would enjoy visiting? Where do they live? How about distant relatives whom you've never met? Do any of them live in places with appealing vacation opportunities?
4. Would any of your hobbies or interests lead you to especially significant places? Are there special annual events—conventions, displays, competitions, performances, etc.—that could be focal points for a trip?
5. Are there any places that friends have wholeheartedly recommended?

6. Is there a sports facility which especially draws you to an area? Do you want to ski at Biarritz or snorkel off the Bahama coast?

Investigate Now

Your answers to the Personal Preference Profile should give you some sense of direction, but keep your list open and flexible. You will get hundreds of ideas for future travel from newspapers and magazines, on television, in discussions with acquaintances, and in every form of advertisement. Even if you're not planning to take a trip right away, you can add possible future excursions to your list and become familiar enough with the different kinds of deals which are offered to be able to make an informed judgment when you are ready.

In addition to finding the best values in transportation and lodgings, the well-informed traveler can take advantage of lesser known, less expensive shops and attractions, can save on local transportation by planning his days efficiently and using public transit whenever possible, and can select the reasonably priced items and entertainments enjoyed by the natives of an area.

The best part of learning about the places you will be visiting is the pleasure you take in the hours of anticipation. By getting all you can out of getting ready for a trip, you'll be increasing the overall value of your vacation.

Building Your Travel Library

Once you've found a few interesting places to consider, a visit to the library or bookstore is in order. There you'll find dozens of books on travel, both domestic and foreign. As you read up on the areas you are specifically researching, be sure to check what the authors have to say about nearby locations. You may find that a brief side trip that adds little to your transportation costs could double the enjoyment of your trip.

Tourist information offices and chambers of commerce are gold mines of information. They provide free maps and brochures packed with inviting photographs as well as calendars listing local special events.

If you are interested in foreign travel, you should send for your free copy of "Sources of Tourist Information on Foreign Countries," available from the U.S. Department of Commerce, U.S. Travel Service, Washington, DC 20030. This publication gives the addresses of all the foreign government tourist information offices located in the United States. Just a letter to any of these offices will bring you a substantial assortment of information on the country and its tourist attractions, and any visa or vaccination requirements.

Another useful piece of literature for your travel library is the U.S. Customs Bureau publication, "Know Before You Go," available free from your local customs office. This booklet gives the basic information the international traveler needs on what can and cannot be brought back into the country, what the limits are on duty-free purchases, and what papers and identification you will need for smooth passage coming and going.

Tourism is also a big business within the United States, and each of the states and many cities have free brochures that cover their own local attractions.

Write to the state information office in the state capital for information.

If you write to a specific hotel for accommodations, don't forget to ask for off-season rates as well as special senior citizen discounts. These sometimes substantial savings could be a major factor in your future vacation plans.

Travel Agents

Most of the services a travel agent performs, including arranging your transportation and hotel accommodations, are done without charge to you. The agent is being paid a percentage of your total bill by the airline or hotel, and his commission will be larger if your arrangements are more expensive. However, if you want a special package prepared to your individual specifications, you will generally have to pay for the agent's expertise.

Even if you are willing to pay whatever is required, it is better to do some research before you approach an agent. If you present him or her with some definite goals you have in mind, whether it's a particular country or just a climate or activity you like, there will be a greater likelihood that the agent will be able to plan a tour that will fulfill your specific desires.

Be sure you find a reliable travel agent. Ask for recommendations from satisfied, well-traveled friends and neighbors, and check to see if the agent you choose belongs to the American Society of Travel Agents (ASTA), the major national trade association in the field.

Group Bargains

Nearly every organization has some program that provides special group travel rates. Whether it's a fraternal order like the Elks, a labor union, a church group, a trade association, or a club, their group arrangements can save you lots of money and give you a set of traveling companions who share your interests.

Ask an officer in any organization you now belong to whether there is a travel committee. If there isn't, you might be able to start one and have a say in choosing future destinations.

Or you could join an organization specifically to help make your future travel plans more successful. Ask about the travel activities of local community groups and civic organizations, and don't forget the organizations that deal with retirement, such as the American Association of Retired Persons. Their active travel service is geared to the needs of older people.

*   *   *

Experiment Now

Instead of just looking ahead to the days when you can travel at your leisure, why not begin to take some minivacations right now? If you plan your current trips with your retirement in mind, you will be exploring now for future, more elaborate journeys.

Perhaps you are thinking of going camping. If you've never tried it before, or haven't done it in years, set aside a two- or three-day weekend and choose a campsite near your home. Read a guide to camping beforehand, rent the equipment you need, and consider going with some friends who are experienced campers. The brief taste may confirm your interest, or it may convince you that another travel plan might suit you better.

Experiment with accommodations, activities, and means of transportation. Even if some of your experiments are out-and-out disasters, you'll get the satisfaction and sense of adventure which comes from trying something new. With luck, you'll discover new, exciting investments for your retirement time.

When you have a pretty good idea of your travel preferences, you can start long-term planning. And do keep in mind the following considerations:

- *Language.* If you are thinking about visiting foreign countries, you might want to pick up the basics of the local language before you get there. Take a conversational language course so that you will have enough background to understand what is going on around you. Ask your librarian about the availability of recorded language courses which you could take home and study.
- *Passport.* A United States passport is required for travel to most foreign countries. You can get an application from the passport agent in most cities, a clerk at a federal or state court, or at many post offices. You must present the completed form along with proof of citizenship, two photographs of the correct size and pose, and a small fee; your passport will be mailed to you within a few weeks. If you are planning

an overseas trip, make sure to mail in your documents early to allow for any occasional slipups in the bureaucratic process. A passport is good for five years and easily renewed by mail.

- *Insurance.* Check with your insurance broker about the extent of your coverage when you are traveling. This is especially important when it comes to health insurance, where there are often strict limitations on paying for illnesses contracted outside this country. Medicare does not cover you outside the United States. There are policies to fill the gap, though, and your broker will provide you with details.

- *Travel Companions.* If you have no spouse, you should consider looking for a suitable travel companion, especially if you are trying to save money. All the attractive prices quoted in the travel literature are based on "double occupancy," meaning that two people will be sharing the room. The price goes up substantially for a single.

- *Medical Considerations.* If you have any physical problems, ask your doctor's opinion on your travel plans before making elaborate arrangements. With today's convenient forms of transportation, there are few conditions that would prohibit you from traveling. You may want to stock up on any special medications you require, particularly if your digestive system might be offended by unusual cuisines. Carry with you a copy of any prescriptions you are now taking, with the generic name of the drug to make it easily recognizable for any pharmacist. Take a copy of your eyeglass prescription as well.

Even if you are severely handicapped, there are multitudes of travel possibilities available for you. Air, bus, and train lines all provide special assistance to those with difficulty getting around; call the appropriate terminal in your area to ask about these programs.

Education, the arts, and extensive traveling may fill the bill, but some people are incurable workaholics. In retirement, work—either paid or volunteer—can be an ideal leisure pursuit. The next chapter outlines some of the many alternatives.

13

YOUR SECOND CAREER:
WORK AS A
LEISURE ACTIVITY

*Work spares us from three great evils: boredom, vice, and
need.*

VOLTAIRE

WORKING TO EARN ADDITIONAL INCOME

It would be quite possible to write an entire book on job opportunities for people over fifty. Actually, with the current trends
toward greater employment opportunities for older Americans
and longer working lives, virtually all the plentiful how-to-get-a-job
books in your public library contain information that applies to your
current job-hunting needs.

What I intend to do here, then, is offer suggestions on how you
can best use the preretirement planning period to prepare a moneymaking form of employment which will fit your retirement needs.

You might want to make this change as soon as you can exercise an early retirement option, or when you reach mandatory retirement age, or simply whenever you no longer want to be a part of the job market as a full-time worker, but still want or need some form of gainful employment.

You have only two disadvantages in working past your sixtieth birthday: your real physical limitations, and popular predudice.

As for the first problem, you should refuse to underestimate your own abilities when looking for a situation that fits your physical prowess. Heavy physical labor has become such a rare requirement in the labor force of modern industrial society that physical strength or speed are now virtually irrelevant to most of the appealing jobs on the market.

The fact that *we* all may know this does not help when it comes to encountering the prejudicial attitudes that may stand between you and continued success as an employee. Public attitudes are becoming somewhat more enlightened, but discriminatory hiring practices have not yet been substantially eliminated. You can fight the prejudice through political action if you so choose. But your personal strategy must be to accept the fact that you—a bright, intelligent, able older person—are going to have more trouble getting a job than your younger colleague. Remember, though, that you have an enormous advantage over many of the older Americans who presently cannot find work—you are planning your future in advance and can build each talent, ability, asset, and experience you have into improved earning potential.

You can always set up your own business when you retire. If you are your own boss, you know that nobody is going to fire you in favor of a younger, less experienced person who'll work for half your salary. However, the perils of self-employment are considerable, and it is certainly less of a headache to remain gainfully employed and leave the responsibilities of owning a company to someone else.

*   *   *

Building a Future from Your Present Job

You can use your current position as a basis for your future employment stance. First, determine whether you want to stay with your present company. To make this decision, ask yourself the following questions:

1. Do I have a legal right to keep my position?

The new law (January 1, 1979) concerning mandatory retirement pushed the minimum legal age at which most companies can force you to retire from sixty-five to seventy. There are significant exceptions, including anyone working in a company with fewer than twenty employees, executives with an annual pension exceeding $27,000, tenured university professors, and certain job categories where age is considered an occupational qualification. Speak to your personnel department and be sure that you understand the pertinent mandatory retirement policy. If you are a federal employee, you can probably relax—there is a mandatory retirement age for only a handful of positions.

2. How will getting older affect my position in the company?

Even though you can't be fired, there's no guarantee that your working conditions won't change in ways which will make your position uncomfortable—possibly untenable.

What do you enjoy about your job? Will that necessarily change in the future? If the challenge of moving up is a major part of your work satisfaction, if you find fulfillment in learning on the job, you will want to avoid a situation where management pushes you out of the mainstream of company movement.

Similarly, if the social aspect of your job is important to you, take a good look at the position you'll hold as an older worker. In some companies, the number of workers over sixty-five is very small, and the younger people may not accept them as equals on a social level.

The only accurate way to assess your future in your present company is to look at the way older workers are currently treated. The time to recognize a potentially disastrous situation is now, when you are young enough to get the most from your situation and then leave with your self-esteem intact and your next moves carefully planned.

3. Will my company be flexible about my changing needs?

What provisions does your company make for part-time work for older employees if they want to cut back on their weekly hours? If the company does utilize part-time help, how much are they paid, and what benefits do they receive?

Businesses have expanded their use of part-time help in the past decade, and these experiments have shown some very positive results. There have been several innovative attempts to make the work week more efficient for both employer and employee, including:

- *Flexitime,* requiring all workers to spend a certain core period together and allowing them to distribute the rest of their work hours at their convenience.
- *Job sharing,* allowing two workers to split the hours and responsibilities of a full-time job between them.
- *Flexible location policies,* allowing part of the week's work to be done at home, when possible.
- *Shortened work week,* permitting employees to work more hours per day for less than five days, eliminating extra time and expense in traveling and permitting more full days off.
- *Increasing use of part-time workers* to handle excess workloads, reducing demands by employers for potentially exhausting overtime commitments. This situation could be especially important to you if you are drawing Social Security benefits while you work, since exceeding the earning limitation will cut down on your government check.

If you are lucky enough to be employed by an enlightened company, you might be able to design your own job role. This would make you feel comfortable in ''retirement'' and let management know how you can help them by remaining with the company.

Creating your own position requires planning well in advance of your retirement date, using your imagination to design a job which will benefit both your employer and yourself, and using your best salesmanship to put the idea over to your superiors. Perhaps you could come in as a part-time consultant—twice a week, or twice a month, or whatever fits your needs—to give advice on problem situations.

Getting What You Can and Leaving

If your company will not fill your future employment needs, you can still use your present situation to make your next work experience successful.

Use Your Pension. First, of course, you must understand your pension plan and how your benefits will vary depending on your actions. Your strategy for a new job may rest on the answer to the following questions:

- *How much will I receive if I leave earlier than mandatory retirement age?* Many companies have arranged their pension programs so that older workers get the incentive to leave early. If you are covered by such a plan, it may pay to take the money and run—to a more inviting job opportunity somewhere else.
- *How will the total benefit be affected by the way in which I take payment?* If you need capital to start a new business, you might prefer a lump sum payment of your pension. If your future plans include a form of employment which does not require much initial investment but offers no guarantee of regular payment (selling on commission, marketing your craft work, etc.), then a regular monthly check might be a welcome source of security. Be sure you fully understand the options available and the effect your decisions will have on your tax situation.

Use Your Training Opportunities. There are some companies that will pay for courses you take to enable you to find a new job or start your own business as part of their preretirement counseling program. Others are obligated to pay for job-related training; you should check with your personnel department to see if you are eligible to take advantage of this contract provision.

By keeping your eyes open to your future needs, you may be able to steer your career in a direction you can follow after you leave the company. For instance, you might be able to shift into a sales position in your present company if you are interested in selling as a retirement career, or try for a slot in the public relations department if the idea of doing part-time p.r. work later on appeals to you. You may be able to learn how to program a computer, correspond with customers, make purchasing decisions, or plan investment strategies while serving your employer's interests at the same time.

Develop Your Contacts. There are many times in your professional life when *who* you know truly is just as important as *what* you know. Be sure that you are not letting valuable connections slip through your fingers. If your business dealings put you in touch with people who potentially could do you some good, make sure they know your name and what your particular skill is. The people with whom you do business outside your company clearly have some need for services in your field of expertise. Perhaps when the time comes you can offer them the opportunity to employ someone with your proven abilities.

As you get close to your retirement day, don't hesitate to let others in your company know that you would like to find another job. Through their business contacts, they may know of a company which would be interested in someone with your background. If you are a good worker, anyone who recommends you for a position is doing another company a favor by providing them with a talented addition to their work force.

Start a New Career in Your Free Time. In other words, moonlight. Labor unions and management may frown, but it is still your right to get a second job if you want one, and with retirement approaching, there is no better way to investigate the opportunities available. If you are considering working as a salesperson when you leave your present job, it should be easy to find a weekend or evening position in the meantime. That way, you can test the waters in a different field to see if you like it, make contacts and secure a future position before you need it, and make a little extra money to add to your retirement nest egg.

Finding a New Job

When it comes to finding a job in your sixties or beyond, all the basic rules you followed throughout your professional life still apply. A resumé is still a resumé, and an interview is still an interview. However, there are certain key issues which are especially relevant to you as an older worker. Try to take a realistic outlook on the following questions:

- *How much money do I want or need to earn?* As I mentioned earlier, the combination of losing part of your Social Security benefits and substituting taxable income may make working to earn a moderate salary uneconomical. If this is the case for you, you might consider alternative ways of using your time, such as volunteer work or increased leisure pursuits, or ways in which you can increase your unearned income.

- *How much responsibility do I want?* If you find satisfaction in holding down a key position in an organization, by all means look for a job where there are decisions to be made. Many retirees prefer to take jobs which will let them enjoy the pleasures of a working environment, earn enough to supplement their other sources of income, but remain free of the pressures which accompany a position of major responsibility. The point is that your employment in your later years should fill your own needs, not some set of expectations you feel other people may have for you.

- *Do I have the skills I need?* If you don't have all the resources and abilities you plan to offer an employer, or feel that your skills might be a bit rusty, you can always take a brushup course in an office or technical skill, practice at home, or enroll in a program to teach you about an entirely new field. It's also conceivable that the company you apply to may offer some training.

- *How convenient can my new job be?* Retirement is the time of life when you can try to make your work conform to your other needs. Now you can take the time to look around at the job possibilities which are located where you want them, and occupy just as many hours as you choose to spend each week. Investigate the requirements and benefits of attractive positions well in advance of your retirement, to increase your chances of finding the one job which fills the greatest number of your personal preferences.

Getting the Job

Once you know what kind of job you want, how are you going to get it?

- *Want ads*. The ads will give you a feeling for the job opportunities and pay scale in your area, and you may find a listing which seems to be directed right at you.
- *Employment agencies*. An older person looking for temporary work is a prime candidate for a private temporary employment agency, particularly if your office skills are up to par. These agencies specialize in filling short-term assignments, and retirees who are looking for occasional work to supplement their incomes should be able to get a fairly steady stream of varied jobs. If the employer is impressed with your performance as a temporary worker, he may offer you a permanent position.

  As for finding a permanent job through a private employment agency, you are just one of the crowd, and in a business which makes a profit by rapidly placing as many people as possible, you can't expect much in the way of personal counseling or understanding of special requirements. There are, however, certain agencies which specialize in placing older workers, and you can find them by looking through the Yellow Pages. In some major cities you will find branches of Mature Temps, a commercial agency which has been extremely successful in placing older (not necessarily retired) workers in temporary jobs, and now has thirteen offices across the country. On a smaller scale there are employment services and job banks for seniors in cities like West Hartford, Connecticut, Boise, Idaho, Lebanon, Ohio, and Vancouver, Washington, serving interested older workers on the city or county level.

Be sure to read any contract which is presented to you when dealing with private employment agencies. Understand whether you or the employer will be paying the agency commission. If you don't like what you read, don't sign.

- *State employment services.* These state agencies are a good source not only for specific job leads but for counseling and information as well. The state employment services have in recent years increased their concern for helping older workers seeking employment and can now give you a good picture of your local job picture. They will know about any federal or state government programs, and the special employment agencies, both profit and nonprofit, which deal specifically with older workers in your area.

- *Schools and trade associations.* If you are a college graduate, your alma mater may have a placement service for its alumni. If the program was initiated after you graduated, you may not even be aware of its existence, so call the office to check out the possibility.

  If you belong to a professional association, or are looking for work in a field which has one, the association may be able to help you. For certain professional positions, like selling real estate or becoming a travel agent, you must contact these associations long before you hope to begin practicing, since there are training and licensing requirements in these fields. To locate the association in any given field, check the *Encyclopedia of Associations* (published by Gale Research), which you will find in the reference section of your public library.

- *Personal contacts.* I have already mentioned building up your business contacts while you are working at your present job. It is worth speaking to nonbusiness contacts as well, whether they are family or friends, friends of friends, or members of clubs or organizations to which you belong. It is important to reach the people who do the hiring, and not just deal with the personnel department. The contacts you already have may help you to achieve this aim. If not, then find out who *does* control the hiring, and write to that person directly. You may be able to win a person in a position of power over to your side, gain a crucial interview, and establish a personal rapport which could pay off in the form of serious consideration for a future position.

Presenting Yourself Well. You have been indoctrinated to believe that older workers are less competent, less desirable, and less welcome in the job market, so it's easy to let yourself feel that you are licked before you even begin. But, as I stressed earlier, the reality of aging is that older people exhibit high productivity and high overall abilities. By looking for work now, you are part of the wave of the future, an example of a definite positive trend toward Americans working longer, continuing to be self-sufficient, and contributing to the general health of the economy.

Age Discrimination

It is against the law for you to be fired, denied a job, denied a promotion, or demoted because of your age, and that protection now extends to your seventieth birthday. As with any other kinds of discrimination, though, it is difficult to prove the reasons behind a company's actions; thus it is hard to win a legal battle against a former employer. If you feel strongly that you have been wronged strictly because of your age, you can fight. The Equal Employment Opportunity Commission, a branch of the federal government, will explain your rights to you if you contact the nearest office. You may also get some help from the Age Discrimination Project of the American Association of Retired Persons, located at 1909 K Street NW, Washington, DC 20049.

If you feel you have a reasonable complaint, you should protest, especially if your pension benefits are jeopardized by the company's unfair action. But do go on with your life at the same time. If the case is decided in your favor, you may be eligible for back pay and reinstatement, but these proceedings can drag on interminably. In the meantime, go out and find yourself a new position, one in which your services are valued. Then if the wheels of justice grind out a decision in your favor, you will have won two victories.

Self-Employment

If you have toyed with the idea of becoming your own boss, then your changing financial needs may provide the perfect atmosphere for fulfilling that ambition. When you work for yourself, you want to make the greatest possible profit with the least possible risk and get enjoyment from your employment. There are agencies and individuals who can help you find success in your new enterprise, but the most important factors determining the future of your business adventure are your own personal attributes.

Do you have what it takes to be your own boss? Rate yourself honestly in the following areas:

- initiative
- positive, pleasant attitude
- leadership ability
- organizing ability
- industry
- responsibility
- ability to make quick, accurate decisions
- sincerity
- perseverance
- high level of physical energy

These are the ten personal qualities which the Small Business Administration suggests are essential for succeeding in a business of your own. To these I would add:

- Courage to face the uncertainty of income and the possibility of losing whatever initial investment the business requires.
- Intelligence to learn how to run a company, manage money, deal with legal and taxation problems, and make the product or service you offer competitive in price and quality with the others on the market.

Getting Help. Even if you intend to become a one-person company, you can't do it all by yourself. You will need advice from your professional colleagues, your lawyer, and your accountant, to help you operate within the appropriate local laws and keep the financial risks involved to a reasonable level.

The first place to turn is the Small Business Administration. In offices located all over the country, the SBA offers free personal advice along with dozens of relevant publications which explain exactly what you will need to know to start your business off on the right foot.

With the help of these sources and your own good judgment, ask yourself the following questions:

- *How much risk will my project involve, and can I afford it?* Even if your plans are to produce an inexpensive item and sell it locally, with little overhead expense, you are still gambling when it comes to bringing in a steady income. And if you do invest substantial capital in starting a business—buying into a franchise operation, say, or opening up a small shop—you will have to consider the possibility of losing not only the sum you invest but the profit you would have made if that capital had been placed elsewhere, in bonds or savings certificates, for example.

  Investigate the business you are considering thoroughly and begin on a small scale. Do your research early, start your business while you are still receiving an income from your first career, and you can build a successful enterprise by using your profits to increase the scope of your sales or services.

  Think profits while minimizing personal risk—you can incorporate, or form a partnership or other legal forms of business organization. For instance, if you include your spouse in your business and arrange a salary for both of you, each of you would be entitled to receive the maximum individual amount of earned income permissible before the Social Security benefits of either of you are affected. Discuss this and other personal financial strategies with your accountant or your lawyer or both.

- *How can I advertise my goods or services most effectively?*
- *What are my best sources for supplies?*
- *Where can I best buy the goods I plan to sell?*
- *Where is the best location for my business?*
- *What is the most efficient way to run my business?*

Look through catalogues to price supplies, speak to wholesalers, check out areas in which you are thinking of setting up shop, and investigate the advertising media available to you. You should consider taking out inexpensive ads in local newspapers or newsletters, distributing fliers, mailing out announcements and, of course, getting a word-of-mouth campaign started.

The best possible way to discover the potential pitfalls in your self-employment scheme is to speak to someone who has done it. If the business you are considering is a large-scale affair, you not only should request advice from the owner of a similar, established firm but should take a job if possible and learn what it looks like from the inside.

- *Where will I get the money to finance my venture?* The Small Business Administration not only has special expertise in this area, but power to assist you as well. Part of the SBA's job is to help find the money to get small ventures on their feet and keep them there. You may be able to secure a loan through the SBA itself, or through a combination of SBA and commercial financing, if you meet their criteria. Contact your local SBA office for further information.

Selling Your Wares. The key to finding a product to make and sell is to keep your eyes open for items that are currently purchased from sources other than big corporations; that you can make yourself with a reasonably small extra investment in tools, materials, or training; that you can improve on in some way, either in quality, design, appearance or price; and that are not already available in such great supply that the market is glutted.

When investigating the market, be sure to consider all the potential customers for your product, including not only the general public but businesses and institutions as well. For the talented ceramics enthusiast this could mean offering to design and produce distinctive, handmade coffee mugs for a local café. The artist who works with mosaic tiles could approach a local school board and propose to construct a mural.

These are a variety of ways to present your goods for sale to the general public.

- *Direct Sales.* Attracting customers can be as simple as showing your friends and neighbors your product and letting their enthusiasm create a word-of-mouth advertising campaign for you. It doesn't cost much to print fliers to be stuffed into mailboxes, or to take out a small ad in the local paper.

  If what you are offering can in any way be construed as a gift item, try to focus your attention on the pre-Christmas rush or on a specific time of the year. An advantage of offering an item with seasonal interest, whether it is for a holiday or for the warm- or cold-weather months, is that you can concentrate your selling efforts in a short period of time and leave yourself free at other times to build up your inventory.

  One way to sell a lot in a short period of time is to organize sales parties in your home. Tupperware parties have been extraordinarily successful all over the nation. One New Jersey retiree I know raises houseplants in her small greenhouse; when she has enough plants on hand, she invites her neighbors and friends to a plant party. She provides a few simple refreshments, displays her wares attractively in her backyard, and regularly clears out her leafy inventory in a single afternoon.

  There may also be organized gatherings that will draw an audience for your product. The flea market phenomenon has become a regular ritual with bargain hunters across the country. If you can find a flea market which offers space at a reasonable price, you stand a good chance of turning a profit there. Be sure to inquire about the future plans of church groups, school groups, and other local organizations for crafts fairs, flea markets, and bazaars.

- *Mail Order*. With the right product, a mail order business can be the best vehicle for selling your work. You are free to deal with the customers when it is convenient for you, and you can attract a national clientele with a single advertisement. You can start small, in your spare time while you are still working, and build up a mailing list of customers and an expertise in effectively advertising your goods without running much risk.

  Selling by mail can be somewhat complicated, however. There are regulations governing procedures for selling through the mail, as well as questions of tax collection and postal regulations. The Small Business Administration has several useful booklets that will explain the procedure for starting a mail order business.

- *Finding a Middleman*. If the thought of selling has no appeal to you, you should look into the possibility of having a local merchant sell your work in his shop. The best arrangement is to have the shopkeeper buy your work outright, pay you directly, and reorder when he needs to. As a beginning producer, though, you are unlikely to find a shop willing to deal on this basis. At the very least, you will probably have to offer to accept returns of unsold goods for a full or partial refund.

  A better way to get your product into a store initially is to offer to sell on consignment. This means that the storekeeper agrees to display your work and, if it sells, to pass the proceeds on to you, after he has taken his cut. The shop's profit on the sale should be no more than thirty to thirty-five percent. If the owner tells you he feels he has a good chance of selling your goods, it is probably worth a try. Just keep in mind that the price you set for your item must include not only your own costs, your profit, and the store's commission, but also a generous allowance for unsold merchandise and damaged, unsalable goods.

Some communities have shops that specialize in selling on commission, particularly those run by local organizations to benefit not only the sponsoring group's coffers but the crafts-people and artisans as well.

Selling Your Services. Your skills and abilities may be a valuable community resource. The retired bookkeeper can find local businesses that need occasional help with their financial records, and the advertising copywriter can put together a newspaper ad for a neighborhood store from time to time. But even if you don't have the type of professional skills that lend themselves to free-lance assignments in the business world, there are many, more general moneymaking opportunities available.

The key to setting yourself up in a personal service business—selling your problem-solving abilities or consulting skills—is to hit upon an idea that meets the specific needs of your neighbors. Take a look at the kind of people around you and try to spot the niche in their lives which you could fill. Could the college students in your neighborhood use your sewing talents on their popped buttons and ripped hems? Would working women welcome your offer to tend their children after school until they get home from the job? Are there enough pet owners in your vicinity who take vacations to support you in a dog-and-cat-sitting operation?

You can advertise your services in much the same way as you would your homemade items. Be sure to consult your lawyer first, and perhaps your insurance broker as well, as to your legal liability.

The following is a list of just a few of the services you might consider. Even if none of them strikes a responsive chord for you, they might help stimulate your thinking.

- Child care—newborn baby nursing, babysitting, day care (check licensing requirements in your state).
- Cleaning—homes, venetian blinds, rugs, etc.
- Consulting—offering businessmen advice based on your experience in the same or a similar field.

- Delivery service—making local deliveries to customers for several local shops.
- Proofreading—for newspapers, magazines, journals, or book publishers in your area.
- Repairing—radios, televisions, appliances.
- Refinishing—furniture, toys, etc.
- Sewing—tailoring, repairs.
- Sitting of all sorts—watching homes, pets, plants, etc., in owners' absence.
- Tax preparation—there are courses to teach you how to prepare other people's returns.
- Tutoring—foreign languages, academic subjects, crafts, hobby skills, etc.
- Typing—college students' papers, authors' manuscripts, etc.

Setting Up Shop. Should you open up your own store? Two out of ten new small businesses fail in the first year. Another two go under in the second year. By the third year, half are gone, and by the fifth year, only four out of ten survive.

Of course there are successes, and you may find yourself in that happy minority, but you will have to put in a great deal of money and time to get there. You will need enough initial capital to buy stock, refurbish a store, and pay the rent for about two years before you can expect it to start paying for itself. You will have to put in hours and hours of hard work—sixty hours a week is a conservative estimate for a retail business in the first years; it is generally more like seventy or eighty.

Is that what you want for your "retirement"? It might be, if you are planning to set up shop in your mid fifties and continue working for fifteen or twenty more years, or if this will be a family venture and your children and grandchildren will be involved with you.

If you are absolutely dedicated to making a go of it, you must protect yourself by learning everything there is to know about your proposed venture before you get in too deeply.

Your local SBA office can provide you with information and suggest courses of study which will prove extremely useful to you as a small businessman. You may also find valuable free advice on running your business through the Service Corps of Retired Executives (SCORE) or the Active Corps of Executives (ACE), both SBA programs, in which professional businessmen volunteer their time and knowledge to analyze struggling new businesses and help solve the problems which may occur. You can also help yourself immeasurably by working in someone else's similar business to get the day-to-day experience.

If you decide to take a shortcut—buying an existing operation or a franchise—you will still have to expend about the same effort as you would if you had started your business from scratch. Buying someone else's business, though, may provide you with established customers and reputation, a viable location, and a store which is properly set up. After you have proved to yourself that you can run the enterprise, you must ask why the owner is trying to sell. It could be that he wants to retire, or move on, or whatever. It might also be that the buying population of the neighborhood is changing, or major competition has entered the area recently, or the store has actually acquired a *bad* reputation over the years. Have your accountant go over the business's financial records very carefully, and then go on and do some detective work on your own. Speak to neighboring store owners, ask people where they buy their goods, talk to the local Chamber of Commerce, and watch the daily operation of the present owner firsthand.

Buying into a franchise is another possibility. You will get some of the same advantages this way as you would if you bought an existing store. You benefit from the advertising campaigns of the franchiser, so that your customers have immediate recognition of your store name and a good idea of what you sell. The franchiser also provides advice and assistance in finding a location, setting up the facilities, providing the merchandise to be sold, and running the business. All of this doesn't come cheap—the minimum equity capital required for a McDonald's franchise is about $100,000.

Of course, there are hundreds of franchises available in dozens of different fields for much smaller investments. You can become a franchised dealer in automotive products, shoes or clothing, cosmetics, foods, lawn and garden supplies, pets, paints, security systems, and swimming pools, to name just a few. A useful guide is *A Business of Your Own: Franchise Opportunities* (Sterling, 1980. Paperback, $7.95) which provides a listing of several hundred companies in the franchise business, with a basic description of their operations, the number of franchises currently operating, the amount of capital you'll need, any financial assistance available through the franchiser, and the services you can expect from the company. The introductory section is particularly helpful because it explains how to protect yourself if you are considering buying a franchise. Your Small Business Administration can also advise you in this area.

VOLUNTEERING

If you have arranged your financial resources so that you don't *have* to earn money in retirement, then you have paved the way for one of the most potentially rewarding experiences there is—volunteering your time for a worthwhile cause. You will be using your valuable skills, giving your time, taking on responsibility, and making commitments, and you will be reimbursed for your time and effort with the kind of emotional satisfaction that is all but unattainable through conventional employment. You will gain a sense of accomplishment and self-assertion by reaching out to others and touching their lives in a positive, meaningful way. Perhaps most crucial to the retiree who does volunteer work is the strong, invigorating sense of being needed.

Roy and Mary Louise Wilson have found a full measure of personal satisfaction in their volunteer activities. Roy holds a doctorate in chemical engineering and worked for over thirty-five years for Standard Oil, before moving on to teach chemistry at Central Washington State University. Mary's background is also in academia; she taught mathematics at Central Washington State and at Purdue University.

When they retired to Sun City, a large retirement community in

Arizona, they were actively seeking a new avenue for their energies and abilities. They had contacted VISTA, a federal program which coordinates volunteer activities in the United States (see page 328) and considered some sort of involvement with the local Indian population. With the help of VISTA they found their opportunity through a local church, which put them in contact with the Southwest Indian School, a nonsectarian Christian school located only a few miles from their new home.

Since that time, about nine years ago, the Wilsons have played an important role in the education of Indian children. They both teach and tutor math, and Roy even pitched in with some carpentry work on a new building at the school.

What do the Wilsons get for all of their hard work and dedication? They have the opportunity to employ the knowledge gained in a lifetime of learning, in an atmosphere where their expertise is appreciated. They expand their own understanding of the world by learning about a different culture firsthand. They have become personally involved—they even went so far as to sponsor one of their students, helping him to meet his expenses and driving him to his new college in Kentucky. The fringe benefits of this sort of volunteer arrangement are limitless.

You don't have to be highly trained or skilled to make an enormously valuable contribution as a volunteer. There are openings in schools, hospitals, museums, charitable organizations, and political groups that will make use of precisely the amount of time and talent you can bring to the job.

Planning Your Volunteer Activities

One way to help ensure a successful volunteer commitment is to do your research early. Some programs pay expenses, some train you, and some allow for travel, while others are neighborhood undertakings. In a few select cases, such as the Peace Corps, there are waiting lists for willing volunteers, and it is necessary to apply early. But there are numerous organizations that always need your help—

whether to wipe out a particular disease, elect a specific candidate, aid the poor and unfortunate, or spruce up your community.

The ideal approach is to get a taste of what volunteer work is like now, by getting involved in your spare time. By making a long-term commitment to a group, you can qualify for a leadership position in the organization when you retire and have more time available, if this suits your purposes. And of course, whatever the scale of your involvement now, the sense of fulfillment which comes from giving will provide a welcome balance to the commercial concerns which may dominate your working life.

Where Are You Needed? On a local level, the following groups and organizations will be interested in hearing from you:

- *Volunteer bureaus.* There are numerous central offices across the country which provide information on volunteer programs. To get in touch with a volunteer bureau in your area, contact the National Center for Voluntary Action at 1214 16th Street NW, Washington, DC 20036 (phone 202-467-5560). This center will have a wide range of options to suggest, based on your personal interests, abilities, and willingness to donate your time.
- *Community social service organizations.* You can contact groups in your area involved in charitable work by checking in your telephone directory under headings such as "Social Service Organizations."
- *Church groups.* Not only do churches and synagogues sponsor volunteer work on their own, but they frequently serve as a clearinghouse for outside programs.
- *Schools.* If you are interested in tutoring or otherwise assisting schoolchildren, contact your local board of education and find out if they have a program utilizing community volunteers.
- *Cultural institutions.* If you wish to volunteer at a museum, a concert facility, a theater group, a public television station, or some other organization, contact them directly. There are many jobs, such as serving as a tour guide, helping out at a gift shop, or helping with fund raising, which may be filled by unpaid staff members. If you can think of a way in which

your personal talent could be put to use, by all means suggest it, even if it is not something which is now being done.

- *Hospitals*. Volunteers are such an integral part of the running of a hospital that you are sure to be welcome, even if you don't feel your skills are very strong. If you can care about other people, sympathize, smile, assist in the simple tasks which are often difficult for the infirm, and find pride and satisfaction in easing pain for others, then hospital volunteer work is for you. Contact the social services supervisor or volunteer coordinator of a hospital near you.

- *Political action*. This can entail anything from working with one of the major political parties to joining an activist group which espouses a specific cause. You may well have to start out stuffing envelopes or canvassing for public opinions, but individuals with the right personal characteristics and a suitable degree of commitment can work their way up to policy-making positions.

And you can never tell where your political involvement will lead. Just ask Oliver V. Phillips, the soft-spoken mayor of Wheat Ridge, Colorado.

Mr. Phillips is blessed with the fertile mind of the inventor—nearly twenty patents have been issued in his name, but that's just the tip of the iceberg. Throughout his working career he used his ingenious problem-solving abilities in aviation (he developed the first electronic altimeter), oil exploration, and related technical fields. His production of inventive products and processes is still prolific—when we met him, he had just finished testing a new carburetor design for automobiles and was eagerly awaiting receipt of the patent. But when he retired, his involvement unexpectedly spread out of the workshop and into the political arena.

Oliver Phillips is a dedicated resident of his Denver suburb, and when he saw it threatened by an ill-advised land development scheme, he and a group of friends set out to see whether a plain old citizen had a say in his town government or not. It seems that an out-of-state development company had purchased a 400-acre plot, including the land comprising Wheat Ridge cemetery, and planned to build a multimillion-dollar shopping center there. The town council, interested only in the sales tax they were going to get from the shops, turned deaf ears to community residents who protested that the project would cost the city a fortune in utilities, sewers, water mains, roads, etc., and wouldn't even pay its own way.

"Couldn't reason with them," Mr. Phillips remembers, so he and a group of concerned citizens set out to gather data. They discovered that the development firm had no real money behind it but planned to carve up the property into separate units and sell them off individually. It took two years of battling, but Phillips's group won on the zoning decision. Since that time, Wheat Ridge and its sister city of Lakewood have bought the property, and it's going to be a park.

Eventually the community drafted Phillips to run for mayor of Wheat Ridge. "I'm just not a politician," he protested. But as the campaign progressed he saw his chances steadily improving. He won the election to the part-time position of mayor at the age of sixty-five.

The infectious enthusiasm which animated Oliver Phillips's recounting of his exploits in the political sphere at least equaled the pleasure he took in describing his earlier career experiences in aviation and industry. His retirement allowed him to devote more time to the needs of his community—and both the man and the community have benefited. Perhaps you, too, have the ability and drive to make your mark in the way your government is run.

Older Americans have a good deal of political clout, and this makes you an especially valuable member of any organization that hopes to win votes or sway public opinion. A larger percentage of older people go out and vote than any other age group—in the 1976 presidential election, 67 percent of eligible voters over age sixty-five went to the polls, as opposed to 45 percent of the general voting population. As the older segment of the population grows, the ballot counters and opinion pollers are finding the needs of older Americans more and more prominently represented on their tally sheets.

One of the organizations that works for the rights of the aging (which, they are quick to point out, includes each of us) is the activist group, the Gray Panthers. The organization, organized in 1970, filled a substantial void with action in areas such as health care, housing, poverty, employment, women's rights, and minority rights. Today's membership represents all sides of the age, sex, race, and religion spectrum. There are local chapters throughout the country, and a national office at 3700 Chestnut Street, Philadelphia, PA 19104.

ACTION PROGRAMS

Several of the most popular national programs are run under the aegis of ACTION, the federal agency that coordinates major volunteer efforts. Your expenses are paid in each of the ACTION programs, and for individuals in a low-income bracket there are two service agencies—Foster Grandparent Program and Senior Companions—that offer a small salary. For further information on the ACTION programs, write to ACTION, 806 Connecticut Avenue NW, Washington, DC 20525, or call, toll-free, 800-424-8580.

- *Peace Corps*. Peace Corps volunteers work in developing foreign countries, teaching in technical and nontechnical fields including education, agriculture, health, and engineering. Volunteers serve a two-year, full-time stint, receive training in the language and culture of the country in which they will serve, and receive a $125-per-month readjustment allowance for each month of service when they return to the United States, as well as reimbursement for their expenses abroad.

  In recent years a larger percentage of Peace Corps members have been over fifty-five than ever before—up from only about 1 percent in 1966 to 5 percent in 1979. Lillian Carter joined the Peace Corps at age sixty-eight and served in India, teaching birth control techniques. If you have a valuable skill and want to see foreign lands as an insider rather than as a tourist, the Peace Corps could be for you.

- *VISTA (Volunteers in Service to America)*. VISTA, the domestic counterpart of the Peace Corps, works in social services, education and health, housing, community planning, and economic development to help fight poverty. Volunteers serve full time for one or two years, after a three-to-five-week training period. VISTA furnishes housing, living allowances, personal expenses, and a readjustment allowance of $75 for each month of service at the end of your commitment.

Here, too, older Americans are becoming an increasingly large segment of the volunteer ranks. Thirteen percent of the VISTA force were over fifty in 1979, more than double the figure of a decade earlier.

- *RSVP (Retired Senior Volunteer Program)*. The RSVP program calls for a part-time commitment within your own community, and is open only to those sixty or older. The services provided in each local area vary widely, including assistance to educational institutions, health care facilities, and various community service organizations.
- *Foster Grandparent Program*. Volunteers spend twenty hours each week providing love, friendship, and companionship to troubled children in hospitals and institutions. Open to people over sixty with low incomes, the program offers a modest stipend along with training in counseling techniques, and the opportunity to help someone who really needs you.
- *Senior Companion Program*. Similar in requirements and payment to the Foster Grandparent Program but aimed at serving the needs of elderly people.

BUSINESS PROGRAMS

- SCORE (Service Corps of Retired Executives) for retirees, and ACE (Active Corps of Executives) are two likely programs for retired (or soon-to-be-retired) executives. They are sponsored by the Small Business Administration and are designed to capitalize on your skills and experience to help struggling younger businessmen. Contact your local Small Business Administration office or the national office at 1441 L Street NW, Washington, DC 20416 (202-382-1891).

NONPROFIT ORGANIZATIONS

- *The International Executive Service Corps* sends volunteers with business expertise abroad to aid foreign businesses in

THE BEST YEARS BOOK

developing countries. The assignments as management advisers generally last two or three months in such fields as food production, health care, construction methods, natural resource development, communications, and port management. The expenses for you and your spouse are reimbursed by the agency. Write to this private, nonprofit organization at 622 Third Avenue, New York, NY 10017, or call 212-490-6800.

- The following are just a few of the private, non-profit organizations operating on a national level with great needs for volunteers:

American National Red Cross
17th and D Streets SW
Washington, DC 20006
202-737-8300

Care
660 First Avenue
New York, NY 10016
212-686-3110

Federation of Protestant
  Welfare Agencies
281 Park Avenue South
New York, NY 10010
212-770-4800

National Conference of
  Catholic Charities
1346 Connecticut Avenue NW
Washington, DC 20036
202-785-2757

National School Volunteer Program
300 North Washington Street
Alexandria, VA 22314
703-836-4880

United Way of America
801 North Fairfax Street
Alexandria, VA 22314

14

CHOOSING YOUR IDEAL ENVIRONMENT: WHERE TO LIVE IN RETIREMENT

To be happy at home is the ultimate result of all ambition, the end to which every enterprise and labor tends, and of which every desire prompts the prosecution.

SAMUEL JOHNSON

O
ne of the most complex, important, and exciting decisions you will make about your retirement is where to live. You now have a pretty good idea of *how* you'd like to spend your time in retirement, so the next question is *where* to do it. The possibilities which were unthinkable when you were chained to a job or needed schools and playgrounds for the kids are suddenly viable. People can choose new, unexpected places to make their home. There are farm couples who lived in small rural communities all their lives who decided to sample city life in their sixties, and we recently met a former druggist from Brooklyn who

wakes each morning to the sound of surf pounding the shore outside his cottage on the Irish seacoast.

Ruth and I used a five-point system in looking for a place where we could put down new roots, and our search extended from Tahiti to Portugal. Since we never felt quite at home in a large city and no longer had family ties to the Midwest, we had a feeling of not having a real home, of not being rooted.

So we began to wonder about totally different places. We both liked Portugal and I liked Tahiti, but they got ruled out for various reasons.

Our five points were climate, people, water, flag, and family location. One of the reasons we chose Arizona was that it was central—at that time, I had one child in New Mexico, a brother in Dallas, and another brother in California. As for the flag, we finally concluded that we didn't want to live under another government, which ruled out Tahiti and Portugal. There are places where water is either impure or scarce. Water is healthy and plentiful in the section of Arizona we chose. People are certainly important—we wanted a nice mix. One of the reasons we like Arizona is that there's no snobbery or sense of hierarchy; there are people of various occupations and all ages. Finally, Arizona's celebrated Sonora desert fully deserves its praise. It's probably the best climate there is—it's dry, and there's year-round outdoor living. I wouldn't want to work hard in the summer sun or play tennis at noon on a 110° August day, but that would be folly anyplace. Arizona scored high on all five points. I believe everybody has to create his own "five points"—or ten, or twenty—and find the locale that fits them most closely.

The alternatives are vast—in fact, they can even be overwhelming. The sheer number of available locales leads some people to throw up their hands and eliminate many exciting ideas. Too many choices can be as bad as no choice at all if you let yourself be daunted by the difficulties of decision making. And this decision will largely determine the economic, social, leisure, personal, and family life opportunities open to you in the future.

*   *   *

THE HOUSING DECISION

Here are three keys to defusing the housing question and to making it part of the enjoyable overall process of retirement planning.

1. *Approach the decision early in the planning process, to give yourself time to consider all the possibilities.*

2. *Determine which areas of consideration are important* to you and to your spouse, and ask the right questions about the locations and types of housing available. By setting priorities together you will establish a useful framework for your explorations.

3. *Make an ongoing activity out of your research.* You are on a shopping spree that can take you around the country—around the world, if you like. Explore all appealing choices, even those that may not be exactly what you want for the long run. The decision you make today is not necessarily binding for the rest of your life. It *is* important—a move is expensive, time-consuming, and emotionally charged—but *not* irrevocable. If you move into your dream retirement home and find it not to be what you bargained for, there is almost always some way out, a new possibility to investigate.

You may be wise *not* to move immediately after retirement. Sometimes two major changes at once—leaving a job and a familiar home—can be a terrible wrench. Maybe you should wait six months or a year; maybe you should pick your new region right now and find a job there instead of waiting until you reach retirement age. But don't feel there is any pressure on you to move on a given day, or to move at all, if it doesn't suit you.

Practicality and Preference

There are several aspects to making a decision on where and how to live in retirement. Some are practical—What can I afford? Shall I continue to work? If so, do I need to remain near my present job? Others are purely a matter of taste—Will my new home be too noisy? too small? too dull? There is a necessary trade-off between the two areas, but the practical considerations lessen as economic and family responsibilities become lighter. In the end, the deciding factor will rest primarily on your personal characteristics and desires.

The first thing to do is to decide what you are looking for. The following Personal Preference Profile is to help you determine what is important to *you*—not what is hailed in a promotional brochure.

In addition to identifying your priorities, this questionnaire will help you spot the differences of opinion between your spouse and yourself. Laying your cards on the table now will prevent the too-frequent situation in which one spouse doesn't even raise a voice in protest and then is stuck in a miserable living situation.

Each of you should answer the questions individually, without conferring, and compare responses later. First go through the list quickly, jotting down your initial responses. Then, perhaps a day later, go through the questions more slowly and thoughtfully, carefully evaluating the places you have lived in the past, and what made them more or less appealing to you. You can make use of the knowledge gained from past experience and add your thoughts on the kind of retirement lifestyle that suits you, to narrow the wide range of housing choices.

Personal Preference Profile: Housing

LOCATION

1.   Do you prefer to live in a city? A suburb? A rural environment?

2.   Would you like to live near your children, grandchildren, or other relatives?

3.   Have you lived in or visited a part of the country or a foreign country where you felt particularly comfortable?

4.   Do you take pleasure in the physical beauty of the area in which you live, or are you fairly indifferent to your surroundings?

5.   Do you have a preference for a particular type of climate?

6.   Has your doctor told you that one type of climate is better for your health than another?

POPULATION

7.   Would you prefer to live in a community restricted to adults, or do you like to have children around?

8.   Are you looking for a neighborhood where a large percentage of the population is made up of people in your own religious or ethnic group, or won't that make a difference to you?

FACILITIES

9.   Are you interested in having an organized set of activities readily available?

10.   Would you prefer your privacy, without the pressure to join in?

11.   What athletic facilities are needed for your current sports interests? How about the sports you would like to try some time in the future?

12.   What spectator sports would you like to be able to attend in person?

13.   Which entertainment and cultural facilities do you frequent? Movie theaters? Concerts? Museums? Plays? Libraries?

14.   Do you plan to continue your education in retirement? If so, are you interested in attending an adult education center? A college or university?

15.   Do any of the hobbies you presently pursue, or intend to take

up, require access to special facilities? Will you need a kiln for ceramics? A library to do research? A supply store to provide parts or equipment?

16.   Is it important to you to have your meals prepared for you?

17.   How security-conscious are you? Will you feel better living in a tightly guarded environment, or will average safety precautions suffice?

ACCOMMODATIONS

18.   Would you feel cramped living in a small space, or would you welcome the freedom from housekeeping?

19.   Does a noisy environment get you on edge?

20.   Do you need extra space to pursue some of your special interests? A sewing room? A workshop? A photographic darkroom? A garden?

21.   Do you have pets? Will they be happy indoors, or do they need space to run and play?

RESPONSIBILITIES

22.   Are you willing to take on home maintenance tasks yourself?

23.   Do you need to feel free to move away or travel a lot, or are you willing to put down roots?

WORK

24.   Is it important to you to live in an area where you will be able to find full- or part-time work?

25.   Are you looking for a place where you will be able to operate a business?

Evaluating Your Personal Preference Profile

In reading through your responses to the preceding questions, you may find a clear trend taking shape. Many people, though, have to make some compromise between what they like and what is available in a single location. Someone who loves Chicago, ballet, privacy, a large living area, and snorkeling is going to have to decide on priorities—for example, saving the snorkeling for vacation and making Chicago the home base. A home in a Chicago suburb would provide access to the city's cultural events and still afford a measure of privacy and larger living quarters than could be found in the city itself for the same price.

When you compare your responses with your spouse, be prepared for some differences. Just as in any other marital decision-making effort, selecting housing together requires some patience, an effort to understand each other's positions, a spirit of mutual respect, and (with any luck) the creativity to fashion a solution that will leave both parties feeling satisfied. Go back over your responses to the Personal Preference Profile and list your areas of concern in order of their priority. This should help you reach a compromise that will fulfill the most important requirements, and allow a trade-off on some of the lower-level choices.

FIVE VITAL ELEMENTS OF RETIREMENT LIVING

The Profile covers those areas where your own taste will be the deciding factor. But there are practical necessities to consider as well. The following five essentials of retirement housing must be considered before you can arrive at a successful decision.

Economics

Chapter 7 showed you how to put together a retirement budget based on your expected level of income and assets, setting aside a specific segment for housing. This sum will of course give you a boundary when it comes to choosing a dwelling but will still allow for plenty of variation and range within certain limits.

You can find a broad price range of housing possibilities in most geographical areas. As a retiree you may be able to move out of areas of high-job concentration and therefore find comparatively luxurious accommodations at a reasonable price. You probably don't need as much space as you did when you were younger, so you might be able to find a smaller, more affordable house in a desirable, higher-rent area.

One of your first questions in determining your choice of housing is whether or not you will treat your home as a form of investment. Owning your own home, condominium, or co-op allows you to build up equity in the property, either as a means of preparing for your own financial future or as an asset to leave to your heirs. Given the tax advantages of home ownership, you may want to invest a substantial portion of your assets in your residence.

If you don't have a large sum of money to tie up in a home, you can live in rental housing or investigate the possibility of a long-term mortgage. After you put down your down payment, you will only be required to pay reasonable fixed monthly charges which would fit into your budget.

You must ask yourself whether you will be able to afford your residential expenses ten or twenty years from now. There is virtually no form of housing that is immune from continuing price escalation, whether it be in the form of increased rents, higher monthly maintenance charges, or bigger bills for heating and upkeep. However, a homeowner with a fixed monthly mortgage payment, a condo or co-op resident whose maintenance charges and other fees are set by an owners' association, or a renter whose dwelling is rent-controlled or rent-stabilized is a step ahead of the game.

Safety

It goes without saying that you will demand the highest standards of sound, sturdy, fire-resistant construction in your home. But these elements alone do not ensure your safety. When you're looking for a place to live in retirement, you should bring a new, more stringent set of requirements to the basic features offered by a prospective residence.

This is the only time I'm going to suggest that you *underestimate* your abilities. Instead of judging the livability of a place by your normal standards of tip-top health and vitality, imagine yourself with less flexibility and energy, and look out for potential obstacles. A flight of stairs may not faze you now, but it is certainly no asset in the home you've selected for your later years. Good common sense is your best guide in assessing the amount of walking, climbing, stretching, and bending a home will require. There are certain specifics, though, that you can demand when you are scouting around for a retirement house.

- Single-story layout. It shouldn't be necessary to climb stairs at any time, and that includes walking up to the front door or down to the basement to reach the fuse box. If you can't avoid stairs, they must have solid, secure handrails, safe, nonskid surfaces, and adequate lighting.
- Bright lighting, natural and electric, all over the house.
- Floors in good repair, with nonskid, nonslip floor coverings.
- Minimal need to walk far to perform regular household tasks.
- Electrical outlets readily accessible—preferably high enough off the floor to avoid stooping down to plug or unplug appliances.
- Good insulation and airtight doors and windows.
- Nonslip tiling in bathroom. Grab bars and no-slip surface in bath tubs and showers.
- Storage spaces and closets accessible without climbing and bending, especially in the kitchen.

- Doors and windows should open and close easily. Windows should be large enough to serve as fire exits in emergency. You should be able to open bathroom doors from the outside in case of emergency.

Shopping and Transportation

You want to be sure that the shopping facilities in any neighborhood you are considering will be adequate. Ideally, you should have a wide choice of stores available to you within walking distance. You shouldn't have to rely on a car—both for economic and practical reasons.

Investigate local transportation facilities. Buses, trains, car services, and taxis in the area may all prove essential to your future comfort. If your family lives far away, you might want to check out the location of the nearest airport as well.

Even if you plan to live in a retirement village which has all the facilities you could ask for on the grounds, you still need the outside world—accessible to you—otherwise you're likely to feel unpleasantly restricted even in the midst of plenty. Most communities have a shuttle bus or limousine service into town—and you may be surprised at how often you use it.

Family Responsibilities

If your children or your parents are dependent on you, then of course this limits your choice of dwelling. However, it is unlikely that your children really need you right next door. You may love them dearly, and have a wonderful time visiting with them and their children, but you cannot expect to gear your entire lifestyle around their presence. Living near your children is undeniably a source of pleasure—as long as you maintain an active, fulfilling life of your own outside your children's home. This is even more important if economic necessity leads you to move in with your children—one of the most potentially explosive family situations known to humankind.

The problem is just as complex if you have an older parent who requires substantial attention. The enormous rise in the number of people who live into their eighties and nineties has made the phenomenon of a retiree with an elderly dependent parent more and more common. Investigate the programs and services in your area that will assist you in caring for your parent without making you feel as if you have abandoned your responsibilities. There are many worthwhile organizations offering home care for the elderly for some part of the day while leaving the family unit intact. There are also, despite the highly publicized scandals of inadequate and criminally negligent nursing homes, many fine full-care facilities which provide skillful personal services to the infirm. To explore the possibilities available in your community, speak to your family doctor, call the local social services administration or senior citizens center, or contact your state office on aging.

No one should shirk his family obligations. However, you owe it to yourself to make the best possible personal choices while considering the needs of your loved ones.

Medical Facilities

Even if you are at the peak of physical health, your retirement home should be within easy reach of competent, reliable medical care. When you investigate any community, including your current neighborhood, be sure that the emergency and long-term medical facilities will be adequate for your continuing needs.

If your health is not particularly good, or if you have any significant impairment, you should give serious consideration to the possibility of moving into a retirement home or life-care facility. These are residences which combine on-premises medical care with personal services such as meals, housekeeping, and laundry service. A retirement home may consist of rental units, individually owned condominium apartments, or separate homes. Life-care facilities generally call for a hefty commitment on your part: an entrance fee of several thousand dollars in addition to monthly charges. In some church-sponsored institutions, you must turn over all your assets to the institution at the time of admission. The policies and provisions of any facility you are contemplating should be thoroughly investigated before you make a decision. Your family doctor should be a good adviser on this topic, as will a local senior citizen center or state council on aging.

TO MOVE OR NOT TO MOVE?

Now that you have a pretty fair idea of your personal preferences and requirements, it's time to ask yourself how your present home measures up. Remember that what you ask from your home and the neighborhood you live in is likely to change substantially in retirement, and while your living accommodations may be perfectly adequate right now, they may not serve as well in the new, different lifestyle you plan to pursue when your working life changes.

Ask yourself:

1. How desirable an area is your present neighborhood? If the community is safe and comfortable, with a stable population and good prospects for the future, that's a powerful incentive to stay. On the other hand, if you moved to a less attractive area to be near your place of business, and never really liked it, this is a good time to look for alternative sites.

2. How important to you are your friendships with people in the neighborhood? Some of your friends and acquaintances will undoubtedly be planning to move themselves. Also, how

many of your social relationships are tied in to your job, and how close do you think you'll be with these people when that bond is broken?

3. Do you treasure the comfortable feeling of dealing with familiar streets and towns, merchants and businesspeople, doctors and other professionals? If you have lived in one place for some time, the knowledge that you are in touch with the best essential services and the most sympathetic people can be very valuable.

4. Do you hold a position in the community which you would forfeit by leaving? If you have worked for a charity, political party, civic or social organization in the past, you may have built up a reputation and risen to a responsible level within that group. Your present commitments can be a powerful factor in keeping you within a community.

5. How do the economics of your current residence measure up? If you have paid off your mortgage, you will have only property taxes, fuel, insurance, and upkeep expenses to contend with, but don't underestimate that financial burden. Be sure to check on any tax breaks coming your way when you reach sixty-five. Your home could be worth more to you as a salable or rentable asset than as a place to live.

6. How do your present living conditions fulfill the personal preferences and necessity items you determined earlier in this chapter? You may be overanxious to compromise on some of the activities you would like to pursue to avoid the inconvenience and emotional upheaval of moving, but remember that a move is only a temporary inconvenience. It takes a certain amount of courage to initiate a change, but many retirees have found that the difficult decision to move has opened up new possibilities which were totally unavailable in their old, familiar homestead. Before you do anything drastic, though, check out your current community. It could be that you aren't aware of the services and opportunities open to retirees in your area, because you never had occasion to take advantage of them in the past. Before writing off your neighborhood, do some exploring.

The decision to stay where you are or move on has probably never been just a matter of choice. When you had to move for business reasons, you simply made the most of the situation. Now, though, you must find good reasons to stay or to go purely on personal grounds. Exploring all your options as thoroughly as possible, and taking as much time as you need, can help in this difficult choice. If you possibly can, keep the door open to return to your present community. Here are some tips to ease the way for this choice:

Guide to Exploring Options

- *Make identifying possible retirement locations a casual but persistent part of your thinking right now*. By watching television reports, reading newspapers and magazines, or taking minivacations with an eye toward the suitability of the areas visited for your retirement, you can painlessly put together a selection of interesting prospects for further investigation.

  You can also profit from the experience of others. Any information you glean from social or business acquaintances about communities where they have lived or visited will of course be colored by their own personal prejudices, but by asking the right questions you can gain some insight into the style and feeling of life in different areas as well as learning about climate, transportation, and other practical matters.

  Our experience in Arizona bears out the wisdom of this advice. Ruth and I were familiar with the state before we moved there, but one thing we didn't anticipate was that we would miss the change in the seasons. The Sonora desert is beautiful—people go out there on vacation and decide they would like to live there forever, and they really mean it. But when you were born and brought up in the Midwest, where you can walk in the shade of the walnut trees in the summer, watch the leaves come down in the fall, enjoy the snow in the winter, and see the first crocus in spring, you miss those experiences. The desert is wonderful but relatively the same from season to season—no over the river and through the woods, no dragging the Yule log, no sense of winter's coming—there just aren't enough climate surprises. And when things are too predictable, especially if you're chained to your environment, there's a danger that you may suffer from boredom.

● *Visit the areas you are considering, and do it more than once.* The only way to get a really accurate impression of a new area is to go there yourself and look around. If you are thinking about living somewhere all year round, you have to see what it's like there during the hot and cold months as well as the temperate ones. Take the time to speak to local residents, judge the local facilities, and look for problem areas within the community. Set up an appointment with a bank officer, for instance, and while discussing the availability of financing for housing in the area, ask questions about local trends in population—its growth or decline; its composition—the prospects for industrialization, and the employment picture. Owners of small businesses and stores are also good sources of information.

● *Subscribe to the local newspaper.* There is no better guide to a community than the local paper. Not only will it give you the news of the region, but the selection of items covered and the slant of the stories will indicate the residents' overriding concerns. Also, you will see the goods and services of the community advertised and will get an idea as to the availability of movies, plays, and other entertainment.

● *Explore the possibilities of keeping your current residence while you try out a new one.* It is not usually feasible to have your cake and eat it too, but in this case it can sometimes be done at relatively modest expense by renting or subletting. You can eliminate a large percentage of the risk involved in uprooting yourself and moving by going to the extra effort of finding a way to keep your home, at least temporarily.

● *Rent accommodations in your new community for a tryout period.* Even if you are planning to purchase a home, you may be able to find an acceptable apartment or house in your new area which you can rent temporarily. This way, you will get the feel of the new place before sinking all your money into a home purchase. By renting furnished accommodations, you can hold off on the expense and bother of shipping your furniture by placing it in storage for a while.

Even retirement villages often include some rental units. If you do have to sign a long-term agreement, you may still be able to negotiate a clause specifying a trial period, thus allowing you the luxury of changing your mind.

- *Turn a vacation home into a retirement residence*. If you are interested in retiring to an area which has many recreational facilities, you may be able to buy a vacation home there now and rent it out for a portion of the year. Not only will you have a desirable home waiting for you in retirement, but you may actually come out slightly ahead financially.

The feasibility of this approach rests on your ability to finance a second home on favorable terms within your current budget, the degree of success you will have finding renters and managing the property, and the trends of property values in the area you select.

Professional Advice for the Final Decision

Many of the pitfalls encountered in buying or renting a retirement home can be avoided simply by taking the time to investigate thoroughly the location and the building in question yourself. Don't take a salesman's word about the nature of the community, the type of recreational opportunities available, the ease of transportation, or the wonderful climate. Go out and check all these yourself, along with any other questions you might have about the area.

If you have any doubts about the fine points of structural soundness and location, invest in a professional inspection service, which will have someone visit your prospective home and give you an expert estimation of its condition from basement to rooftop, alerting you to those problems which might not show up immediately, like a deteriorating roof or a poorly constructed foundation.

Any purchase agreement, whether it is for a private dwelling or a share in a condominium or co-op, should be reviewed by a qualified attorney of your choosing, as should a lease. If you are moving far from your home state, it may be advisable to speak to an attorney who practices in your new area, who will be familiar with local zoning, financing, construction, and contractual regulations.

CHOOSING YOUR NEW LOCATION

Despite the publicity, most older Americans do *not* choose to move to the Sunbelt retirement states. It is true that Florida has the greatest percentage of citizens over sixty-five, but the next nine are Arkansas, Iowa, Missouri, South Dakota, Nebraska, Rhode Island, Kansas, Pennsylvania, and Oklahoma.

In fact, it apparently takes quite a bit of motivation to get retirees to move at all—in the period from 1975 to 1978, only about 17 percent of the people between fifty-five and sixty-four, 15 percent between sixty-five and seventy-four, and 12 percent from seventy-five up had changed homes, and only about 5 percent of those crossed state lines.

If you *have* decided to look for a new, more suitable place to call home, you don't have to go far, nor do you have to stick with the retirement trend of Arizona, Florida, or California. The goal is to find a place that suits your own personal needs, and you may be able to do that right near your present home.

Although it's virtually impossible to make one set of individual desires and demands and transfer that to a map, *Money* magazine decided to try it and engaged specialists in economic forecasting to find the ten best retirement states for the 1980s. Their choices were made on the basis of economic trends, as well as cultural, recreational, and climatological ones. The results, as published in the July 1979 issue of *Money,* are as follows:

The 10 best . . .

For at least the next 10 years, retirement income is likely to buy more good living in this group of states than elsewhere in the U.S. The ranking is based primarily on long-range projections by Chase Econometrics. Though all 10 states are in the South and West, where the inflation rate has lately outgalloped the Northeast's, Chase thinks they'll keep a cost-of-living advantage except perhaps in the biggest cities. In addition, taxes and unemployment are likely to stay low. Housing is available, sometimes at surprisingly low prices, in towns with adequate medical care and public services.

1. *Utah*. Low energy costs, moderate cost of living, healthy job growth; cold winters in much of the state.

2. *Louisiana*. Very warm and inexpensive. Real estate taxes extremely low. Less job growth than in Utah.

3. *South Carolina*. Low living costs and taxes; doctor shortage in many counties.

4. *Nevada*. An abundance of new housing and jobs; no state income or inheritance taxes; cost of living no lower than the U.S. average.

5. *Texas*. Service jobs plentiful; housing costs moderate outside Houston and Dallas; urban living costs rising fast.

6. *New Mexico*. Job supply growing, energy costs low, cheap housing abundant; social services thinly spread.

7. *Alabama*. Cheapest and warmest of the 10, but not much growth in jobs; medical care lacking in many areas.

8. *Arizona*. Good, inexpensive housing, warm climate, fine medical care; but increasingly high taxes and rapidly rising living costs.

9. *Florida*. Warm climate, excellent medical services, no income tax; living costs very high in coastal areas; property taxes rising.

10. *Georgia*. Mild climate; very low living costs even in Atlanta; slower job growth than elsewhere in the top 10; poor medical services in some areas.

. . . and the worst

50. *Massachusetts*. Highest cost of living in the nation for retired people; residential utility bills average $1,600 a year;

high taxes; dividends and interest taxed at double the rate for earned income; high unemployment; part-time job market dominated by college students. Offsetting advantages: great medical and cultural institutions. All of New England, New York, and New Jersey fall in the bottom 10 for similar reasons; Connecticut, best among them, has no income tax.

This is not, of course, the definitive word on where to retire, but it does suggest some interesting directions for your own exploration. You'll need to do some library research and general reading of your own, as well as some traveling, to get a true picture of what each region has to offer.

Regional Wrap-ups

What About Climate?

NORTHEASTERN STATES:
Maine, New Hampshire, Vermont, New York, Pennsylvania, Connecticut, New Jersey, Rhode Island, and Massachusetts.
Cool summers . . . severe winters . . . abundant snowfall . . . southernmost region experiences warmer summers and milder winters . . . coastal states experience frequent winter storms, which occasionally move inland.

	Temp.				Annual In. Rain/Snow		Clear Days per Year
	Jan.		July				
City	Hi	Lo	Hi	Lo			
Williamsport, PA	36	21	85	62	41	44	77
Hartford, CT	35	17	85	62	43	56	81
Atlantic City, NJ	43	27	84	66	42	17	87
Boston, MA	37	23	82	65	43	43	99

MIDEASTERN STATES:

Virginia, West Virginia, Kentucky, Tennessee, South Carolina, North Carolina, Maryland, and Delaware.

Warm, humid summers throughout . . . mountain areas cooler . . . winters are mild and snowfall generally light . . . northern coastal area and mountains have more severe winter weather . . . well-defined seasons . . . thunderstorms are prevalent through-out the year.

City	Temp. Jan. Hi	Jan. Lo	July Hi	July Lo	Annual In. Rain/Snow		Clear Days per Year
Norfolk, VA	50	32	88	70	45	8	97
Lexington, KY	43	26	88	67	45	17	84
Nashville, TN	49	31	91	70	45	12	103
Columbia, SC	58	36	93	71	47	1	111
Charleston, SC	61	38	89	72	49		109
Wilmington, NC	58	37	89	71	51	2	106

MIDDLE STATES:

Ohio, Minnesota, Iowa, Wisconsin, Missouri, Indiana, Michigan, and Illinois.

Warm summers . . . cold winters . . . areas bordering Great Lakes have generally colder winters, heavier snowfall, and more moderate summer temperatures.

City	Temp. Jan. Hi	Jan. Lo	July Hi	July Lo	Annual In. Rain/Snow		Clear Days per Year
Duluth, MN	18	1	77	54	29	78	79
Des Moines, IA	29	11	87	65	30	32	93
Green Bay, WI	25	9	82	59	26	41	89
St. Louis, MO	40	24	89	67	35	17	98
Indianapolis, IN	37	21	86	64	39	21	98
Columbus, OH	38	22	87	63	37	29	81
Lansing, MI	31	17	83	60	31	48	69

SOUTH-CENTRAL STATES:
Texas, New Mexico, Arkansas, and Louisiana.
Summers in coastal areas are warm, humid, and rainy, with possible tornadoes and tropical storms . . . central Texas experiences dry winters and humid summers; cooler temperatures occur in high western elevations . . . sunshine is abundant in New Mexico, although winters are cooler and snowfall heavier in high elevations.

City	Jan. Hi	Jan. Lo	July Hi	July Lo	Annual In. Rain	Annual In. Snow	Clear Days per Year
Corpus Christi, TX	67	47	94	75	28		95
San Antonio, TX	62	42	94	74	28		101
Brownsville, TX	71	52	93	76	27		90
Roswell, NM	55	21	95	62	12	11	178
Albuquerque, NM	46	24	91	66	8	10	188
Little Rock, AR	51	31	93	71	49	6	117
New Orleans, LA	64	45	91	73	54		106

NORTHWESTERN STATES:
Washington, Oregon, and Alaska.
More moderate temperatures and abundant winter rainfall along coast . . . cooler temperatures inland . . . snowfall can be heavy in mountain regions . . . Alaska interior experiences extremes of temperature.

City	Jan. Hi	Jan. Lo	July Hi	July Lo	Annual In. Rain	Annual In. Snow	Clear Days per Year
Seattle, WA	46	37	75	56	34	8	56
Yakima, WA	37	19	89	53	8	25	120
Medford, OR	42	28	88	56	20	9	108
Portland, OR	45	36	79	58	37	8	70
Fairbanks, AK	-2	-21	73	50	12	70	69

SOUTHWESTERN STATES:

California, Arizona, Nevada, and Hawaii.

Moderate temperatures along coast . . . northern California experiences generally cooler temperatures and rain in all seasons . . . Hawaii is sub-tropical . . . remainder of region is marked by abundant sunshine, low humidity . . . extreme temperatures in desert and mountain regions. . . heavy snowfall in high elevations.

City	Jan. Hi	Jan. Lo	July Hi	July Lo	Annual In. Rain	Annual In. Snow	Clear Days per Year
Los Angeles, CA	64	45	76	62	13		162
San Diego, CA	65	45	77	63	10		148
San Francisco, CA	55	42	72	54	19		183
Flagstaff, AZ	40	14	81	50	18	79	182
Phoenix, AZ	64	35	105	75	7		223
Tucson, AZ	63	37	99	74	11	1	221
Reno, NV	45	16	89	46	7	26	166
Honolulu, HI	79	66	85	73	32	0	190

SOUTHEASTERN STATES:

Mississippi, Alabama, Florida, and Georgia.

Hot, humid summers moderating inland and along Atlantic coast . . . mild winters, colder and wet in northern inland sections . . . generally abundant rainfall with thunderstorms likely in summer months . . . possibility of tornadoes and hurricanes throughout area.

City	Jan. Hi	Jan. Lo	July Hi	July Lo	Annual In. Rain	Annual In. Snow	Clear Days per Year
Jackson, MS	58	37	93	72	51	1	109
Mobile, AL	62	44	92	73	68		91
Birmingham, AL	57	36	93	71	54	1	102
Tampa, FL	71	51	90	73	52		106
Daytona Beach, FL	70	49	88	72	50		97
Miami, FL	76	58	89	75	60		93
Savannah, GA	63	41	91	71	49		99
Atlanta, GA	52	37	87	71	47	2	108

THE PLAINS STATES:

North Dakota, South Dakota, Nebraska, Kansas, and Oklahoma.
Northern portion marked by extremely cold winters and occasional heavy snowfall . . . extremes of wet and dry trends through center areas . . . hailstorms and dust storms can occur . . . usually hot summers except in North Dakota and mountain areas . . . thunderstorms and tornadoes may occur throughout area.

City	Temp. Jan. Hi	Jan. Lo	July Hi	July Lo	Annual In. Rain	Annual In. Snow	Clear Days per Year
Bismarck, ND	20	0	86	58	15	39	92
Omaha, NE	32	13	90	67	28	32	104
Wichita, KS	42	22	92	69	28	15	127
Oklahoma City, OK	46	28	93	72	31	9	138

INTER-MOUNTAIN STATES:

Idaho, Montana, Wyoming, Utah, and Colorado.
Generally cool climate . . . colder temperatures and heavier snowfall in mountain regions . . . windstorms and hail can occur in northernmost states . . . light precipitation in southern portion.

City	Temp. Jan. Hi	Jan. Lo	July Hi	July Lo	Annual In. Rain	Annual In. Snow	Clear Days per Year
Boise, ID	36	22	91	59	11	22	110
Helena, MT	29	8	84	52	11	49	73
Casper, WY	33	14	87	56	12	69	111
Salt Lake City, UT	37	18	94	60	14	56	117
Denver, CO	42	15	88	57	15	58	115

STATE-BY-STATE TAX GUIDE

Table 12 summarizes the major taxes imposed by each state, along with special tax considerations for retirees. There may be additional

Table 12. State Tax Guide

	State Income Tax	Sales Tax	Advantages for Retirees
ALABAMA	Ranges from 1.5% on first $1,000 to 5% on $5,000 up.	4% (higher in some areas).	Personal exemptions: $1,500 singles, $3,000 couples, $300 dependents. Property tax exemptions for 65+ with income under $5,000. No inheritance tax. Estate tax credits based on federal formula.
ALASKA	For singles: 3% on first $2,000, up to 14.5% over $200,000. Double for marrieds filing jointly.	None statewide, but localities range from 1% to 5%.	Property tax exemption for 65+ on principle residence. Special treatment of retirement income, pensions, annuities from qualified plans approved by IRS.
ARIZONA	2% on first $1,000, increased by 3% per $1,000 up to 8% for $6,000 up.	4% (cities may impose more).	Extra $1,101 income tax exemption for 65+. Inheritance tax exemption: $100,000. Net estate rates: from 0.8% below $50,000, graduating to 16% on $10 million.
ARKANSAS	1% on first $2,999, up to 7% on $25,000+. Tax exempt: singles with less than $3,000, marrieds $4,000.	3% (cities may impose added 1%).	Tax-exempt: first $6,000 of retirement annuities. For 65+ and widows 62+ possible income-tax credit for property taxes paid. Inheritance tax: same exemptions as under federal laws.

State	Income Tax	Sales Tax	Other Provisions
CALIFORNIA	For singles: 1% on first $2,000 to 11% maximum on $15,500+. No tax for couples or surviving spouse under $10,000.	6% (added 0.5% transit tax in some counties).	Homeowners' $1,750 property tax exemption. Graduated percentage of assistance to residents 62+ if income not over $12,000. Inheritance tax: exempts ½ interest on spouse-community property and separate property plus $60,000.
COLORADO	2.5% on first $1,000, up to 8% on $10,000 +2% surtax on dividends, interest.	3% (added taxes by cities may not exceed 7%).	Certain pension income tax exempt for age 55+. Property tax concessions for 65+. Inheritance tax exemptions: up to $75,000 family members.
CONNECTICUT	7% tax on capital gains income. Dividends taxed 1% to 9% if income is $20,000+.	7% (exempt: utilities, fuel, medicines).	Property tax concession for 65+ if income below $6,000. Inheritance tax exemptions: $100,000 spouse; $20,000 parents, children; $6,000 brother, sister.
DELAWARE	1.6% for first $1,000 up to 19.8% for $100,000+. Fixed personal exemption: $600.	None.	Up to $2,000 exemption for age 60+ with income under $10,000. Pensions excludable from tax to annual maximum $2,000. Inheritance tax exemptions: $70,000 spouse; $3,000 parents, children.
FLORIDA	None.	4%. Exemptions: rent, groceries, medicines.	Homeowners' $5,000 homestead exemption; added $5,000 for 65+ occupying residence for 5 previous years. Inheritance tax: same exemptions as federal law.

Table 12.   State Tax Guide (Continued)

	State Income Tax	Sales Tax	Advantages for Retirees
GEORGIA	1% on first $1,000, up to 6% on $10,000+ income depending on marital status.	3%. Some local taxes 1% more.	Extra $700 personal tax exemption for 65+. Homestead exemption $4,000 for 65+. NO with income under $4,000. Inheritance tax credits based on federal formula.
HAWAII	Ranges from 2.25% on first $500 up to 11% on $30,000+. Extra $750 exemption for 65+.	4%.	Taxpayers 65+ may claim double excise credit. Taxpayers 60+ double homeowners' $24,000 exemption; age 70+ to 2.5 times the exemption. Medical expenses for 65+ fully deductible if itemized.
IDAHO	Ranges from 2% on first $2,000, up to 7.5% on $10,000+.	3%.	Extra $30 tax credit for 65+. Property tax concession of $200 for 65+. Surviving spouse's community property exempt; other exemptions $30,000–50,000.
ILLINOIS	2.5% on individuals, trusts, estates. $1,000 exempted for each personal federal exemption	4%.	Residents 65+ with income under $10,000 can get rebate on property and sales taxes. Renters may claim percentage as property tax. Inheritance tax exemption: $40,000 spouse, children, up to $270,000.

State	Income Tax	Sales Tax	Provisions
INDIANA	2% of resident's adjusted gross income.	4%.	Homeowners 65+ get $1,000 deduction in assessed value of total income not over $10,000. Transfers between spouses not subject to inheritance taxes.
IOWA	From 0.5% to 13% of excess over specified sums.	3%.	Additional $15 tax credit for 65+. For 65+ (or surviving spouses 55+) with annual income under $10,000, property tax reimbursement up to $1,000. Some reimbursement to renters 65+. No inheritance tax if share under $80,000.
KANSAS	Graduated specified sums, plus 2% on first $2,000 up to 9% over $25,000.	3% (0.5%+ in some counties and cities).	For 65+ first $2,000 of military retirement-income tax-exempt. For 58+, unmarried widows 52+, or disabled: homestead property tax relief if income under $12,800; renters included $20 food sales-tax refund for 58+ if income under $10,000.
KENTUCKY	Ranges from 2% on first $3,000 to 6% over $8,000.	5%.	If 65+ property taxes exempted on first $10,200 value if owner-occupied. Inheritance tax exemptions: $50,000 surviving spouse; $5,000 lineal heirs.
LOUISIANA	Ranges from 2% on first $10,000 to 6% on over $50,000.	3% (plus some local excise).	$400 personal state income-tax exemption for 65+. $5,000 homestead exemption for all homeowners. Inheritance tax exemptions: $5,000 spouse, lineal heirs; $1,000 collateral descendents.

Table 12. State Tax Guide (Continued)

	State Income Tax	Sales Tax	Advantages for Retirees
MAINE	1% on first $2,000; graduated surcharges plus 2% to 10% of excess over specified sums.	5%.	Householders age 62+ with incomes not over $5,000 and unmarried widows, widowers age 55+ with disability entitled to tax refund not exceeding $400. Inheritance tax exemptions $50,000 spouse; $25,000 parents, children; $1,000 brothers, sisters.
MARYLAND	Ranges from 2% on first $1,000 to 5% on over $3,000.	5%.	Extra $800 personal tax exemption for 65+. Up to $5,200 may be excluded by residents 65+ receiving pension, annuity, or endowment (but not including Social Security, Railroad benefits). Inheritance tax: 1% on entire share; no tax if value below $150.
MASSACHUSETTS	10.75% on interest, dividends, capital gains; 5⅛% on all other income.	5%.	Income from other states' annuities, pensions, or retirement fund exempt on reciprocal basis. $4,500 property-tax concession for 70+ under $6,000 (single), $7,000 (married) if in state 10 years. Inheritance tax: general $30,000 exemption. Marital deduction up to ½ adjusted gross estate.

MICHIGAN	4.6% on taxable income.	4%.	Property tax credit for seniors. Retirement pensions exempt with $7,500 max. singles, $10,000 couples. Inheritance tax exemptions: $65,000 spouse, $10,000 lineal heirs.
MINNESOTA	Ranges from 1.6% on first $500 to 17% on over $40,000	4% (higher in some cities).	Extra $20 tax-credit for 65+ on state income tax. $800 maximum credit or refund for age 65+ on property tax. Inheritance tax exemptions: $60,000 spouse; $30,000 dependent child, $6,000 adult child.
MISSISSIPPI	3% on first $5,000; 4% on over $5,000.	5%.	$1,500 personal exemption from state income tax for age 65+. Pensions, annuities tax exempt up to $5,000. Inheritance tax exempts property to value of $120,666.
MISSOURI	Ranges from 1.5%. Under $1,000 to 6% over $9,000.	Basic 3⅛%. Municipalities may add 0.5% to 1%, plus 0.5% for mass transit.	Age 65+ who rent or own homes entitled to some property tax credit if household income less than $7,500 and resided in state preceding year. Inheritance tax exemptions: $20,000 spouse; $15,000 lineal heirs; $5,000 brothers, sisters.
MONTANA	Ranges from 2% on first $1,000 to 11% on over $35,000.	None.	Extra $650 exemption from income tax for 65+. Property tax concessions for 62+ widows, widowers. No inheritance tax.

Table 12. State Tax Guide (Continued)

	State Income Tax	Sales Tax	Advantages for Retirees
NEBRASKA	18% of federal income tax before tax credits.	0.5% (1% higher in some cities).	Age 65+ entitled to 100% homestead exemption on first $15,000 of actual value if single, divorced, widowed, with less than $3,200 income, or $4,800 if married. Inheritance tax exemptions: $10,000 spouse, lineal heirs.
NEVADA	None.	3% (½% additional in 13 counties).	Property tax concessions to homeowners and renters age 62+ if income not over $11,000. No inheritance or estate tax. New legislation pending.
NEW HAMPSHIRE	5% on interest and dividend income. Statutory exemption: $600.	None.	Extra $600 state income-tax exemption for age 65+. No inheritance tax for spouse, lineal heirs: but 15% tax on property passing to brothers, sisters, others.
NEW JERSEY	2% on first $20,000 of taxable income. 2.5% thereafter.	5%.	Extra $1,000 personal income exemption for 65+. Age 62+ entitled to exclude up to $7,500 pension benefits; $10,000 if married. Property tax concessions: $160 deduction for 65+ with income under $5,000. Inheritance tax exemptions: $15,000 spouse,

lineal heirs; no tax for others if share less than $500.

State	Income Tax	Sales Tax	Other
NEW MEXICO	Graduated surcharges plus 0.8% to 9% of excess over specified sums.	3.75%.	Some annuities deductible from base income; $200 property exemption to head of household. Maximum property tax liability $40. Progressive rates according to income. Estate tax credits based on federal formula.
NEW YORK	Ranges from 2% on first $1,000 to 15% on over $30,000.	4% to 8% depending on locality.	Exemptions on property according to individual county's assessments. General tax credit on all estates; gross tax is $2,750.
NORTH CAROLINA	Ranges from 3% on first $2,000 to 7% on over $10,000.	4% (except for 3% in 3 counties).	For homeowners age 65+, first $7,500 in tax value of property owned and occupied is exempt if income $9,000 or less. Inheritance tax exemptions: $20,000 spouse; $2,000 adult child, others.
NORTH DAKOTA	1% up to $3,000, then ranges from 2% to 7.5% for $30,000 or over.	3% (2% on farm equipment).	$750 personal tax exemption for 65+. Renters age 65+ with under $8,000 income eligible for up to $175 refund. Inheritance tax credit based on federal formula.
OHIO	0.5% to $5,000, then from 1% to 3.5% over specified sums.	4% (up 0.5% or 1% in 39 counties).	Homeowners 65+ with total income $10,000 qualify for tax relief. Inheritance tax exemptions: $30,000 spouse; $7,000 minor child; $3,000 adult child.

Table 12. State Tax Guide (Continued)

	State Income Tax	Sales Tax	Advantages for Retirees
OKLAHOMA	0.5% on first $2,000, then to 6% on over $15,000.	2%.	Military retirement benefits exempt up to first $1,500. Some property tax relief. Inheritance tax exemptions: $60,000 parents, lineal heirs. Exempts property passing to spouses.
OREGON	Ranges from 4% on first $1,000, to over $10,000.	None.	Exemption up to $3,400 for federal pensions. Inheritance tax exemptions: $70,000 for spouses (increasing to $100,000 in 1981).
PENNSYLVANIA	2.2% on total taxable income.	6%.	All retirement-income tax exempt. Rebates on property taxes on sliding scale for 65+ under $7,500 income. Inheritance tax exemptions: $2,000 spouse, lineal heirs.
RHODE ISLAND	19% of taxpayer's federal income-tax liability.	6%.	Tax rates set locally may exempt property of 65+. Inheritance tax exemptions: $50,000 spouse, lineal heirs; $5,000 brothers, sisters.

	Income Tax	Sales Tax	Other
SOUTH CAROLINA	2% on first $2,000, increasing to 7% on $10,000+.	4%.	Up to $1,200 of pension is exempt for 65+. On property taxes, first $10,000 tax-exempt for 65+. Inheritance tax exemptions: $120,000 gross estate; taxes 5% on $40,000 net estate to 7% on $100,000+.
SOUTH DAKOTA	None.	4% (cities may levy additional tax).	Age 65+ (and the disabled) with under $4,625 income single or $7,375 for multi-member home qualify for tax refund based on income. Inheritance tax exemptions: $80,000 spouse, $30,000 lineal heirs.
TENNESSEE	No tax on earned income; 4% to 6% on dividends.	4.5% (cities, counties may impose added 2.25%).	Income from stocks and bonds of pension and profit-sharing trusts eligible for some deductions if 65+. Inheritance tax exemptions: $120,000 or more for spouse, lineal heirs; $30,000 others.
TEXAS	None.	4% (in most cities an extra 1%).	State homestead exemption of $3,000. Inheritance tax exemptions: $200,000 prorated among all Class A beneficiaries, in proportion to amount passed.
UTAH	Ranges from 2¼% under $750 to 7¾% for over $7,500.	4% (with counties adding 0.75% more).	Pensions, annuities from qualified investments, rent, dividends by age 65+ deductible as retirement income. $147,000 exemption on estate tax.

Table 12. State Tax Guide (Continued)

	State Income Tax	Sales Tax	Advantages for Retirees
VERMONT	25% of taxpayer's federal income tax.	3%.	65+ entitled to tax credits on income up to $6,000. Inheritance tax exemption: 30% of federal estate tax.
VIRGINIA	Ranges from 2% on first $3,000 to 5.75% on over $12,000.	4%.	Added $400 exemption (or total $1,000) for 65+ on state income tax. On property taxes, counties, cities, towns authorized to provide reductions for owned/occupied by 65+. As of Jan. 1, 1980, all inheritance tax exemptions abolished in favor of death-tax credit based on federal formula.
WASHINGTON	None.	5% (plus 0.5% for mass transit in some cities).	Property tax concessions for homeowners 61+ if family income less than $11,000. Property tax deferrals follow sliding rate. Inheritance tax exemptions: $5,000 spouse, lineal heirs; $1,000 brothers, sisters. New legislation pending.
WEST VIRGINIA	Ranges from 2.1% for under $2,000 to 9.6% for over $200,000.	3%.	Residents 65+ may deduct up to $8,000 from any pension, annuity. Inheritance tax exemptions: $30,000 spouse, $10,000 lineal heirs.

WISCONSIN	Ranges from 3.4% for $3,000 and under, to 10% for $40,000+.	4%.	First $1,180 of Civil Service annuity exempt for age 62+ with less than $600 earned income. Inheritance exemptions: $250,000 spouse, $10,000 lineal heirs. Residence sales exclusion: $100,000 for 50+.
WYOMING	None.	3% (optional 1% sales tax in many counties).	Residents 65+ (and the disabled) qualify for refund and exemption of sales taxes. Inheritance tax exemptions: $200,000 spouse; $33,300 lineal heirs, brothers, sisters; $16,500 grandchild, half-bloods.

Note: Since state taxes are subject to change, be sure to check with the department of finance or taxation of states you are considering, to get the most up-to-date regulations.

Table 13. Indexes of Comparative Costs Based on a Higher Budget for a Retired Couple, Autumn 1978 (U. S. Urban Average Costs = 100)

Area		Total Budget	Total Consumption	Food Total	Food at Home
	Urban United States	100	100	100	100
	Metropolitan Areas	104	104	101	101
	Nonmetropolitan Areas	88	88	95	98
	Boston	125	125	106	106
	Buffalo	107	107	100	101
	Hartford	109	109	102	105
	Lancaster	96	96	101	102
Northeast	New York	117	117	111	108
	Philadelphia	104	104	110	108
	Pittsburgh	102	102	104	102
	Portland	102	102	103	106
	Nonmetropolitan Areas	96	96	101	102
	Cedar Rapids	100	100	92	91
	Champaign-Urbana	104	104	99	100
	Chicago	100	100	102	104
	Cincinnati	96	96	102	105
	Cleveland	103	103	100	100
	Dayton	98	98	98	100
	Detroit	106	106	99	99
North Central	Green Bay	100	100	90	93
	Indianapolis	99	99	97	97
	Kansas City	102	102	105	103
	Milwaukee	103	103	98	96
	Minneapolis	100	100	100	97
	St. Louis	98	98	105	105
	Wichita	99	99	94	97
	Nonmetropolitan Areas	89	89	97	100
	Atlanta	91	91	98	96
	Austin	96	96	92	89
	Baltimore	98	98	99	96
	Baton Rouge	91	91	100	102
	Dallas	98	98	95	91
South	Durham	93	93	94	96
	Houston	100	100	98	94
	Nashville	94	94	91	93
	Orlando	91	91	87	88
	Washington	107	107	101	102
	Nonmetropolitan Areas	85	85	94	96
	Bakersfield	94	94	94	97
	Denver	100	100	102	101
	Los Angeles–Long Beach	101	101	101	97
	San Diego	96	96	95	91
West	San Francisco–Oakland	106	106	103	102
	Seattle-Everett	106	106	101	101
	Honolulu	113	113	127	127
	Nonmetropolitan Areas	89	89	94	98
	Anchorage	134	134	127	129

SOURCE: U. S. Bureau of Labor Statistics.
NOTE: Listings for cities include both the city proper and the greater metropolitan area. "Philadelphia," for example, includes the city of Philadelphia, Pennsylvania, and its surrounding suburbs.

	Housing						Other Family Consumption
Total	**Renter Costs**	**Homeowner Costs**	**Transportation**	**Clothing**	**Personal Care**	**Medical Care**	**Other Family Consumption**
100	100	100	100	100	100	100	100
108	111	108	102	99	99	101	108
77	67	76	93	103	103	98	76
156	138	211	110	103	90	97	112
113	126	114	108	116	92	94	107
117	112	124	108	100	124	97	115
92	82	88	99	100	84	93	103
136	132	165	96	91	104	101	111
109	122	107	92	80	92	99	107
101	84	106	104	89	92	97	110
101	93	99	103	117	83	96	102
93	77	120	101	104	97	98	75
100	101	98	103	116	99	99	107
103	97	101	104	129	107	99	105
99	114	87	94	98	98	101	108
89	68	90	96	110	83	99	106
103	96	108	102	110	118	97	112
97	89	90	97	106	86	100	110
113	121	120	101	109	99	101	110
104	101	93	98	109	97	99	110
98	76	100	101	108	92	99	106
98	84	96	106	110	106	102	105
107	95	115	101	117	99	98	109
99	93	97	99	101	102	96	113
89	65	80	113	94	90	96	105
97	90	87	104	111	100	100	111
79	72	82	90	113	109	97	77
80	70	63	96	100	98	99	105
93	92	82	105	103	89	100	108
95	90	77	100	99	103	100	105
75	63	58	103	103	106	98	106
96	120	81	107	90	96	103	106
88	70	82	98	93	95	103	105
100	114	91	104	100	105	105	103
90	93	76	102	113	87	98	102
85	69	75	99	100	87	100	107
112	103	120	109	91	119	104	113
72	58	64	95	93	98	98	75
87	88	70	109	79	90	109	102
95	89	82	102	116	92	98	110
98	163	65	113	87	95	108	99
92	121	74	105	88	93	106	106
102	112	82	118	102	120	108	111
109	114	105	104	103	112	104	110
109	136	90	107	94	108	102	119
79	79	72	89	116	115	100	78
148	175	150	122	141	168	126	91

Family Consumption

local taxes in an area you are considering. Since tax regulations do change from time to time, contact the department of finance or taxation in the state capital to get the most up-to-date tax information.

Comparative Cost Indexes for a Retired Couple in Selected U.S. Cities

Table 13 indicates the relative levels of expense on basic budget items of a hypothetical retired couple living in different regions. The figures are based on autumn 1978 prices: a lower-level budget ($5,514), an intermediate-level budget ($7,846), and a higher-level budget ($11,596). Although the expenses in each category vary widely according to the particular budget, the relative expense of each category remains approximately the same. The index for the higher-budget couple is shown here. The actual expense figures for the other budgetary levels are available from the Bureau of Labor Statistics.

The figures represent variations above and below the *average urban costs,* which are set at an index of 100. You can use these statistics to compare total costs and also to examine items which are particularly important to your lifestyle. In Boston, for instance, home ownership is far more expensive than the national average (211) and renting (138) is more reasonable, while in Los Angeles the situation is reversed.

Retire in a Foreign Country?

The almighty dollar does not buy what it used to, and this is particularly true when you spend it abroad. If you are planning to move to Spain, or Greece, or some other sunny spot, and maintain the standard of living you enjoy in the United States, it will cost you about the same amount and in some cases astronomically more.

I've already told you the reasons Ruth and I decided against putting down new roots in a foreign country, and they were largely matters of personal preference. But another minus factor for most people is that Medicare will not pay your medical bills when you live abroad. And what about your legal status as a long-term resident? How would you be taxed? Would you be prohibited from holding a job if you wanted one? What other requirements and restrictions would you be subject to? For answers, contact the embassy or consulate of the country you are considering. Your love of another land or culture or your desire to be near close relatives may override the negatives, but you should know exactly what you may encounter before you make a permanent move abroad.

Is a Retirement Community Right for You?

The number of retirement communities has grown rapidly in recent years. These developments may include any form of housing, ranging from luxurious town houses and detached homes to modestly priced mobile homes. The key factor in retirement communities is not the type of building available but the age restriction on the population and the special services provided. The sociological significance of segregating older citizens from the rest of the population is a problematic issue, but beyond the scope of our discussion here. The important question right now is whether this type of living will fill your personal needs in retirement.

The facilities of these developments are often very impressive. The atmosphere is like that of a country club with every recreational facility imaginable, from sports and hobbies to clubs and organizations to adult education and entertainment opportunities. And the concentration of people of the same age group, with similar interests and enthusiasms, promotes a very active, busy lifestyle.

There is also a practical advantage to the retirement community. Because the developments were planned with the specific requirements of older people in mind, the shopping and transportation within the grounds are very convenient, the security system is excellent, and living quarters are laid out to best advantage, minimizing safety hazards and maximizing work-saving features. There are often medical facilities available as well.

Still, it is not certain that you are the type of individual who will be happy living in this environment. The virtues of the situation are readily apparent; however, let me inject a caveat.

Consider the following questions:

- *Will you be happy living exclusively with people your own age?* It is hard to know whether you will miss the sound of children playing in the street or the occasional chat with a young neighbor until you have experienced the difference of *not* having them around.
- *Is it worth the money to you?* All of the recreational facilities cost money, and the maintenance fees or rentals are based on the total cost of the entire community package. If you are not a golfer, you still pay your share of the cost of keeping the greens trimmed. Of course you needn't participate in all the activities to get your money's worth, but if you are not a joiner, you might be better off elsewhere.
- *How do you feel about obeying regulations?* In an attempt to be free of other people's noisy grandchildren and poor taste in decorating, retirement communities usually enforce stringent rules. These vary from one development to another, but you can expect to encounter restrictions on your visitors' use of the facilities and possibly their length of stay, your right to sell or sublet your property, your freedom to paint the exterior of your home, and so on.

For many people, the rules offer welcome boundaries. Living in a retirement village can be the epitome of their leisure dreams, the ultimate extended vacation. For others, the country club seems more like summer camp, and they tire of it quickly. How can you decide? Here are a few steps to follow in evaluating retirement communities:

1. See if you can stay there for a week or two as a visitor. This might be possible if you know someone who lives in a retire-

ment village and would be willing to take you in as a guest. Some developers also offer programs which let you vacation on the premises at a very reasonable fee as a prospective customer. Inquire about the possibility well in advance—there is usually a long wait for this inexpensive vacation opportunity.

2. Ask friends and neighbors who have spent time in a retirement village about their experiences.

3. Check on the reputation of the developer. This can be done through the local Better Business Bureau and Chamber of Commerce. If the developer has been in business for a number of years, you should be able to visit some of his or her other projects and see how they have fared.

4. Try to avoid retirement communities which are too isolated from the outside world. You may find that, once firmly established as a resident, you never want to leave the grounds, but it is always a good idea to have access to schools and colleges, jobs, cultural opportunities, religious institutions, and stores.

WHAT TYPE OF HOUSING FOR YOU?

Shopping for a new home is essentially the same process at any age. The odds are that you already have experience with a home purchase, so let's turn our attention here to three types of home ownership which have been highly touted in recent years as the ideal for a retiree—condominiums, cooperatives, and mobile homes. These housing choices do offer distinct alternatives to the more traditional single family home or rental apartment, and bear individual consideration.

* * *

Condominiums and Cooperatives

The choice used to be simple—if you wanted to own your home you bought a single-family house—if you wanted to rent, you moved into an apartment. To get the best of both worlds, however, you can select a condominum or a cooperative, where you own your residence in a multifamily building or development, and the grounds and facilities are owned jointly by all the residents. The facilities provided vary widely. Some condominiums and cooperatives are simply existing apartment buildings which have been changed over to a new system of ownership, while others are brand-new apartments, villas, or town houses in carefully planned retirement villages, with full leisure opportunities for those who wish to take advantage of them.

Once the condo or co-op is completed, it is usually run by the people who live there through an owner's association. As long as your owners' association runs efficiently (and many hire professional management consultants), your home will be part of a community aiming for the greatest comfort at the lowest possible expense.

How do condominiums and cooperatives differ? When you buy into a condominium, you purchase your own living unit and agree to pay your share of the expenses for maintaining the common areas. You will be assessed directly for real estate taxes, be responsible for obtaining your own mortgage, and enjoy the same tax benefits as any other home owner.

In a cooperative, you buy a share of stock rather than an actual apartment. All facilities are owned jointly by the cooperative, and your share of stock entitles you to occupy a unit within the development. The co-op is taxed as a single unit, with each tenant assessed for his share, and there is an overall mortgage held by the co-op Each shareholder is allowed to take a proportionate income-tax deduction for mortgage payments and property taxes.

There are certain disadvantages to co-op ownership as compared to a condominium, but they are fairly minor. You may find it a little more difficult to sell or rent your unit in a co-op, since any transaction will have to be approved by the owners' association. Also, if someone living in a co-op defaults on his payments, the rest of the residents must absorb the cost in their own maintenance fees. However, you should judge any prospective condo or co-op on its own merits and compare the restrictions involved against the desirability of the facilities provided.

Making the Purchase. The purchase agreements for condominiums and cooperatives are quite complicated, so you must go over the documents involved with a lawyer who is familiar with the local real estate laws. Condominiums are controlled by state, not federal, laws, and these vary widely from one area to another.

Some of the basic considerations in buying a condo or co-op are:

- What limits are there on monthly charges?
- What restrictions are imposed on your personal life? Visitors? Pets?
- Will you be able to rent or sell the property as you like? Are you permitted to will it to your heirs?
- Exactly how will the development be managed? By professionals, or by the residents themselves? How much control will the developer retain over the project once it is completed?

Mobile Homes

The mobile home is smaller, more convenient, and less expensive than the traditional single-family house and is not the temporary shelter you may think it is. Many people think of mobile homes as trailers, hitched to cars. Nothing could be further from the truth—there is a world of difference between a trailer or recreational vehicle and a mobile home. Mobile homes, also called manufactured homes, are mobile, but usually just for the one trip from the factory to the home site.

The modern manufactured home is made of the same kinds of materials used in conventional site-built construction, but it is assembled in a factory, using assembly line techniques. The manufacturers can keep the price of their homes down by employing efficient construction methods and buying raw materials in large quantities.

Economy is a major factor in the popularity of manufactured homes. For a couple with modest requirements, a 14-by-60-foot manufactured home should provide all the space they need, and prices averaged about $15,000 for a unit that size in 1979. That includes the basic structure, major appliances, free-standing and built-in furniture, carpeting and tile, and drapes and curtains, in addition to standard heating and hot water facilities.

Convenience is a major factor in mobile home living. The homes are designed for minimal maintenance and maximum efficiency in the use of interior space. You will be able to customize your purchase, to pick and choose options much as you would when buying a car from a dealer, and have the factory deliver a home which is virtually ready to live in. Your cleaning and upkeep chores will be far less than in a traditional home. In addition, if you buy it new you will generally get a warranty that covers you for defects in the building and furnishings for a period of time.

In the past ten years, enormous strides have been taken by government, financial institutions, local zoning boards, and the manufactured housing industry itself in the following areas:

- *Safety*. Questionable construction standards were once a major problem in buying a mobile home. The federal government stepped in, and in 1976 the Department of Housing and Urban Development instituted a strict set of standards. The requirements for structural soundness, fire safety, electrical, plumbing, heating, and cooling systems, anchoring provisions, and layout specifications assure you that the manufactured home you buy will be at least as safe as a standard site-built model—and more fuel-efficient.

- *Location*. Local planning boards used to ostracize mobile homes and place heavy zoning restrictions on them. This is still true in some communities, but the trend today is to integrate manufactured housing in the town. The key to this change is monetary—mobile homes used to be regarded as personal property for tax purposes, like an automobile, and hence the local authorities could not collect property taxes on them. When manufactured homes became more popular and better made, and were anchored to fixed foundations, they were put into the same taxable category as other real estate.

Developers are now establishing entire suburban communities using manufactured housing. As a matter of fact, about half of the manufactured home shipments today are to mobile home parks, many of which are equivalent in facilities to other retirement communities.

There are some contractual considerations to life in a mobile home park. For instance, your lease should specify your liability to rent increases on the site of your home, and responsibility for upkeep of the park. You may be able to find a mobile home development which is run as a cooperative, where the residents have control over their own living conditions. The books and booklets listed at the end of this section will give you a full picture of the ins and outs of mobile home purchase and living arrangements.

- *Financing.* As the categorization of mobile homes changes from personal property to real estate, the terms for financing change, too. Previously, you had to take out the same type of loan to buy a mobile home as you did for a car, instead of being able to assume a mortgage at more favorable interest rates. Financial institutions are now frequently offering regular mortgage terms to manufactured housing buyers. Manufactured home mortgages are also eligible for FHA or Veterans Administration loan guarantees.

Another issue which seems to be turning in favor of mobile homes is the question of depreciation. A mobile home used to plummet in value as quickly and as drastically as does an automobile. Today there are signs that this is changing, at least in the case of the more attractive, larger homes in permanent residential communities. The Manufactured Housing Institute cites a recent study by Foremost Corporation of America, the largest insurer of mobile homes in the United States, which reported that a mobile home bought in 1973 appreciates in value by 5 to 15 percent per year, with hot real estate markets like southern California reporting up to 23 percent annual appreciation. It is too early to state that mobile homes generally appreciate in value, but it is safe to say that they definitely do not *depreciate* to the same degree that they used to. You will increase your chances of maintaining your original investment or building up equity by selecting a quality manufactured home in an established, desirable neighborhood that offers the same advantages—such as transportation, schools, medical facilities, and tax rate—that control the asking price of any other form of real estate.

For further information about manufactured homes, write for the following publications:

- "Quick Facts on Manufactured Housing," a booklet available free from the Manufactured Housing Institute, 1745 Jefferson Davis Highway, Suite 511, Arlington, VA 22202.
- "Tips on Buying a Mobile Home," a free booklet from the Council of Better Business Bureaus, 1150 17th Street NW, Washington, DC 20036.
- "Buying and Financing a Mobile Home," a free government publication available from the Superintendent of Documents, U.S. Government Printing Office, Washington, DC 20402.

FOR FURTHER READING

Books

Tuck, Curt, *The Fannie Mae Guide to Buying, Financing, and Selling Your Home;* Dolphin Doubleday paperback, rev. ed. 1978.
This joint effort of the Federal National Mortgage Association and the National Association of Real Estate Editors was written to give the layman a framework for buying or selling a home.
Dickinson, Peter A., *Sunbelt Retirement;* E. P. Dutton paperback, 1978.

A complete guide to the ins and outs of retirement in each of the very popular "sunbelt" states.

U.S. Government Publications

The following government publications may be obtained from the Consumer Information Center, Pueblo, CO 81009. Enclose check or money order for the amount indicated, if any:

- *Buying Lots from Developers.* What to ask about a property and contract before you sign; information the developer must give you under the law. $1.
- *Finding and Keeping a Healthy House.* How to identify and protect your home from water damage, wood decay, and destructive insects such as termites, beetles, and carpenter ants. $1.25.
- *Home Buyer's Vocabulary.* Defines terms you need to understand when buying. Free.
- *Home Buying Veteran.* Useful for nonveterans as well; choosing a neighborhood, a lot, a house; checklist for inspecting a house; financing. Free.
- *House Construction: How to Reduce Costs.* How to save in location, style, interior arrangements, and selection of materials and utilities. $.80.
- *Questions and Answers on Condominiums.* What to ask before buying. Free.
- *Remodeling a House—Will It Be Worthwhile?* What to consider when deciding whether a wood-frame house is worth restoring. Free.
- *Rent or Buy?* How to compare costs and returns of renting with owning a home; includes charts for estimating the monthly costs of each. $.80.
- *Selecting and Financing a Home.* Brief comparison of renting with buying; how to figure what you can afford; how to

apply for a loan; what to look for in homeowners insurance. $1.10.

- *Selling Property: Brokers, Title, Closing, and Taxes.* Advantages and disadvantages of using a real estate broker; some costs of selling; tax implications. Free.
- *When You Move—Do's and Don'ts.* Planning, what to expect during the move, and how to handle a loss or damage claim; tips for the do-it-yourselfer. Free.
- *Wise Home Buying.* Information on choosing a real estate broker, locating a house, inspecting an old house, and financing the purchase of a home. Free.

A CONCLUDING WORD

IN the foregoing chapters we have attempted to cover every plannable aspect of retirement. I hope that you will find ongoing value in this book as a reference work, as you seek answers and directions for maximizing health, comfort, satisfaction, and security in your retirement years.

America seems to be moving toward abolishing unfair age discrimination, and some day there may be no "retirement" in the sense we use the word today. There will be a gradual withdrawal from heavy work schedules, and wide latitude as to when and at what pace this takes place. There will be fifty-year-olds gradually phasing out of the work force, or abruptly changing careers, and there will be eighty-five- and ninety-five-year-olds staying in their occupations at full blast or on diminished schedules, or going on to new careers, or abandoning work for full-time leisure—all largely at the option of the individual concerned.

When all the myths, injustices, and prejudices are retired, age will be seen in its true light: as a triumph over the forces of decay and dissolution, a time for well-earned reward and respect, and a time for choice as to one's satisfactions, including the right to savor the memories, the friends, the kin, the accomplishments, honors, skills, techniques, and landmarks that have accumulated in the course of a lifetime. When age is viewed in this light by the whole community, it will be seen that *there is no aging problem*.

There will still be problems—individual problems of impairment, poverty, loneliness, poor health, loss of mobility, vision, memory. But these will be regarded and dealt with apart from the issue of age. Doctors will diagnose and treat the health disorders without commenting, "You shouldn't expect too much at your age." Poverty will not come to the aged as a class, for society will insure that those whose work has been done are not made to suffer from inadequate pension resources, shrinking with inflation. The loneliness will be mitigated by care and compassion. And sensory and muscular decline will be offset by technology made available to those who need it at any age.

There is no aging problem except that created by social injustice. We refuse to employ the aged and infer from their joblessness that they are unemployable. We deny them the dignity of being taken seriously as students and then say they are uneducable.

We force them into poverty and then, studying their expenditures, conclude they don't need much money. We shame them into impotence and declare they are not interested in sex. When they are righteously indignant at neglect or unfairness, or confused through overmedication, or simply reluctant to conform, we write them off as "senile." When they hurt from illness or injury we say it is because they are old, as though being old is a disease.

There is nothing wrong with getting old or being old. There is always something wrong with being ill or injured.

There is nothing wrong with retirement and retiring. There *is* something wrong and destructive about being forced into uselessness because of a calendar age. Regardless of which route brings you to retirement, you can cushion the shock with proper forethought and turn the experience into a positive, rewarding phase of your life.

When we were very young the bulk of the world was bounded by our nursery walls—and time was a matter of the moment: there was

no significant past to reflect on, and the future was the next toy we
reached for or the expected appearance of our mother. Slowly this
time realm expanded: as schoolchildren we learned that people die,
and an old person was once a child, and that we would one day be
old. We gradually came to know that we had come into the world at
some point in the past and that we would leave it at some point in the
future. With middle age we get a handle on the brevity of life and the
limitations of what we could have accomplished in any case: we may
feel bitter or we may feel self-satisfied, but now for the first time we
take stock. And contrary to popular myth, now we can develop the
attitudes that make advanced age a time of great joy.

In knocking down myths about aging and in trying to undo the
wrong our culture has laid on its elders, there is the danger of appear-
ing to say "Aging is a figment of our imaginations: if we think positively and live right, we can go on indefinitely as though we are
thirty-five." To infer such nonsense from anything in this book
would be to have misread it. No one lives forever. There are physical
and mental differences between a forty-year-old and an eighty-year
old, just as there are between a twelve-year-old and a twenty-four-
year-old. The longer we live, the more time we expose ourselves to
the risks of accident and disease. And in addition, entropic forces
inexorably render our systems less efficient, less able to keep us immune and integrated, and the balancing act at last comes to an end.

Once we accept all this, the points this book has sought to make
(and the reason for compiling tips and techniques for keeping the best
years best) are these:

(a) There is no fixed timetable for decline of powers or impairment
of faculties. (For example, while age forty-two is the *statistical* turning point for the need for reading glasses, a given individual may
reach the point earlier, or later, or not at all—there is no absolute cer-
tainty a person will ever need glasses. At age ninety-five, Scott Nearing read to me from a fairly fine-print book in his library—without
glasses.)

(b) Impairment and limitations, gradual or sudden, can be dealt
with less painfully than we generally tend to think. There are happy
people who are not tall, not wealthy, not beautiful, not even in pos-
session of sound physical health—there are happy people who do not

see well, or hear well, or get around easily. Up to a point, losses of this kind can be accommodated by average people with no net loss of happiness.

(c) The risks of encountering these losses can be modified, as can the risks of being miserable if they occur. *Something* can be done about any condition. We live in an age where, although there are still incurable diseases, there is no longer such a thing as a hopeless disease. There may be irreversible impairments, but there are growing numbers of ways to offset them and to go on functioning.

(d) We need not shackle ourselves with the expectations of a society that mistreats and misunderstands age. We can raise hell. For we are at the dawn of an era in which elders are beginning to move toward center stage again; and society will gain by reinstating the respect that went dormant when citizens became consumers.

And finally we can begin reasonably to expect in our later years justice and comfort. If we can get these at any age, there is little else we need to ask for.

HUGH DOWNS

RETIREMENT PLANNING CHECKLIST

The checklist which follows is a concise summary of the steps you will want to take to plan most effectively for your retirement. You will find the background information for carrying out each step in the pages of *The Best Years Book*.

Retirement planning at its best is a gradual, long-term, and ongoing process. Whatever your age today, it is not too early to begin the tasks included in this checklist. And it's a good idea to review the checklist periodically, to measure your progress toward meeting your retirement goals. By the time you are a year or two away from retirement, you will have an active well-thought-out program for each of the following areas.

*　　*　　*

Personal

1._____I have decided when I would like to retire.

2._____I have discussed my tentative plans, expectations, and hopes for retirement with my spouse.

3._____I have listed the location of all my important documents (will, insurance policies, birth certificate, etc.) and assets (savings account passbooks, stock certificates, deeds) and gone over the list with my spouse.

4._____I have listed all of my important advisers, including my lawyer, accountant, stockbroker, etc., and introduced my spouse to them.

Financial and Legal Affairs

1._____I have estimated the amount of money I will need in retirement.

2._____I have determined how much of this amount will be provided by my pension and Social Security.

3._____I have computed my present net worth and how much my assets will be worth at the time I retire.

4._____I have explored my investment options—IRA and Keogh plans, mutual funds, stocks and bonds, etc.

5._____I have explored ways I can make money by working in retirement.

6._____I have completed a valid, up-to-date will and reviewed it with my lawyer recently.

7._____I have evaluated my life insurance coverage in light of
my current and future family needs.

8._____I have checked into the provisions of my medical insurance coverage, including the way in which it inte-
grates (or fails to integrate) with Medicare, and the
possibility of continuing a company-sponsored policy
after retirement.

Housing

1._____I have decided on some possible retirement locations.

2._____I have researched these areas in detail, and visited
them whenever possible.

3._____I have explored the possibility of living in a retirement community.

4._____I have examined my present community to determine
how suitable it would be as a retirement location.

5._____I have explored the different forms of housing
available—single-family homes, apartments, cooperatives and condominiums, and manufactured houses.

Health and Fitness

1._____ I have had a recent physical checkup.

2._____ I have improved my eating habits to minimize health risks.

3._____ I have incorporated a regular program of exercise in my schedule.

4._____ I have assessed my personal habits and their effects on my health, and made efforts to improve them where necessary.

5._____ I have read up on the techniques of preventive medicine, and have established a cooperative health care partnership with my personal physician.

Leisure Time

1._____ I have considered how much additional time I will have to use as I please after I retire.

2._____ I have thought about which of my present activities I would like to continue in retirement, and how much time I will devote to them.

3._____ I have explored other possible activities which I might be interested in pursuing, and begun whatever classes or training would help me get more enjoyment from these activities.

4._____I have inquired about the possibility of continuing at my present job past age sixty-five or seventy, either full-time or part-time.

5._____I have considered the possibility of finding a new, more attractive position, as a paid worker or a volunteer, or of starting my own business, and have taken steps toward fulfilling any of my ambitions in this area.

INDEX

I